The Combined Gospel of
Jesus Christ

T0369302

"…Go ye into all the world, and preach the gospel to every creature. He that believeth and is baptized shall be saved; but he that believeth not shall be damned." **Mark 16:15-16.**

Abner Smith

DEDICATION

$\mathbf{God}$ the Father decided approximately 2,013 years ago, to execute the most important decision that has ever confronted mankind, since the creation of the world. He decided, to send his firstborn *(Colossians 1:15)*, who we all know as Jesus Christ (4 B.C. – 30 A.D.), into a sinful world. For that purpose, I dedicate this book to God the Father, Jesus Christ, and the Holy Spirit.

For four hundred years, nothing new was added to the Bible. The prophets fell silent. During this time, Middle Eastern empires rose and fell, and the tiny nation of Israel suffered under the domination of greater powers like Greece and Rome.

And then something momentous happened. A baby was born, unlike any, who had ever come before. That baby was named Jesus Christ or Immanuel. God fertilized his son seed with the Holy Spirit, before descending it down into the womb of the Virgin Mary. God chose the springtime to bring forth his single seed of salvation for mankind. The springtime is a season when the rain comes down and waters the trees and all the vegetation. The rain coupled with the fertility of the soil creates beautiful growth, that spring forth from the ground, and from the limbs of trees. Jesus anointed mission was to preach the gospel to the poor; heal the brokenhearted, preach deliverance to the captives, and recovering of sight to the blind, to set at liberty them that are bruised. To preach the acceptable year of the Lord and die for all mankind sins on the cross. His death would redeem all mankind who believe, and is baptized, back to his Father.

Jesus was God firstborn creature, and was the first Supreme Being from heaven, to die. God allowed Jesus to create all things, including Lucifer, and all the angels of heaven and man *(Colossians 1:15-17; Ephesians 3:9; John 1:1-14)*. God the Father Firstborn son (God the Son/Jesus Christ) did not suffer contamination or sin.

God the Son creation got contaminated with sin, by the temptation of Lucifer in heaven, and on earth. The angels of heaven were tempted by Lucifer and two thirds of them prevailed, but one third failed, and was removed from heaven to earth, with Satan. *(Revelation 12:4-9)*. Eve and Adam was tempted in their earthly home, called the Garden of Eden. They failed the temptation and like Satan and the evil angels, they were removed from their Garden home. Ironically, Jesus volunteered to leave his heavenly home to be tempted by Satan, on behalf of mankind. The temptation of Jesus Christ completed the temptation of all of God's heavenly host. Jesus was tempted in the same fashion as we are, with an incarnate body. It was extremely difficult, for God the Father, to allow his only begotten Son to descend to earth and die for man. However, like Jesus, God so loved the world, and trusted his son enough, to allow his mission to occur.

Biblical history teaches us, that a failure to accurately know the scriptures, through reading and studying, is what led to the crucifixion of Jesus Christ. The high priest, chief priest, and scribes, were unaware, that the man they were accusing of blasphemy, was truly the Son of God. From the location of his birth, to his sermons, healings, and extraordinary miracles, had all proclaimed him, as the promise Messiah, written of by the prophets.

The prophecies of the scriptures were being fulfilled before their eyes, but they had not carefully studied the scriptures, therefore, they did not believe. Many in the congregation they preached to, was just as lost regarding the scripture concerning Jesus Christ. So the high priest sent the son of God, to the gentiles slaughter house of Pilate, to be crucified. Similar to what happen to the lambs that were brought before the tabernacle and the temple, and slain for the sins of men, before the high priest. Pilate reluctantly had his soldiers mock, spitefully entreat, spit on, and scourged Jesus, before crucifying him to death, on the cross at Calvary.

I sincerely respect the works of God disciples and inspired servants; Matthew, Mark, Luke, and John. My efforts here is not to smear, or any way detract from their sacred work; which is truly divine, inspired, uplifting, and essential to prosperity. I decided to combine their accounts, and the first 30 verses of Acts, for a future act.

I learned from serving in the military, that you can have four people at the scene of an incident, and they would write what they saw, differently. To get an accurate picture of what transpired, you would have to consolidate their reports and make one statement. I used that same approach to complete this book. Master, please forgive me, if I have missed a crossing of a t, or a dotting of an i.

Special thanks to: My uncle, the genius of our family, Dr. Molefi K. Asante for his guidance and assistance. Pastor Dr. Lewis W. Edwards, my boyhood minister, for his teaching and material support. Sisters Elnora, Carolyn, and Carla Newton for their editing support.

Explanation of Time and Text

1. The charts below, makes it easier for you to understand the difference between our current time and the Roman/Jewish time.

2. Working day started early and ended at the beginning of evening *(Matthew 20:1; 3-6, 8, 12)*. During Roman/Jewish time a day was divided by the Jews into 12 hours *(John 11:9)*. It began at 6:01 am (6:01 to 7am, 1st hour) and ended at 6:00 pm.

Current Time	7 am	8 am	9 am	10 am	11 am	12 am
Jewish Time	1st Hour	2nd Hour	3rd Hour	4th Hour	5th Hour	6th Hour

Current Time	1 pm	2 pm	3 pm	4 pm	5 pm	6 pm
Jewish Time	7th Hour	8th Hour	9th Hour	10th Hour	11th Hour	12th Hour

4. The night started at 6:01 pm and ended at 6:00 am. It was divided into four periods of Watch, that equaled 12 hours, as indicated below *(Matthew 14:25; Mark 6:48; 13:35; Luke 12:38)*.

Jewish Night	1st Watch Evening	2nd Watch Midnight	3rd Watch Cockcrowing	4th Watch Morning
Hours	6:01 – 9 pm	9:01 – 12 pm	12:01 – 3 am	3:01 – 6 am

Note: Jews accepts the creation chronology of a day, as represented by evening and morning (Genesis 1:5, 8).

The meaning behind the text of the Combined Gospel:
1. Bold Black, Italics, and Underline: *Is God the Father speaking*. Here are the Chapters where God speaks to Jesus in the presence of others; Chapter 2 (2-2.g), Chapter 5 (5-16.h), and Chapter 8 (8-1.g).
2. Bold Black and Italics represent: *An angel speaking.*
3. Bold Black: **Is Jesus speaking.** He was born on earth as a man (incarnate), lower than the angels *(Psalm 8:5)*.
4. Italics in parenthesis: *(My addition for various reasons).*

Table of Contents

Appendixes

The Combined Gospel of Jesus Christ

Chapter One
The First Coming

1-1. Jesus Christ Gospel.

a. The beginning of the gospel of Jesus Christ, the Son of God.

b. In the beginning was the Word, and the Word was with God, and the Word was God.

c. The same was in the beginning with God. All things were made by him; and without him was not any thing made that was made.

d. In him was life; and the life was the light of men. And the light shineth in darkness; and the darkness comprehended it not.

1-2. John's birth announced to Zacharias.

a. Forasmuch as many have taken in hand to set forth in order a declaration of those things which are most surely believed among us.

b. Even as they delivered them unto us, which from the beginning were eyewitnesses, and ministers of the word; It seemed good to me also, having had perfect understanding of all things from the very first, to write unto thee in order, most excellent Theophilus. That thou mightest know the certainty of those things, wherein thou hast been instructed.

c. There was in the days of Herod, the king of Judaea, a certain priest named Zacharias, of the course of Abia: and his wife was of the daughters of Aaron, and her name was Elisabeth.

d. And they were both righteous before God, walking in all the commandments and ordinances of the Lord blameless.

e. And they had no child, because that Elisabeth was barren, and they both were now well stricken in years.

f. And it came to pass, that while he executed the priest's office before God in the order of his course. According to the custom of the priest's office, his lot was to burn incense when he went into the temple of the Lord.

g.   And the whole multitude of the people were praying without at the time of incense.

h. And there appeared unto him an angel of the Lord standing on the right side of the altar of incense. And when Zacharias saw him, he was troubled, and fear fell upon him.

i. But the angel said unto him, *Fear not, Zacharias: for thy prayer is heard; and thy wife Elisabeth shall bear thee a son, and thou shalt call his name John.*

j. *And thou shalt have joy and gladness; and many shall rejoice at his birth. For he shall be great in the sight of the Lord, and shall drink neither wine nor strong drink; and he shall be filled with the Holy Ghost, even from his mother's womb.*

k. *And many of the children of Israel shall he turn to the Lord their God.*

l. *And he shall go before him in the spirit and power of Elias, to turn the hearts of the fathers to the children, and the disobedient to the wisdom of the just; to make ready a people prepared for the Lord.*

m. And Zacharias said unto the angel, Whereby shall I know this? For I am an old man, and my wife well stricken in years.

n. And the angel answering said unto him, *I am Gabriel, that stand in the presence of God; and am sent to speak unto thee, and to shew thee these glad tidings.*

o. *And, behold, thou shalt be dumb, and not able to speak, until the day that these things shall be performed, because thou believest not my words, which shall be fulfilled in their season.*

p.   And the people waited for Zacharias, and marvelled that he tarried so long in the temple.

q. And when he came out, he could not speak unto them: and they perceived that he had seen a vision in the temple: for he beckoned unto them, and remained speechless.

r. And it came to pass, that, as soon as the days of his ministration were accomplished, he departed to his own house.

s. And after those days his wife Elisabeth conceived, and hid herself five months, saying, thus hath the Lord dealt with me in the days wherein he looked on me, to take away my reproach (*shame or disgrace that somebody incurs*) among men.

1-3. Jesus birth announced to Mary.

a. And in the sixth month the angel Gabriel was sent from God unto a city of Galilee, named Nazareth. To a virgin espoused (*to marry or give somebody in marriage*) to a man whose name was Joseph, of the house of David; and the virgin's name was Mary.

b. And the angel came in unto her, and said, *Hail, thou that art highly favored, the Lord is with thee: blessed art thou among women.*

c. And when she saw him, she was troubled at his saying, and cast in her mind what manner of salutation (*greeting*) this should be.

d. And the angel said unto her, *Fear not, Mary: for thou hast found favour with God. And, behold, thou shalt conceive in thy womb, and bring forth a son, and shalt call his name JESUS.*

e. *He shall be great, and shall be called the Son of the Highest: and the Lord God shall give unto him the throne of his father David: And he shall reign over the house of Jacob for ever; and of his kingdom there shall be no end.*

f. Then said Mary unto the angel, How shall this be, seeing I know not a man?

g. And the angel answered and said unto her, *The Holy Ghost shall come upon thee, and the power of the Highest shall overshadow thee: therefore also that holy thing which shall be born of thee shall be called the Son of God.*

h. *And, behold, thy cousin Elisabeth, she hath also conceived a son in her old age: and this is the sixth month with her, who was called barren. For with God nothing shall be impossible.*

i. And Mary said, Behold the handmaid of the Lord; be it unto me according to thy word. And the angel departed from her.

1-4. Mary visit's with Elisabeth.

a. And Mary arose in those days, and went into the hill country with haste, into a city of Juda; And entered into the house of Zacharias, and saluted Elisabeth.

b. And it came to pass, that, when, Elisabeth heard the salutation of Mary, the babe leaped in her womb; and Elisabeth was filled with the Holy Ghost:

c. And she spake out with a loud voice, and said, Blessed art thou among women, and blessed is the fruit (*offspring*) of thy womb.

d. And whence is this to me, that the mother of my Lord should come to me? For, lo, as soon as the voice of thy salutation sounded in mine ears, the babe leaped in my womb for joy.

e. And blessed is she that believed: for there shall be a performance of those things which were told her from the Lord.

1-5. The song of Mary.

a. And Mary said, My soul doth magnify the Lord. And my spirit hath rejoiced in God my Saviour.

b. For he hath regarded the low estate of his handmaiden: for, behold, from henceforth all generations shall call me blessed.

c. For he that is mighty hath done to me great things; and holy is his name. And his mercy is on them that fear him from generation to generation.

d. He hath showed strength with his arm; he hath scattered the proud in the imagination of their hearts.

e. He hath put down the mighty from their seats, and exalted them of low degree.

f. He hath filled the hungry with good things; and the rich he hath sent empty away.

g. He hath holpen (*helped*) his servant Israel, in remembrance of his mercy. As he spake to our fathers, to Abraham, and to his seed for ever.

1-6. John the Baptist birth; Mary return to Nazareth.

a. And Mary abode with her about three months, and returned to her own house.

b. Now Elisabeth's full time came that she should be delivered; and she brought forth a son.

c. And her neighbours and her cousins heard how the Lord had showed great mercy upon her; and they rejoiced with her.

d. And it came to pass, that on the eight day they came to circumcise the child; and they called him Zacharias, after the name of his father.

e. And his mother answered and said, Not so; but he shall be called John.

f. And they said unto her, There is none of thy kindred that is called by this name.

g. And they made signs to his father, how he would have him called.

h. And he asked for a writing table, and wrote, saying, His name is John. And they marvelled all.

i. And his mouth was opened immediately, and his tongue loosed, and he spake, and praised God.

j. And fear came on all that dwelt round about them: and all these sayings were noised abroad throughout all the hill country of Judaea.

k. And all they that heard them laid them up in their hearts, saying, What manner of child shall this be! And the hand of the Lord was with him.

1-7. The song of Zacharias.

a. And his father Zacharias was filled with the Holy Ghost, and prophesied, saying, blessed be the Lord God of Israel; for he hath visited and redeemed his people.

b. And hath raised up an horn of salvation for us in the house of his servant David. As he spake by the mouth of his holy prophets, which have been since the world began.

c. That we should be saved from our enemies, and from the hand of all that hate us.

d. To perform the mercy promised to our fathers, and to remember his holy covenant. The oath which he sware to our father Abraham.

e. That he would grant unto us, that we, being delivered out of the hand of our enemies, might serve him without fear. In holiness and righteousness before him, all the days of our life.

f. And thou, child, shalt be called the prophet of the Highest: for thou shalt go before the face of the Lord to prepare his ways.

g. To give knowledge of salvation unto his people by the remission of their sins. Through the tender mercy of our God; whereby the dayspring from on high hath visited us.

h. To give light to them that sit in darkness and in the shadow of death, to guide our feet into the way of peace.

i. And the child grew, and waxed strong in spirit, and was in the deserts till the day of his showing unto Israel.

j. There was a man sent from God, whose name was John. The same came for a witness, to bear witness of the light, that all men through him might believe.

k. He was not that Light, but was sent to bear witness of that Light. That was the true Light, which lighteth every man that cometh into the world.

1-8. Jesus birth.

a. He was in the world, and the world was made by him, and the world knew him not. He came unto his own, and his own received him not.

b. But as many as received him, to them gave he power to become the sons of God, even to them that believe on his name.

c. Which were born, not of blood, nor of the will of the flesh, nor of the will of man, but of God.

d. And the Word was made flesh, and dwelt among us, (and we beheld his glory, the glory as of the only begotten of the Father), full of grace and truth.

e. Now the birth of Jesus Christ was on this wise: When as his mother Mary was espoused to Joseph, before they came together, she was found with child of the Holy Ghost.

f. Then Joseph her husband, being a just man, and not willing to make her a public example, was minded to put her away privily.

g. But while he thought on these things, behold, the angel of the Lord appeared unto him in a dream, saying, *Joseph, thou son of David, fear not to take unto thee Mary thy wife: for that which is conceived in her is of the Holy Ghost.*

h. *And she shall bring forth a son, and thou shalt call his name JESUS: for he shall save his people from their sins.*

i. Now all this was done, that it might be fulfilled which was spoken of the Lord by the prophet, saying, behold, a virgin shall be with child, and shall bring forth a son, and they shall call his name Emmanuel, which being interpreted is, God with us. (Fulfilled Prophecy: *"Therefore the Lord himself shall give you a sign; Behold, a virgin shall conceive, and bear a son, and shall call his name Immanuel."* Isaiah 7:14*).*

j. Then Joseph being raised from sleep did as the angel of the Lord had bidden him, and took unto him his wife. And knew her not till she had brought forth her firstborn son.

k. And it came to pass in those days, that there went out a decree from Caesar Augustus, that all the world should be taxed. (And this taxing was first made when Cyrenius was governor of Syria).

l. And all went to be taxed, every one into his own city.

m. And Joseph also went up from Galilee, out of the city of Nazareth, into Judaea, unto the city of David, which is called Bethlehem; (because he was of the house and lineage of David:).

n. To be taxed with Mary his espoused wife, being great with child.

o. And so it was, that, while they were there, the days were accomplished that she should be delivered.

p. And she brought forth her firstborn son, and he called his name JESUS.

q. And wrapped him in swaddling clothes, and laid him in a manger; because there was no room for them in the inn.

1-9. The first fourteen generations of the genealogy of Jesus Christ from Abraham to David.

The book of the generation of Jesus Christ, the son of David, the son of Abraham. **Abraham** begat Isaac; and Isaac begat Jacob; and Jacob begat Judas and his brethren; and Judas begat Phares and Zara of Thamar; and Phares begat Esrom; and Esrom begat Aram; and Aram begat Aminadab; and Aminadab begat Naasson; and Naasson begat Salmon; and Salmon begat Booz of Rachab; and Booz begat Obed of Ruth; and Obed begat Jesse; and Jesse begat **David** the king;

1-10. The second fourteen generations from David until
(before a time or event) **the carrying away to Babylon.**
  and **David** the king begat Solomon of her that had
been the wife of Urias; and Solomon begat Roboam; and
Roboam begat Abia; and Abia begat Asa; and Asa begat
Josaphat; and Josaphat begat Joram; and Joram begat
Ozias; and Ozias begat Joatham; and Joatham begat
Achaz; and Achaz begat Ezekias; and Ezekias begat
Manasses; and Manasses begat Amon; and Amon begat
Josias;

1-11. The third fourteen generations from the carrying
away to Babylon unto Jesus Christ.
  and Josias begat **Jechonias** and his brethren, about
the time they were carried away to Babylon: And after
they were brought to Babylon, Jechonias begat Salathiel;
and Salathiel begat Zorobabel; and Zorobabel begat
Abiud; and Abiud begat Eliakim; and Eliakim begat Azor;
and Azor begat Sadoc; and Sadoc begat Achim; and
Achim begat Eliud; and Eliud begat Eleazar; and Eleazar
begat Matthan; and Matthan begat Jacob; and Jacob begat
Joseph the husband of Mary, of whom was born **Jesus,**
who is called Christ. So all the generations from
Abraham to David are fourteen generations; and from
David until *(before a time or event)* the carrying away into
Babylon are fourteen generations; and from the carrying
away into Babylon unto Christ are fourteen generations.

1-12. Jesus birth announced to the shepherds.
  a. And there were in the same country shepherds
abiding in the field, keeping watch over their flock by
night.

b. And, lo, the angel of the Lord came upon them, and the glory of the Lord shone round about them: and they were sore afraid.

c. And the angel said unto them, *Fear not: for, behold, I bring you good tidings of great joy, which shall be to all people.*

d. *For unto you is born this day in the city of David a Saviour, which is Christ the Lord.*

e. *And this shall be a sign unto you; Ye shall find the babe wrapped in swaddling clothes, lying in a manger.*

f. And suddenly there was with the angel a multitude of the heavenly host praising God, and saying, *Glory to God in the highest, and on earth peace, good will toward men.*

g. And it came to pass, as the angels were gone away from them into heaven, the shepherds said one to another, Let us now go even unto Bethlehem, and see this thing which is come to pass, which the Lord hath made known unto us.

h. And they came with haste, and found Mary, and Joseph, and the babe lying in a manger.

i. And when they had seen it, they made known abroad the saying which was told them concerning this child.

j. And all they that heard it wondered at those things which were told them by the shepherds.

k. But Mary kept all these things, and pondered them in her heart.

l. And the shepherds returned, glorifying and praising God for all the things that they had heard and seen, as it was told unto them.

1-13. Jesus presented in the temple for circumcision.

a. And when eight days were accomplished for the circumcising of the child, his name was called JESUS, which was so named of the angel before he was conceived in the womb.

b. And when the days of her purification according to the law of Moses were accomplished (*40 days later*), they brought him to Jerusalem, to present him to the Lord. (As it is written in the law of the Lord, Every male that openeth the womb shall be called holy to the Lord;).

c. And to offer a sacrifice according to that which is said in the law of the Lord, a pair of turtledoves, or two young pigeons.

d. And, behold, there was a man in Jerusalem, whose name was Simeon; and the same man was just and devout, waiting for the consolation of Israel: and the Holy Ghost was upon him.

e. And it was revealed unto him by the Holy Ghost, that he should not see death, before he had seen the Lord's Christ.

f. And he came by the Spirit into the temple: and when the parents brought in the child Jesus, to do for him after the custom of the law.

g. Then took he him up in his arms, and blessed God, and said, Lord, now lettest thou thy servant depart in peace, according to thy word. For mine eyes have seen thy salvation.

h. Which thou hast prepared before the face of all people. A light to lighten the Gentiles, and the glory of thy people Israel.

i. And Joseph and his mother marvelled at those things which were spoken of him.

j. And Simeon blessed them, and said unto Mary his mother, Behold, this child is set for the fall and rising again of many in Israel; and for a sign which shall be spoken against; (Yea, a sword shall pierce through thy own soul also,) that the thoughts of many hearts may be revealed.

k. And there was one Anna, a prophetess, the daughter of Phanuel, of the tribe of Aser: she was of a great age, and had lived with an husband seven years from her virginity.

l. And she was a widow of about fourscore and four years, which departed not from the temple, but served God with fastings and prayers night and day.

m. And she coming in that instant gave thanks likewise unto the Lord, and spake of him to all them that looked for redemption in Jerusalem.

n. And when they had performed all things according to the law of the Lord, (*they departed back to the site of JESUS birth in the manger and was visited by the MAGI, see* Matthew 2:1-14).

1-14. The visit and return of the MAGI (*MAGI - men with supernatural or magical powers*).

a. Now when Jesus was born in Bethlehem of Judaea in the days of Herod the king, behold, there came wise men from the east to Jerusalem, Saying, Where is he that is born King of the Jews?

b. For we have seen his star in the east, and are come to worship him.

c. When Herod the king had heard these things, he was troubled, and all Jerusalem with him.

d. And when he had gathered all the chief priests and scribes of the people together, he demanded of them where Christ should be born.

e. And they said unto him, In Bethlehem of Judaea: for thus it is written by the prophet. And thou Bethlehem, in the land of Juda, are not the least among the princes of Juda: for out of thee shall come a Governor, that shall rule my people Israel (Fulfilled Prophecy: *"But thou, Bethlehem Ephratah, though thou be little among the thousands of Judah, yet out of thee shall he come forth unto me that is to be ruler in Israel; whose goings forth have been from of old, from everlasting."* Micah 5:2*)*.

f. Then Herod, when he had privily called the wise men, inquired of them diligently what time the star appeared.

g. And he sent them to Bethlehem, and said, Go and search diligently for the young child; and when ye have found him, bring me word again, that I may come and worship him also.

h. When they had heard the king, they departed; and, lo, the star, which they saw in the east, went before them, till it came and stood over where the young child was.

i. When they saw the star, they rejoiced with exceeding great joy.

j. And when they were come into the house, they saw the young child with Mary his mother, and fell down, and worshipped him: and when they had opened their treasures, they presented unto him gifts; gold, and frankincense, and myrrh.

k. And being warned of God in a dream *that they should not return to Herod,* they departed into their own country another way.

1-15. The flight into Egypt.

a. And when they were departed, behold, the angel of the Lord appeareth to Joseph in a dream, saying, *Arise, and take the young child and his mother, and flee into Egypt, and be thou there until I bring thee word: for Herod will seek the young child to destroy him.*

b. When he arose, he took the young child and his mother by night, and departed into Egypt.

c. And was there until the death of Herod: that it might be fulfilled which was spoken of the Lord by the prophet, saying, Out of Egypt have I called my son (Fulfilled Prophecy: *"When Israel was a child, then I loved him, and called my son out of Egypt."* Hosea 11:1).

d. Then Herod, when he saw that he was mocked of the wise men, was exceeding wroth, and sent forth, and slew all the children that were in Bethlehem, and in all the coasts thereof, from two years old and under, according to the time which he had diligently inquired of the wise men.

e. Then was fulfilled that which was spoken by Jeremy the prophet, saying, in Rama was there a voice heard, lamentation, and weeping, and great mourning, Rachel weeping for her children, and would not be comforted, because they are not (Fulfilled Prophecy: *"Thus saith the LORD; a voice was heard in Ramah, lamentation, and bitter weeping; Rahel weeping for her children refused to be comforted for her children, because they were not."* Jeremiah 31:15).

1-16. From Egypt to Nazareth.

a. But when Herod was dead, behold, an angel of the Lord appeareth in a dream to Joseph in Egypt, Saying, *Arise, and take the young child and his mother, and go into the land of Israel: for they are dead which sought the young child's life.*

b. And he arose, and took the young child and his mother, and came into the land of Israel.

c. But when he heard that Archelaus did reign in Judaea in the room of his father Herod, he was afraid to go thither: notwithstanding, being warned of God in a dream, he turned aside into the parts of Galilee.

d. And he came and dwelt in their own city called Nazareth: that it might be fulfilled which was spoken by the prophets, He shall be called a Nazarene. (Fulfilled Prophecy: *"Nevertheless the dimness shall not be such as was in her vexation, when at the first he lightly afflicted the land of Zebulun and the land of Naphtali, and afterward did more grievously afflict her by the way of the sea, beyond Jordan, in Galilee of the nations."* Isaiah 9:1).

1-17. The boy Jesus in the temple for the passover.

a. And the child grew, and waxed strong in spirit, filled with wisdom: and the grace of God was upon him.

b. Now his parents went to Jerusalem every year at the feast of the passover. And when he was twelve years old, they went up to Jerusalem after the custom of the feast.

c. And when they had fulfilled the days, as they returned, the child Jesus tarried behind in Jerusalem; and Joseph and his mother knew not of it.

d. But they, supposing him to have been in the company, went a day's journey; and they sought him among their kinsfolk and acquaintance.

e. And when they found him not, they turned back again to Jerusalem, seeking him.

f. And it came to pass, that after three days they found him in the temple, sitting in the midst of the doctors, both hearing them, and asking them questions.

g. And all that heard him were astonished at his understanding and answers. And when they saw him, they were amazed: and his mother said unto him, Son, why hast thou thus dealt with us? Behold, thy father and I have sought thee sorrowing.

h. And he said unto them, **How is it that ye sought me? Wist ye know that I must be about my Father's business?**

i. And they understood not the saying which he spake unto them. And he went down with them, and came to Nazareth, and was subject (*cause to have an unpleasant experience*) unto them: but his mother kept all these sayings in her heart.

j. And Jesus increased in wisdom and stature, and in favour with God and man.

The Combined Gospel of Jesus Christ

Chapter Two
Jesus Baptism

2-1. John ministry.

a. Now in the fifteenth year of the reign of Tiberius Caesar, Pontius Pilate being governor of Judaea, and Herod being tetrarch of Galilee, and his brother Philip tetrarch of Ituraea and of the region of Trachonitis, and Lysanias the tetrarch of Abilene,

b. Annas and Caiaphas being the high priests, the word of God came to John the son of Zacharias in the wilderness.

c. And it came to pass in those days, that Jesus came from Nazareth of Galilee to Jordan unto John, to be baptized of him.

d. In those days came John the Baptist, preaching in the wilderness of Judaea, and saying, Repent ye: for the kingdom of heaven is at hand.

e. John bare witness of him, and cried, saying, this was he of whom I spake, He that cometh after me is preferred before me: for he was before me.

f. And of his fulness have all we received, and grace for grace. For the laws was given by Moses, but grace and truth came by Jesus Christ.

g. No man hath seen God at any time; the only begotten Son, which is in the bosom of the Father, he hath declared him.

h. John did baptize in the wilderness, and he came into all the country about Jordan, preaching the baptism of repentance for the remission of sins;

i. And there went out unto him all the land of Judaea, and they of Jerusalem, and all the region round about Jordan, and were all baptized of him in the river of Jordan, confessing their sins.

j. For this is he that was written in the book of the words spoken of by the prophet Esaias, saying, behold I send my messenger before thy face, which shall prepare thy way before thee, The voice of one crying in the wilderness, Prepare ye the way of the Lord, make his paths straight.

k. And the same John had his raiment of camel's hair, and a leathern girdle of a skin about his loins; and his meat was locusts and wild honey.

l. And they which were sent were of the Pharisees. But when he saw many of the Pharisees and Sadducees come to his baptism, he said to the multitude that came forth to be baptized of him, O generation of vipers, who hath warned you to flee from the wrath to come?

m. Bring forth therefore fruits worthy of repentance, and begin not to say within yourselves, we have Abraham to our father: for I say unto you, That God is able of these stones to raise up children unto Abraham.

n. And now also the axe is laid unto the root of the trees: every tree therefore which bringeth not forth good fruit is hewn down, and cast into the fire.

o. And the people asked him, saying, What shall we do then? He answered and said unto them, He that hath two coats, let him impart to him that hath none; and he that hath meat, let him do likewise.

p. Then came also publicans to be baptized, and said unto him, Master, what shall we do? And he said unto them, Exact no more than that which is appointed you.

q. And the soldiers likewise demanded of him, saying, and what shall we do? And he said unto them, Do violence to no man, neither accuse any falsely; and be content with your wages.

r. And this is the record of John, when the Jews sent priests and Levites from Jerusalem to ask him, Who art thou? And he confessed, and denied not; but confessed, I am not the Christ.

s. And they asked him, What then? Art thou Elias? And he saith, I am not. Art thou that prophet? And he answered, No.

t. Then said they unto him, Who art thou? That we may give an answer to them that sent us. What sayest thou of thyself? He said, I am the voice of one crying in the wilderness, Make straight the way of the Lord, as saith the prophet Esaias.

u. Every valley shall be filled, and every mountain and hill shall be brought low; and the crooked shall be made straight, and the rough ways shall be made smooth; and all flesh shall see the salvation of God. (Fulfilled Prophecy: *"The voice of him that crieth in the wilderness, Prepare ye the way of the LORD, make straight in the desert a highway for our God. Every valley shall be exalted, and every mountain and hill shall be made low: and the crooked shall be made straight, and the rough places plain: And the glory of the LORD shall be revealed, and all flesh shall see it together: for the mouth of the LORD hath spoken it."* Isaiah 40:3-5).

v. And as the people were in expectation, and all men mused in their hearts of John, whether he were the Christ, or not; and they asked him, and said unto him, Why baptizest thou then, if thou be not that Christ, nor Elias, neither that prophet?

w. John answered, saying unto them all, I indeed baptize you with water unto repentance; but there standeth one among you, whom ye know not; He it is, who coming after me is mightier than I and preferred before me, the latchet of whose shoes I am not worthy to stoop down and unloose; he shall baptize you with the Holy Ghost, and with fire.

x. Whose fan is in his hand, and he will thoroughly purge his floor, and will gather the wheat into his garner; but the chaff he will burn with fire unquenchable.

y. And many other things in his exhortation preached he unto the people.

z. These things were done in Bethabara beyond Jordan, where John was baptizing.

2-2. The baptism of Jesus.

a.   Now the next day when all the people were baptized, John seeth Jesus coming unto him, and saith, Behold the Lamb of God, which taketh away the sin of the world.

b.   This is he of whom I said, After me cometh a man which is preferred before me: for he was before me.

c.   And I knew him not: but that he should be made manifest to Israel, therefore am I come baptizing with water.

d.   But John forbad him, saying, I have need to be baptized of thee, and comest thou to me?

e.   And Jesus answering said unto him, **Suffer it to be so now: for thus it becometh us to fulfill all righteousness.**   Then he suffered him.

f.   And Jesus, when he was baptized, went up straightway, coming up out of the water and praying: and lo, the heavens were opened unto him, and he saw the Holy Ghost Spirit of God descending from heaven in a bodily shape like a dove, and lighting upon him: and it abode upon him.

g.   And lo a voice came from heaven, saying, _**This is my beloved Son, in whom I am well pleased.**_

h.   And John bare record, saying, I saw the spirit descending from heaven like a dove, and it abode upon him.

i.   And I knew him not: but he that sent me to baptize with water, the same said unto me, Upon whom thou shalt see the Spirit descending, and remaining on him, the same is he which baptizeth with the Holy Ghost.

j.   And I saw, and bare record that this is the Son of God.

2-3. Jesus genealogy from Jesus to Maath (First fourteen generations).

And Jesus himself began to be about thirty years of age, being (as was supposed) the son of Joseph, which was the son of Heli, Which was the son of Matthat, which was the son of Levi, which was the son of Melchi, which was the son of Janna, which was the son of Joseph, which was the son of Mattathias, which was the son of Amos, which was the son of Naum, which was the son of Esli, which was the son of Nagge, which was the son of Maath,

2-4. Jesus genealogy from Mattathias to Er (Second fourteen generations).

Which was the son of Mattathias, which was the son of Semei, which was the son of Joseph, which was the son of Juda, which was the son of Joanna, which was the son of Rhesa, which was the son of Zorobabel, which was the son of Salathiel, which was the son of Neri, which was the son of Melchi, which was the son of Addi, which was the son of Cosam, which was the son of Elmodam, which was the son of Er,

2-5. Jesus genealogy from Jose to Nathan (Third fourteen generations).

Which was the son of Jose, which was the son of Eliezer, which was the son of Jorim, which was the son of Matthat, which was the son of Levi, which was the son of Simeon, which was the son of Juda, which was the son of Joseph, which was the son of Jonan, which was the son of Eliakim, which was the son of Melea, which was the son of Menan, which was the son of Mattatha, which was the son of Nathan,

2-6. Jesus genealogy from David to Abraham (Fourth fourteen generations).

Which was the son of <u>David</u>, Which was the son of <u>Jesse</u>, which was the son of <u>Obed</u>, which was the son of <u>Booz</u>, which was the son of <u>Salmon</u>, which was the son of <u>Naasson</u>, which was the son of <u>Aminadab</u>, which was the son of <u>Aram</u>, which was the son of <u>Esrom</u>, which was the son of <u>Phares</u>, which was the son of <u>Juda</u>, which was the son of <u>Jacob</u>, which was the son of <u>Isaac</u>, which was the son of <u>Abraham</u>,

2-7. Jesus genealogy from Thara to Enoch (Fifth fourteen generations).

Which was the son of <u>Thara</u>, Which was the son of <u>Nachor</u>, which was the son of <u>Saruch</u>, which was the son of <u>Ragau</u>, which was the son of <u>Phalec</u>, which was the son of <u>Heber</u>, which was the son of <u>Sala</u>, which was the son of <u>Cainan</u>, which was the son of <u>Arphaxad</u>, which was the son of <u>Sem</u>, which was the son of <u>Noe</u>, which was the son of <u>Lamech</u>, which was the son of <u>Mathusala</u>, which was the son of <u>Enoch</u>,

2-8. Jesus genealogy from Jared to God (Seven generations).

Which was the son of <u>Jared</u>, which was the son of <u>Maleleel</u>, which was the son of <u>Cainan</u>, which was the son of <u>Enos</u>, which was the son of <u>Seth</u>, which was the son of <u>Adam</u>, which was the son of <u>God</u>.

2-9. The temptation in the wilderness.

a. And Jesus being full of the Holy Ghost returned from Jordan, and immediately was led by the Spirit into the wilderness, with the wild beasts, to be tempted of the devil.

b. And when the tempter came to him, he said, If thou be the Son of God, command that these stones be made bread.

c. And Jesus answered him, saying, **It is written, Man shall not live by bread alone, but by every word that proceeded out of the mouth of God.**

d. Then the devil taketh him up into the holy city of Jerusalem, and set him on a pinnacle of the temple, and said unto him, If thou be the Son of God, cast thyself down from hence: For it is written, He shall give his angels charge over thee, to keep thee. And in their hands they shall bear thee up, lest at any time thou dash thy foot against a stone (The devil studied and quoted the scripture written by David that said, *"For he shall give his angels charge over thee, to keep thee in all thy ways. They shall bear thee up in their hands, lest thou dash thy foot against a stone."* Psalm 91:11-12).

e. Jesus said unto him, **It is written again, Thou shalt not tempt the Lord thy God.**

f. Again, the devil taketh him up into an exceeding high mountain, and showed him all the kingdoms of the world in a moment of time, and the glory of them.

g. And the devil said unto him, All this power will I give thee, and the glory of them: for that is delivered unto me; and to whomsoever I will give it. If thou therefore wilt fall down and worship me, all shall be thine.

h. Then saith Jesus unto him, **Get thee behind me, Satan: for it is written, Thou shalt worship the Lord thy God, and him only shalt thou serve.**

i. Then the devil had ended all his temptation; he departed from him for a season. Being forty days tempted of the devil.

j. And in those days he did eat nothing for forty days and nights: and when they were ended, he was afterward an hungered.

k. And, behold, angels came and ministered unto him.

2-10. Andrew and John follow Jesus.

a. Again the next day after John stood, and two of his disciples; (Controversy: *This has to be, the next day after he had spent forty days in the wilderness. The majority of the gospels* (Matthew 4:1-2; Mark 1:12-13, and Luke 4:1-2), *clearly states Jesus was baptized and (immediately) led by the spirit into the wilderness for forty days to be tempted of the Devil. John who lived in the wilderness (John 1:35), saw Jesus walking in the wilderness).* And looking upon Jesus as he walked, he saith, Behold the Lamb of God!

b. And the two disciples heard him speak, and they followed Jesus.

c. Then Jesus turned, and saw them following, and saith unto them, **What seek ye?** They said unto him, Rabbi, (which is to say, being interpreted, Master,) where dwellest thou? He saith unto them, **Come and see.**

d. They came and saw where he dwelt, and abode with him that day: for it was about the tenth hour (*4:00 PM*).

e. One of the two which heard John speak and followed him, was Andrew, Simon Peter's brother *(Biblical scholars has credited the other disciple as being John; throughout his gospel he did not mention his name; see Chapter 12-1(g); 12-9(i).*

f. He first findeth his own brother Simon, and saith unto him, We have found the Messias, which is, being interpreted, the Christ. And he brought him to Jesus.

g. And when Jesus beheld him he said, **Thou art Simon the son of Jona: thou shalt be called Cephas, which is by interpretation, A stone.**

2-11. Philip and Nathaniel follow Jesus.

a. The day following Jesus would go forth into Galilee, and findeth Philip, and saith unto him, **Follow me.** Now Philip was of Bethsaida, the city of Andrew and Peter.

b. Philip findeth Nathaniel, and saith unto him, We have found him, of whom Moses in the law, and the prophets, did write, Jesus of Nazareth, the son of Joseph.

c. And Nathaniel said unto him, Can there any good thing come out of Nazareth? Philip saith unto him, Come and see.

d. Jesus saw Nathaniel coming to him, and saith of him, **Behold an Israelite indeed, in whom is no guile!**

e. Nathaniel saith unto him, Whence knowest thou me? Jesus answered and said unto him, **Before that Philip called thee, when thou wast under the fig tree, I saw thee.**

f. Nathaniel answered and saith unto him, Rabbi, thou art the Son of God, thou art the King of Israel.

g. Jesus answered and said unto him, **Because I said unto thee, I saw thee under the fig tree, believest thou? thou shalt see greater things than these.**

h. And he saith unto him, **Verily, verily, I say unto you, Hereafter ye shall see heaven open, and the angels of God ascending and descending upon the Son of man.**

2-12. Water made into wine (First Miracle).

a. And the third day there was a marriage in Cana of Galilee, and the mother of Jesus was there: And both Jesus was called, and his disciples, to the marriage.

b. And when they wanted wine, the mother of Jesus saith unto him, They have no wine.

c. Jesus saith unto her, **Woman, what have I to do with thee? Mine hour is not yet come.**

d. His mother saith unto the servants, Whatsoever he saith unto you, do it.

e. And there were set there six waterpots of stone, after the manner of the purifying of the Jews, containing two or three firkins *(brewing measure)* apiece.

f. Jesus saith unto them, **Fill the waterpots with water.** And they filled them up to the brim. And he saith unto them, **Draw out now, and bear unto the governor of the feast.** And they bare it.

g. When the ruler of the feast had tasted the water that was made wine, and knew not whence it was: (but the servants which drew the water knew;) the governor of the feast called the bridegroom, And saith unto him, Every man at the beginning doeth set forth good wine; and when men have well drunk, then that which is worse: but thou hast kept the good wine until now.

h. This beginning of miracles did Jesus in Cana of Galilee, and manifested forth his glory; and his disciples believed on him.

i. After this he went down to Capernaum, he, and his mother, and his brethren, and his disciples; and they continued there not many days.

2-13. The first cleansing of the temple (1st passover after baptism, A.D. 28).

a. And the Jews' passover was at hand, and Jesus went up to Jerusalem. And found in the temple those that sold oxen and sheep and doves, and the changers of money sitting.

b. And when he had made a scourge of small cords, he drove them all out of the temple, and the sheep, and the oxen; and poured out the changers' money and overthrew the tables;

c. And said unto them that sold doves, **Take these things hence; make not my Father's house an house of merchandise.**

d. And his disciples remembered that it was written, The zeal of thine house hath eaten me up (Fulfilled Prophecy: *"For the zeal of thine house hath eaten me up; and the reproaches of them that reproached thee are fallen upon me."* Psalms 69:9).

e. Then answered the Jews and said unto him, What sign showest thou unto us, seeing that thou doest these things?

f. Jesus answered and said unto them, **Destroy this temple, and in three days I will raise it up.**

g. Then said the Jews, Forty and six years was this temple in building, and wilt thou rear it up in three days?

h. But he spake of the temple of his body. When therefore he was risen from the dead, his disciples remembered that he had said this unto them; and they believed the scripture, and the word which Jesus had said.

i. Now when he was in Jerusalem at the Passover, in the feast day, many believed in his name, when they saw the miracles which he did.

j. But Jesus did not commit himself unto them, because he knew all men. And needed not that any should testify of man: for he knew what was in man.

2-14. Nicodemus visits Jesus at night.

a. There was a man of the Pharisees, named Nicodemus, a ruler of the Jews: The same came to Jesus by night, and said unto him, Rabbi, we know that thou art a teacher come from God: for no man can do these miracles that thou doest, except God be with him.

b. Jesus answered and said unto him, **Verily, verily, I say unto thee, Except a man be born again, he cannot see the kingdom of God.**

c. Nicodemus saith unto him, How can a man be born when he is old? can he enter the second time into his mother's womb, and be born?

d. Jesus answered, **Verily, verily, I say unto thee, Except a man be born of water and of the Spirit, he cannot enter into the kingdom of God. That which is born of the flesh is flesh; and that which is born of the Spirit is spirit. Marvel not that I said unto thee, Ye must be born again.**

e. **The wind bloweth where it listeth, and thou hearest the sound thereof, but canst not tell whence it cometh, and whither it goeth: so is everyone that is born of the Spirit.**

f. Nicodemus answered and said unto him, How can these things be?

g. Jesus answered and said unto him, **Art thou a master of Israel, and knowest not these things?** Verily, verily, I say unto thee, We speak that we do know, and testify that we have seen; and ye receive not our witness. If I have told you earthly things, and ye believe not, how shall ye believe, If I tell you of heavenly things?

h. And no man hath ascended up to heaven, but he that came down from heaven, even the Son of man which is in heaven.

i. And as Moses lifted up the serpent in the wilderness, even so must the Son of man be lifted up: That whosoever believeth in him should not perish, but have eternal life.

j. For God so loved the world, that he gave his only begotten Son, that whosoever believeth in him should not perish, but have everlasting life.

k. For God sent not his Son into the world to condemn the world; but that the world through him might be saved.

l. He that believeth in him is not condemned: but he that believeth not is condemned already, because he hath not believed in the name of the only begotten Son of God.

m. And this is the condemnation, that light is come into the world, and men loved darkness rather than light, because their deeds were evil.

n. For every one that doeth evil hateth the light, neither cometh to the light, lest his deeds should be reproved.

o. But he that doeth truth cometh to the light, that his deeds may be made manifest, they that are wrought in God.

2-15. Jesus ministry in Judaea; John's testimony of Jesus Christ.

a. After these things came Jesus and his disciples into the land of Judaea; and there he tarried with them, and baptized.

b. And John also was baptizing in Aenon near to Salim, because there was much water there: and they came, and were baptized. For John was not yet cast into prison.

c. Then there arose a question between some of John's disciples and the Jews about purifying.

d. And they came unto John, and said unto him, Rabbi, he that was with thee beyond Jordan, to whom thou barest witness, behold, the same baptizeth, and all men come to him.

e. John answered and said, a man can receive nothing, except it be given him from heaven.

f. Ye yourselves bear me witness, that I said, I am not the Christ, but that I am sent before him.

g. He that hath the bride is the bridegroom: but the friend of the bridegroom, which standeth and heareth him, rejoiceth greatly because of the bridegroom's voice: this my joy therefore is fulfilled.

h. He must increase, but I must decrease. He that cometh from above is above all: he that is of the earth is earthly, and speaketh of the earth: he that cometh from heaven is above all.

i. And what he hath seen and heard, that he testifieth; and no man receiveth his testimony. He that hath receiveth his testimony hath set to his seal that God is true.

j. For he whom God hath sent speaketh the words of God: for God giveth not the Spirit by measure unto him.

k. The Father loveth the Son, and hath given all things into his hand. He that believeth on the Son hath everlasting life: and he that believeth not the Son shall not see life; but the wrath of God abideth on him.

l. When therefore the Lord knew how the Pharisees had heard that Jesus made and baptized more disciples than John, (Though Jesus himself baptizeth not, but his disciples,) He left Judaea, and departed again unto Galilee.

2-16. A woman of Samaria at Jacob's well.

a. And he must needs go through Samaria. Then cometh he to a city of Samaria, which is called Sychar, near to the parcel of ground that Jacob gave to his son Joseph. Now Jacob's well was there, Jesus therefore, being wearied with his journey, sat thus on the well: and it was about the sixth hour (*12:00 AM*).

b. There cometh a woman of Samaria to draw water: Jesus saith unto her, **Give me to drink.** (For his disciples were gone away unto the city to buy meat.).

c. Then saith the woman of Samaria unto him, How is it that thou, being a Jew, askest drink of me, which am a woman of Samaria? for the Jews have no dealing with the Samaritans.

d. Jesus answered and saith unto her, **If thou knewest the gift of God, and who it is that saith to thee, Give me to drink; thou wouldest have asked of him, and he would have given thee living water.**

e. The woman saith unto him, Sir, thou hast nothing to draw with, and the well is deep: from whence then hast thou that living water? Art thou greater than our father Jacob, which gave us the well, and drank thereof himself, and his children, and his cattle?

f. Jesus answered and saith unto her, **Whosoever drinketh of this water shall thirst again: But whosoever drinketh of the water that I shall give him shall never thirst; but the water that I shall give him shall be in him a well of water springing up into everlasting life.**

g. The woman saith unto him, Sir, give me this water, that I thirst not, neither come hither to draw.

h. Jesus saith unto her, **Go, call thy husband, and come hither.** The woman answered and said, I have no husband.

i. Jesus said unto her, **Thou hast well said, I have no husband: For thou hast had five husbands; and he whom thou now hast is not thy husband: in that saidst thou truly.**

j. The woman saith unto him, Sir, I perceive that thou art a prophet. Our fathers worshipped in this mountain; and ye say, that in Jerusalem is the place where men ought to worship.

k. Jesus saith unto her, **Woman, believe me, the hour cometh, when ye shall neither in this mountain, nor yet at Jerusalem, worship the Father. Ye worship ye know not what: we know what we worship: for salvation is of the Jews.**

l. **But the hour cometh, and now is, when the true worshippers shall worship the Father in spirit and in truth: for the Father seeketh such to worship him. God is a spirit: and they that worship him must worship him in spirit and in truth.**

m. The woman saith unto him, I know that Messias cometh, which is called Christ: when he is come, he will tell us all things. Jesus saith unto her, **I that speak unto thee am he.**

n. And upon this came his disciples, and marvelled that he talked with the woman: yet no man said, What seekest thou? Or, Why talkest thou with her?

o. The woman then left her waterpot, and went her way into the city, and saith to the men. Come, see a man, which told me all things that ever I did: is not this the Christ?

p. Then they went out of the city, and came unto him. In the mean while his disciples prayed him, saying, Master, eat.

q. But he said unto them, **I have meat to eat that ye know not of.** Therefore said the disciples one to another, Hath any man brought him ought to eat?

r. Jesus saith unto them, **My meat is to do the will of him that sent me, and to finish his work. Say not ye, There are yet four months, and then cometh harvest? behold, I say unto you, Lift up your eyes, and look on the fields; for they are white already to harvest.**

s. And he that reapeth receiveth wages, and gathered fruit until life eternal: that both he that soweth and he that reapeth may rejoice together.

t. And herein is that saying true, One soweth and another reapeth. I sent you to reap that whereon ye bestowed no labour: other men laboured, and ye are entered into their labours.

2-17. The Samaritans conversion.

a. And many of the Samaritans of that city believed on him for the saying of the woman, which testified, He told me all that ever I did.

b. So when the Samaritans were come unto him, they besought him that he would tarry with them: and he abode there two days.

c. And many more believed because of his own word; And said unto the woman, Now we believe, not because of thy saying: for we have heard him ourselves, and know that this is indeed the Christ, the Saviour of the world.

d. Now after two days he departed thence, and went into Galilee. For Jesus himself testified, that a prophet hath no honour in his own country.

e. Then when he was come into Galilee, the Galilaeans received him, having seen all the things that he did at Jerusalem at the feast: for they also went unto the feast.

2-18. The healings of the nobleman's son (Second miracle).

a. So Jesus came again into Cana of Galilee, where he made the water wine.

b. And there was a certain nobleman, whose son was sick at Capernaum. When he heard that Jesus was come out of Judaea into Galilee, he went unto him, and besought him that he would come down, and heal his son: for he was at the point of death.

c. Then said Jesus unto him, **except ye see signs and wonders, ye will not believe.** The nobleman saith unto him, Sir, come down ere (*before*) my child die.

d. Jesus saith unto him, **Go thy way; thy son liveth.** And the man believed the word that Jesus had spoken unto him, and he went his way (*It was the seventh hour*).

e. And as he was now going down, his servants met him (*a day later*), and told him, saying, Thy son liveth.

f. Then inquired he of them the hour when he began to amend. And they said unto him, Yesterday at the seventh hour the fever left him.

g. So the father knew that it was at the same hour, in the which Jesus said unto him, Thy son liveth: and himself believed, and his whole house.

h. This is again the second miracle that Jesus did, when he was come out of Judaea into Galilee.

2-19. John the Baptist cast into prison.

a. For John had said unto Herod, It is not lawful for thee to have thy brother's wife. Therefore Herodias had a quarrel against him, and would have killed him; but she could not.

b. For Herod feared John, knowing that he was a just man and an holy, and observed him; and when he had heard him, he did many things, and heard him gladly.

c. But Herod the tetrarch, being reproved by him for Herodias his brother Philip's wife, and for all the evils which Herod had done. Added yet this above all, that he shut up John in prison.

d. For Herod himself had sent forth and laid hold upon John, and bound him and shut up John in prison for Herodias sake, his brother Philip's wife: for he had married her.

e. And when he would have put him to death, he feared the multitude, because they counted him as a prophet.

2-20. Jesus heals on the Sabbath (2nd passover after baptism, A.D. 29).

a. After this there was a feast of the Jews; and Jesus went up to Jerusalem. Now there is at Jerusalem by the sheep market a pool, which is called in the Hebrew tongue Bethesda, having five porches.

b. In these lay a great multitude of impotent *(without the strength or power to do anything effective or helpful)* folk, of blind, halt, withered, waiting for the moving of the water.

c. For an angel went down at a certain season into the pool, and troubled the water: whosoever then first after the troubling of the water stepped in was made whole of whatsoever disease he had.

d. And a certain man was there, which had an infirmity thirty and eight years.

e. When Jesus saw him lie, and knew that he had been now a long time in that case, he saith unto him, **Wilt thou be made whole?**

f. The impotent man answered him, Sir, I have no man, when the water is troubled, to put me into the pool: but while I am coming, another steppeth down before me.

g. Jesus saith unto him, **Rise, take up thy bed, and walk.**

h. And immediately the man was made whole, and took up his bed, and walked: and on the same day was the sabbath.

i. The Jews therefore said unto him that was cured, It is the sabbath day: it is not lawful for thee to carry thy bed.

j. He answered them, He that made me whole, the same said unto me, Take up thy bed, and walk.

k. Then asked they him, What man is that which said unto thee, Take up thy bed, and walk?

l. And he that was healed wist not who it was: for Jesus had conveyed himself away, a multitude being in that place.

m. Afterward Jesus findeth him in the temple, and said unto him, **Behold, thou art made whole: sin no more, lest a worse thing come unto thee.**

n. The man departed, and told the Jews that it was Jesus, which had made him whole.

o. And therefore did the Jews persecute Jesus, and sought to slay him, because he had done these things on the sabbath day.

p. But Jesus answered them, **My Father worketh hitherto, and I work.**

q. Therefore the Jews sought the more to kill him, because he not only had broken the sabbath, but said also that God was his Father, making himself equal with God.

2-21. The Son's witness to the Father.

a. Then answered Jesus and said unto them, **Verily, verily, I say unto you, The Son can do nothing of himself, but what he seeth the Father do: for what things soever he doeth, these also doeth the Son likewise.**

b. **For the Father loveth the Son, and showeth him all things that himself doeth: and he will show him greater works than these, that ye may marvel. For as the Father raiseth up the dead, and quickened them; even so the Son quickened whom he will.**

c. **For the Father judgeth no man, but hath committed all judgment unto the Son. That all men should honour the Son, even as they honour the Father. He that honoureth not the Son honoureth not the Father which hath sent him.**

d. **Verily, verily, I say unto you, He that heareth my word, and believeth on him that sent me, hath everlasting life, and shall not come into condemnation; but is passed from death into life.**

e. **Verily, verily, I say unto you, The hour is coming, and now is, when the dead shall hear the voice of the Son of God: and they that hear shall live.**

f. For as the Father hath life in himself; so hath he given to the Son to have life in himself; And hath given him authority to execute judgment also, because he is the Son of man.

g. Marvel not at this: for the hour is coming, in the which all that are in the graves shall hear his voice. And shall come forth; they that have done good, unto the resurrection of life; and they that have done evil, unto the resurrection of damnation.

2-22. The Father's witness to the Son.

a. I can of mine own self do nothing: as I hear, I judge: and my judgment is just; because I seek not mine own will, but the will of the Father which hath sent me.

b. If I bear witness to myself, my witness is not true. There is another that beareth witness of me; and I know that the witness which he witnessed of me is true.

c. Ye sent unto John, and he bare witness unto the truth. But I receive not testimony from man, but these things I say, that ye might be saved. He was a burning and shining light: and ye were willing for a season to rejoice in his light.

d. But I have greater witness than that of John: for the works which the Father hath given me to finish, the same works that I do, bear witness of me, that the Father hath sent me. And the Father himself, which hath sent me, hath borne witness of me.

e. Ye have neither heard his voice at any time, nor seen his shape. And ye have not his word abiding in you: for whom he hath sent, him ye believe not.

f. Search the scriptures; for in them ye think ye have eternal life: and they are they which testify of me. And ye will not come to me, that ye might have life. I receive not honour from men.

g. But I know you, that ye have not the love of God in you. I am come in my Father's name, and ye receive me not: if another shall come in his own name, him ye will receive.

h. How can ye believe, which receive honour one of another, and seek not the honour that cometh from God only?

i. Do not think that I will accuse you to the Father: there is one that accuseth you, even Moses, in whom ye trust. For had ye believed Moses, ye would have believed me: for he wrote of me. But if ye believe not his writings, how shall ye believe my words?

The Combined Gospel of Jesus Christ

Chapter Three
Early Galilean Ministry

3-1. Jesus first rejection at Nazareth.

a. Now when Jesus had heard that John was cast into prison, he returned in the power of the Spirit into Galilee.

b. Jesus came into Galilee, preaching the gospel of he kingdom of God, and saying, **The time is fulfilled, and the kingdom of God is at hand: repent ye, and believe the gospel:** and there went out a fame of him through all the region round about.

c. And he taught in their synagogues, being glorified of all.

d. And he came to Nazareth where he had been brought up: and, as his custom was, he went into the synagogue on the sabbath day, and stood up for to read. And there was delivered unto him the book of the prophet Esaias (*by the minister*).

e. And when he had opened the book, he found the place where it was written **The Spirit of the Lord is upon me, because he hath anointed me to preach the gospel to the poor; he hath sent me to heal the brokenhearted, to preach deliverance to the captives, and recovering of sight to the blind, to set at liberty them that are bruised. To preach the acceptable year of the Lord** (*and then he stood up and started reading it*). And he closed the book, and he gave it again to the minister, and sat down.

f. And the eyes of all them that were in the synagogue were fastened on him.

g. And he began to say unto them, **This day is this scripture fulfilled in your ears** (Fulfilled Prophecy: *"The spirit of the Lord God is upon me; because the LORD hath anointed me to preach good tidings unto the meek; he hath sent me to bind up the brokenhearted, to proclaim liberty to the captives, and the opening of the prison to them that are bound; to proclaim the acceptable year of the LORD, and the day of vengeance of our God; to comfort all that mourn."* Isaiah 61:1-2).

h. And all bare witness, and wondered at the gracious words which proceeded out of his mouth. And they said, is not this Joseph's son?

i. And he said unto them, **ye will surely say unto me this proverb, Physician, heal thyself: whatsoever we have heard done in Capernaum, do also here in thy country.**

j. And he said, **Verily I say unto you, No prophet is accepted in his own country. But I tell you of a truth, many widows were in Israel in the days of Elias, when the heaven was shut up three years and six months, when great famine was throughout all the land; But unto none of them was Elias sent, save unto Sarepta, a city of Sidon, unto a woman that was a widow.**

k. **And many lepers were in Israel in the time of Eliseus the prophet; and none of them was cleansed, saving Naaman the Syrian.**

l. And all they in the synagogue, when they heard these things, were filled with wrath. And rose up, and thrust him out of the city, and led him, unto the brow *(top edge of a hill)* of the hill whereon their city was built, that they may cast him down headlong.

m. But he passing through the midst of them went his way.

3-2. Jesus departs Nazareth to Capernaum.

a. And leaving Nazareth, he came and dwelt in Capernaum, which is upon the sea coast, in the borders of Zabulon and Nephthalim.

b. That is might be fulfilled which was spoken by Esaias the prophet saying, the land of Zabulon, and the land of Nephthalim, by the way of the sea, beyond Jordan, Galilee of the Gentiles.

c. The people which sat in darkness saw great light; and to them which sat in the region and shadow of death light is sprung up (Fulfilled Prophecy: *"Nevertheless the dimness shall not be such as was in her vexation, when at the first he lightly afflicted the land of Zebulun and the land of Naphtali, and afterwards did more grievously afflict her by the way of the sea, beyond Jordan, in Galilee of the nations. The people that walked in darkness have seen a great light: they that dwell in the land of the shadow of death, upon them hath the light shined."* Isaiah 9:1-2).

d. From that time Jesus began to preach, and to say, **Repent: for the kingdom of heaven is at hand.**

3-3. Jesus calls four disciples.

a. Now as Jesus, walked by the sea of Galilee, he saw two brethren, Simon called Peter, and Andrew his brother, casting a net into the sea: for they were fishers.

b. And it came to pass, that, as the people pressed upon him to hear the word of God, he stood by the lake of Gennesaret, and saw two ships standing by the lake: but the fisherman were gone out of them, and were washing their nets.

c. And he entered into one of the ships, which was Simon's, and prayed him that he would thrust out a little from the land.

d. And he sat down, and taught the people out of the ship.

e. Now when he had left speaking, he said unto Simon, **Launch out into the deep, and let down your nets for a draught.**

f. And Simon answering said unto him, Master, we have toiled all the night, and have taken nothing: nevertheless at thy word I will let down the net.

g. And when they had this done, they inclosed a great multitude of fishes: and their net brake.

h. And they beckoned unto their partners, which were in the other ship, that they should come and help them.

i. And they came, and filled both the ships, so that they began to sink.

j. When Simon Peter saw it, he fell down at Jesus' knees, saying, Depart from me; for I am a sinful man, O Lord. For he was astonished, and all that were with him, at the draught of the fishes which they had taken.

k. And so was also James, and John, the sons of Zebedee, which were partners with Simon.

l. And Jesus said unto him, **Fear not; from henceforth thou shalt catch men.**

m. And when they had brought their ships to land, he saith unto them, **Follow me, and I will make you fishers of men.**

n. And they straightway left their nets, they forsook all, and followed him.

o. And going on from thence, he saw other two brethren, James the son of Zebedee, and John his brother, in a ship with Zebedee their father, mending their nets.

p. And straightway he called them and they immediately left the ship and their father with the hired servants and followed him.

q. And Jesus went about all Galilee, teaching in their synagogues, and preaching the gospel of the kingdom, and healing all manner of sickness and all manner of disease among the people.

r. And his fame went throughout all Syria: and they brought unto him all sick people that were taken with divers diseases and torments, and those which were possessed with devils, and those which were lunatick, and those that had the palsy; and he healed them.

s. And there followed him great multitudes of people from Galilee, and from Decapolis, and from Jerusalem, and from Judaea, and from beyond Jordan.

3-4. The unclean spirit cast out.

a. And they went into Capernaum a city of Galilee; and straightway on the sabbath day he entered into the synagogue, and taught.

b. And they were astonished at his doctrine: for his word was with power, he taught them as one that had authority, and not as the scribes.

c. And in the synagogue there was a man, which had a spirit of an unclean devil, and cried out with a loud voice. Saying, Let us alone; what have we to do with thee, thou Jesus of Nazareth? art thou come to destroy us? I know thee who thou art; the Holy One of God.

d. And Jesus rebuked (*to criticize or reprimand sharply*) him, saying, **Hold thy peace, and come out of him** (*this was the rebuke*).

e. And when the devil had torn him and thrown him in the midst, and cried with a loud voice, he came out of him, and hurt him not.

f. And they were all amazed, and spake among themselves, saying, What a word is this! for with authority and power he commandeth the unclean spirits, and they do obey him, and they come out.

g. And immediately his fame spread abroad throughout all the region round about Galilee.

3-5. Simon Peter's Mother in law healed; devils cast out.

a. And he arose out of the synagogue, and entered into Simon's Peter and Andrew house, with James and John.

b. And Simon's wife mother lay sick with a great fever; and they besought him for her.

c. And he came and stood over her, and rebuked the fever; and took her by the hand, and lifted her up; and immediately the fever left her, and she arose, and ministered unto him.

d. Now at even when the sun was setting, they brought unto him all that were diseased, and them that were possessed with devils; And all the city was gathered together at the door and he laid his hands on every one of them, and healed many that were sick of diver diseases, and cast out many devils.

e. He cast out the spirits with his word and devils also came out of many, crying out, and saying, Thou art Christ the Son of God.

f. And he rebuking them suffered them not to speak: for they knew that he was Christ.

g. That it might be fulfilled which was spoken by Esaias the prophet, saying, himself took our infirmities, and bare our sickness (Fulfilled Prophecy: *"Surely he hath borne our griefs, and carried our sorrows: yet we did esteem him stricken, smitten of God, and afflicted."* Isaiah 53:4).

3-6. Jesus preach in Galilee.

a. And in the morning, rising up a great while before day, he went out, and departed into a solitary place, and there prayed.

b. And Simon and they that were with him followed after him.

c. And when they had found him, they said unto him, All men seek for thee; When he was come down from the mountain, great multitudes followed him.

d. And the people sought him and came unto him, and stayed him, that he should not depart from them.

e. And he said unto them (*the people*), **I must preach the kingdom of God to other cities also, for therefore am I sent.**

f. And he said unto them (*the disciples*), **Let us go into the next towns, that I may preach there also: for therefore came I forth.**

g. And he preached in their synagogues throughout all Galilee, and cast out devils.

3-7. The leper cleansed.

a. And it came to pass, when he was in a certain city (*in Galilee*) there came a leper to him, full of leprosy, beseeching him, and kneeling down to him, and fell on his face and worshipped him, saying unto him, Lord, If thou wilt, thou canst make me clean.

b. And Jesus, moved with compassion, put forth his hand, and touched him, and saith unto him, **I will; be thou clean.** And as soon as he had spoken, immediately the leprosy departed from him, and he was cleansed.

c. And he straitly charged him, and saith unto him, **See thou say nothing to any man: but go thy way, show thyself to the priest, and offer for thy cleansing those things which Moses commanded, for a testimony unto them;** and forthwith sent him away.

d. But he went out, and began to publish it much, and to blaze abroad the matter, insomuch that Jesus could no more openly enter into the city, but was without in desert places: and great multitudes came together to him from every quarter to hear, and to be healed by him of their infirmities.

e. And he withdrew himself into the wilderness, and prayed.

3-8. A man with palsy healed.

a. And he entered into a ship, and passed over, and came into his own city.

b. And again he entered into Capernaum after some days; and it was noised that he was in the house.

c. And it came to pass on a certain day, as he was teaching, that there were Pharisees and doctors of the law sitting by, which were come out of every town of Galilee, and Judaea, and Jerusalem: many were gathered together, insomuch that there was no room to receive them, no, not so much as about the door: and he preached the word unto them, and the power of the Lord was present to heal them.

d. And, behold, men brought in a bed, a man which was taken with a palsy, which was borne of four (*the bed supported by four men*): and they sought means to bring him in, and to lay him before him. (Controversy: Luke 5:24 *said it was a couch*. Matthew 9:6 and Mark 2:11-12 *said it was a bed, therefore, I went with a bed (Luke 5:18 said a bed)*).

e. And when they could not find by what way they might bring him in because of the multitude, they went upon the housetop and uncovered the roof where he was: and when they had broken it up, they let him down through the tiling with the bed, wherein the sick of the palsy lay, into the midst, before Jesus.

f. And when he saw their faith, he said unto the sick of the palsy; **son be of good cheer; thy sins be forgiven thee.**

g. And the scribes and the Pharisees began to reason in their hearts, saying, This man blasphemeth, Why do this man thus speaketh blasphemies? Who can forgive sins, but God only?

h. And immediately when Jesus perceived their thoughts in his spirit, that they so reasoned within themselves, he said unto them, **Wherefore think ye evil in your hearts? Why reason ye these things in your hearts? Whether is easier to say to the sick of the palsy, Thy sins be forgiven thee; or to say, Arise and take up thy bed, and walk?**

i. **But that ye may know that the Son of man hath power upon earth to forgive sins, (then saith he to the sick of the palsy,) I say unto thee, Arise, and take up thy bed, and go thy way into thine own house.**

j. And immediately he arose before them, took up the bed whereon he lay, and went forth before them all, and departed to his own house, glorifying God.

k. But when the multitudes saw it, they were all amazed, and they glorified God, which had given such power unto men and were filled with fear, saying, we never saw it on this fashion, we have seen strange things to day.

3-9. Matthew called; The feast at Matthew house.

a. And he went forth again by the sea side; and all the multitude resorted unto him, and he taught them.

b. And as Jesus passed forth from thence, he saw a publican, Levi the son of Alphaeus sitting at the receipt of custom named Matthew, and he said unto him, **Follow me.** And he left all, rose up, and followed him.

c. And Levi made him a great feast in his own house: And it came to pass, as Jesus sat at meat in the house, behold, a great company of publicans and sinners came and sat down also together with him and his disciples; for they were many, and they followed him.

d. And when the scribes and Pharisees saw him eat with publicans and sinners, they said unto his disciples, Why eateth you and your Master with publicans and sinners?

e. But when Jesus heard that, he said unto them, **They that are whole have no need of the physician, but they that are sick.**

f. **But go ye and learn what that meaneth, I will have mercy, and not sacrifice: for I am not come to call the righteous, but sinners to repentance.**

3-10. The Parable of new cloth and new wine.

a. Then came to him the disciples of John, saying, Why do we and likewise the disciples of the Pharisees fast often and make prayers, but thy disciples fast not?

b. And Jesus said unto them, **Can the children of the bridechamber fast while the bridegroom is with them? as long as they have the bridegroom with them, they cannot fast.**

c. **But the days will come, when the bridegroom shall be taken from them, and then shall they fast in those days.**

d. And he spoke also a parable unto them; **No man also seweth a piece of new cloth on an old garment, else the new piece that filled it up taketh away from the old, and the rent is made worse.**

e. **And no man putteth new wine into old bottles: else the new wine will burst the bottles, and be spilled, and the bottles shall perish.**

f. **But new wine must be put into new bottles; and both are preserved. No man also having drunk old wine straightway desireth new: for he saith, The old is better.**

3-11. Jesus the Lord of the Sabbath.

a. And it came to pass on the second sabbath after the first, that Jesus went on the sabbath day through the corn fields; and his disciples were an hungered, and began to pluck the ears of corn, and to eat; rubbing them in their hands.

b. But when the Pharisees saw it, they said unto him, Behold, thy disciples do that which is not lawful to do upon the sabbath day.

c. But he said unto them, **Have ye not read what David did, when he was an hungered, and they that were with him; How he entered into the house of God in the days of Abiathar the high priest, and did eat the showbread, and gave also to them which were with him; which was not lawful for him to eat, neither for them that were with him, but only for the priests?**

d. **Or have ye not read in the law, how that on the sabbath days the priests in the temple profane** (*to treat something sacred with disrespect*) **the sabbath, and are blameless? But I say unto you, That in this place is one greater than the temple.**

e. **But if ye had known what this meaneth, I will have mercy, and not sacrifice, ye would not have condemned the guiltless.**

f. And he said unto them, **The sabbath was made for man, and not man for the sabbath. Therefore the Son of man is Lord even of the sabbath day.**

3-12. Jesus heals the man withered hand.

a. And when he was departed thence, he entered again into their synagogue and taught: And, behold, there was a man which had his hand withered.

b. And the scribes and the Pharisees watched him, whether he would heal him on the sabbath day; that they might find an accusation against him.

c. But he knew their thoughts, and said to the man which had the withered hand, **Rise up, and stand forth in the midst.** And he arose and stood forth.

d. And they asked him, saying, Is it lawful to heal on the sabbath days? That they might accuse him.

e. And he said unto them, **What man shall there be among you, that shall have one sheep, and if it fall into a pit on the sabbath day, will he not lay hold on it, and lift it out. How much then is a man better than a sheep? Wherefore it is lawful to do well on the sabbath days.**

f. Then said Jesus unto them, **I will ask you one thing; Is it lawful on the sabbath days to do good, or to do evil? to save life or to destroy it?** But they held their peace.

g. And when he had look round about upon them all with anger, being grieved for the hardness of hearts.

h. Then saith he to the man, **Stretch forth thine hand.** And he stretched it forth; and it was restored whole, like as the other.

i. And they were filled with madness; and communed one with another what they might do to Jesus.

j. Then the Pharisees went forth, and straightway held a council with the Herodians against him, how they might destroy him.

3-13. Jesus heals many by the sea.

a. But when Jesus knew it, he withdrew himself from thence with his disciples to the sea: and a great multitude, when they had heard what great things he did, followed him from Galilee, and from Judaea, and from Jerusalem, and from Idumaea, and from beyond Jordan; and they about Tyre and Sidon,

b. And he healed them all; and charged them that they should not make him known.

c. That it might be fulfilled which was spoken by Esaias the prophet, saying, Behold my servant, whom I have chosen; my beloved, in whom my soul is well pleased: I will put my spirit upon him, and he shall show judgment to the Gentiles. He shall not strive, nor cry; neither shall any man hear his voice in the streets. A bruised reed shall he not break, and smoking flax shall he not quench, till he send forth judgment unto victory. And in his name shall the Gentiles trust (Fulfilled Prophecy: *"Behold my servant, whom I uphold; mine elect, in whom my soul delighteth; I have put my spirit upon him: he shall bring forth judgment to the Gentiles. He shall not cry, nor lift up, nor cause his voice to be heard in the street. A bruised reed shall he not break, and the smoking flax shall he not quench: he shall bring forth judgment unto truth."* Isaiah 42:1-3.).

d. And he spake to his disciples, that a small ship should wait on him because of the multitude, lest they should throng him.

e. For he had healed many; insomuch that they pressed upon him for to touch him, as many as had plagues.

f. And unclean spirits, when they saw him, fell down before him, and cried, saying, Thou art the Son of God.

g. And he straitly charged them that they should not make him known.

3-14. The chosen twelve.

a. And it came to pass in those days, that he went out into a mountain to pray, and continued all night in prayer to God.

b. And when it was day, he called unto him his disciples: and they came unto him: and of them he chose twelve to ordain, whom also he named apostles; that they should be with him, and that he might send them forth to preach.

c. He gave them power against unclean spirits, to cast them out, and to heal all manner of sickness and all manner of disease.

d. Now the names of the twelve apostles are these; The first, Simon, (whom he also surnamed Peter,) and Andrew his brother; James the son of Zebedee, and John his brother; and he surnamed them Boanerges, which is, The sons of thunder; and Philip, and Bartholomew; Thomas, and Matthew the publican; James the son of Alphaeus, and Labbaeus, whose surname was Thaddaeus called Judas the brother of James; Simon the Canaanite called Zelotes, and Judas Iscariot, who also betrayed him:

e. And they went into an house. And the multitude cometh together again, so that they could not so much as eat bread.

3-15. The beatitudes.

a. And he came down with them, and stood in the plain, and the company of his disciples, and a great multitude of people out of all Judaea and Jerusalem, and from the sea coast of Tyre and Sidon, which came to hear him, and to be healed of their diseases; And they were vexed with unclean spirits: and they were healed.

b. And the whole multitude sought to touch him: for there went virtue out of him, and healed them all.

c. And seeing the multitude, he went up into a mountain: and when he was set, his disciples came unto him:

d. And he lifted up his eyes on his disciples, and he opened his mouth, and taught them, saying, **Blessed are the poor in spirit: for their's is the kingdom of heaven.**

e. **Blessed are they that mourn: for they shall be comforted. Blessed are ye that weep now: for ye shall laugh.**

f. **Blessed are the meek** *(those who showing mildness or quietness of nature)*, **for they shall inherit the earth.**

g. **Blessed are they which do hunger and thirst after righteousness: for they shall be filled.**

h. **Blessed are the merciful: for they shall obtain mercy.**

i. **Blessed are the pure in heart: for they shall see God.**

j. **Blessed are the peacemakers: for they shall be called the children of God.**

k. Blessed are they which are persecuted for righteousness' sake: for their's is the kingdom of heaven.

l. Blessed are ye, when men shall hate you, and when they shall separate you from their company, and shall reproach you, and cast out your name as evil, and persecute you, and shall say all manner of evil against you falsely, for the Son of man's sake.

m. Rejoice ye, and be exceeding glad in that day and leap for joy, for great is your reward in heaven: for so persecuted their fathers the prophets which were before you.

n. But woe unto you that are rich! for ye have receive your consolation.

o. Woe unto you that are full! for ye shall hunger.

p. Woe unto you that laugh now! for ye shall mourn and weep.

q. Woe unto you, when all men shall speak well of you! for so did their fathers to the false prophets.

3-16. The law of love.

a. But I say unto you which hear, Love your enemies, do good to them which hate you, Bless them that curse you, and pray for them which despitefully use you.

b. And unto him that smiteth thee on the one cheek offer also the other; and him that taketh away thy cloak (outer garment) forbid not to take thy coat also.

c. Give to every man that asketh of thee; and of him that taketh away thy goods ask them not again.

d. And as ye would that men should do to you, do ye also to them likewise.

e. For if ye love them which love you, what thank have ye? For sinner also love those that love them.

f. And if ye do good to them which do good to you, what thank have ye? For sinners also do even the same.

g. And if ye lend to them of whom ye hope to receive, what thank have ye? for sinners also lend to sinners, to receive as much again.

h. But love ye your enemies, and do good, and lend, hoping for nothing again; and your reward shall be great, and ye shall be the children of the Highest; for he is kind unto the unthankful and to the evil. Be ye therefore merciful, as your Father also is merciful.

3-17. Judging others.

a. Judge not, and ye shall not be judged. For with what judgment ye judge, ye shall be judged: and what measure ye mete, it shall be measured to you again.

b. Condemn not, and ye shall not be condemned: forgive, and ye shall be forgiven.

c. Give, and it shall be given unto you; good measure, pressed down, and shaken together, and running over, shall men give into your bosom. For with the same measure that ye mete withal it shall be measured to you again.

d. And he spake a parable unto them, **Can the blind lead the blind? shall they not both fall into the ditch?**

e. The disciple is not above his master: but everyone that is perfect shall be as his master.

f. And why beholdest thou the mote that is in thy brother's eye, but considerest not the beam that is in thine own eye?

g. Either how canst thou say to thy brother, Brother, let me pull out the mote that is in thine eye, when thou thyself beholdest not the beam that is in thine own eye? Thou hypocrite, cast out first the beam out of thine own eye, and then shalt thou see clearly to pull out the mote that is in thy brother's eye.

h. Give not that which is holy unto the dogs, neither cast ye your pearls before swine, lest they trample them under their feet, and turn again and rend you.

3-18. The wise and foolish builders.

a. And why call ye me, Lord, Lord, and do not the things which I say? Therefore whosoever cometh to me, and heareth these sayings of mine, and doeth them, I will liken him unto a wise man, which built his house and digged deep, and laid the foundation on a rock.

b. And the rain descended, and when the flood arose, the stream beat vehemently (*done forcefully*) upon that house, and could not shake it; and the winds blew, and beat upon that house; and it fell not: for it was founded upon a rock.

c. And every one that heareth these sayings of mine, and doeth them not, shall be likened unto a foolish man, that without a foundation built an house upon the earth.

d. And the rains descended, and the floods came, and the winds blew, and beat upon that house; against which the streams did beat vehemently, and immediately it fell; and great was the fall and the ruin of that house.

e. And it came to pass, when Jesus had ended these sayings, the people were astonished at his doctrine: For he taught them as one having authority and not as the scribes.

3-19. Teaching about salt and light.

a. **Ye are the salt of the earth: but if the salt has lost his savour, wherewith shall it be salted? It is henceforth good for nothing, but to be cast out, and to be trodden under foot of men.**

b. **Ye are the light of the world.**

c. **A city that is set on the hill cannot be hid. Neither do men light a candle, and put it under a bushel, but on a candlestick; and it giveth light unto all that are in the house.**

d. **Let your light so shine before men, that they may see your good works, and glorify your Father which is in heaven.**

3-20. The higher righteousness.

a. **Think not that I come to destroy the law, or the prophets: I am not come to destroy, but to fulfil. For verily I say unto you, Till heaven and earth pass, one jot or one tittle shall in no wise pass from the law, till all be fulfilled.**

b. **Whosoever therefore shall break one of these least commandments, and shall teach men so, he shall be called the least in the kingdom of heaven: but whosoever shall do and teach them, the same shall be called great in the kingdom of heaven.**

c. **For I say unto you, That except your righteousness shall exceed the righteousness of the scribes and Pharisees, ye shall in no case enter into the kingdom of heaven.**

3-21. Anger and reconciliation.

a. Ye have heard that it was said by them of old time, Thou shalt not kill; and whosoever shall kill shall be in danger of the judgment: But I say unto you, That whosoever is angry with his brother without a cause shall be in danger of the judgment: and whosoever shall say to his brother, Raca, shall be in danger of the council: but whosoever shall say, Thou fool, shall be in danger of hell fire.

b. Therefore if thou bring thy gift to the altar, and there rememberest that thou brother hath ought against thee; Leave there thy gift before the altar, and go thy way; first be reconciled to thy brother, and then come and offer thy gift.

c. Agree with thine adversary quickly, whiles thou art in the way with him; lest at any time the adversary deliver thee to the judge, and the judge deliver thee to the officer, and thou be cast into prison.

d. Verily, I say unto thee, Thou shalt by no means come out thence, till thou hast paid the uttermost farthing.

3-22. Adultery and divorce.

a. Ye have heard that it was said by them of old time, Thou shalt not commit adultery: But I say unto you, That whosoever looketh on a woman to lust after her hath committed adultery with her already in his heart.

b. And if thy right eye offend thee, pluck it out, and cast it from thee: for it is profitable for thee that one of thy members should perish, and not that thy whole body should be cast into hell.

c. And if thy right hand offend thee, cut it off, and cast it from thee: for it is profitable for thee that one of thy members should perish, and not that thy whole body should be cast into hell.

d. It hath been said, Whosoever shall put away his wife, let him give her a writing of divorcement. But I say unto you, That whosoever shall put away his wife, and married another committeth adultery: saving for the cause of fornication, causeth her to commit adultery: and whosoever shall marry her that is divorced committeth adultery.

3-23. Oaths and retaliation.

a. Again, ye have heard that it hath been said by them of old time, Thou shalt not forswear thyself, but shalt perform under the Lord thine oaths: But I say unto you, Swear not at all; neither by heaven; for it is God's throne: Nor by the earth; for it is his footstool: neither by Jerusalem; for it is the city of the great King. Neither shalt thou swear by thy head, because thou canst not make one hair white or black.

b. But let your communication be, Yea, yea; Nay, nay: for whatsoever is more than these cometh of evil.

c. Ye have heard that it hath been said, An eye for an eye, and a tooth for a tooth: But I say unto you, That ye resist not evil: but whosoever shall smite thee on the right cheek, turn to him the other also.

d. And if any man will sue thee at the law, and take away thy coat, let him have thy cloak also. And whosoever shall compel thee to go a mile, go with him twain. Give to him that asketh thee, and from him that would borrow of thee turn not thou away.

3-24. Neighbors and enemies.

a. Ye have heard that it hath been said, Thou shalt love thy neighbor, and hate thine enemy. But I say unto you, Love your enemies, bless them that curse you, do good to them that hate you, and pray for them which despitefully use you, and persecute you: That ye maybe the children of your Father which is in heaven: for he maketh his sun to rise on the evil and on the good, and sendeth rain on the just and on the unjust.

b. For if ye love them which love you, what reward have ye? do not even the publicans the same?

c. And if ye salute your brethren only, what do ye more than others? do not even the publicans so?

d. Be ye therefore perfect, even as your Father which is in heaven is perfect.

3-25. Almsgiving in secret.

a. Take heed that ye do not your alms (*charitable donations*) before men, to be seen of them: otherwise ye have no reward of your Father which is in heaven.

b. Therefore when thou doest thine alms, do not sound a trumpet before thee, as the hypocrites do in the synagogues and in the streets, that they may have glory of men, Verily I say unto you, They have their reward.

c. But when thou doest alms, let not thy left hand know what thy right hand doeth. That thine alms may be in secret: and thy Father which seeth in secret himself shall reward thee openly.

The Combined Gospel of Jesus Christ

Chapter Four
Middle Galilean Ministry

4-1. The demoniac and blind healed; The Pharisees slander.

a. Then was brought unto him one possessed with a devil, blind, and dumb: and he healed him, insomuch that the blind and dumb both spake and saw.

b. And it came to pass, when the devil was gone out, and all the people were amazed, and said, is not this the son of David?

c. And when his friends heard of it, they went out to lay hold on him: for they said, He is beside himself.

d. And others, tempting him, sought of him a sign from heaven.

e. But when the Pharisees and the scribes which came down from Jerusalem heard it, they said, This fellow doth not cast out devils, but by Beelzebub the prince of the devils casteth he out devils. He hath an unclean spirit.

f. And Jesus knew their thoughts, and he called them unto him, and said unto them in parables, **Every kingdom divided against itself is brought to desolation; and every city or house divided against itself shall not stand:**

g. **And if Satan cast out Satan, he is divided against himself; how shall then his kingdom stand? but hath an end.**

h. **And if I by Beelzebub cast out devils, by whom do your children cast them out? therefore, they shall be your judges.**

i. But if I cast out devils by the Spirit of God, then the Kingdom of God is come unto you.

j. When a strong man armed keepeth his place, his goods are in peace: But when a stronger than he shall come upon him, and overcome him, he taketh from him all his armour wherein he trusted, and divideth his spoils.

k. Or else how can one enter into a strong man's house, and spoil his goods, except he first bind the strong man? And then he will spoil his house.

l. He that is not with me is against me; and he that gathered not with me scattered abroad.

m. When the unclean spirit is gone out of a man, he walketh through dry places, seeking rest; and finding none, he saith, I will return unto my house whence I came out.

n. And when he cometh, he findeth it swept and garnished.

o. Then goeth he, and taketh to him seven other spirits more wicked than himself; and they enter in, and dwell there: and the last state of that man is worst than the first.

p. Wherefore I say unto you, All manner of sin and blasphemy shall be forgiven unto men: but the blasphemy against the Holy Ghost shall not be forgiven unto men.

q. And whosoever speaketh a word against the Son of man, it shall be forgiven him: but whosoever speaketh against the Holy Ghost, it shall not be forgiven him, neither in this world, neither in the world to come, but is in danger of eternal damnation.

r. Either make the tree good, and his fruit good; or else make the tree corrupt, and his fruit corrupt: for the tree is known by his fruit.

s. O generation of vipers, how can ye, being evil, speak good things? For out of the abundance of the heart the mouth speaketh.

t. A good man out of the good treasure of the heart bringeth forth good things: and an evil man out of the evil treasure bringeth forth evil things.

u. But I say unto you, That every idle word that men shall speak, they shall give account thereof in the day of judgment.

v. For by thy words thou shalt be justified, and by thy words thou shalt be condemned.

w. And it came to pass, as he spake these things, a certain woman of the company lifted up her voice, and said unto him, Blessed is the womb that bare thee, and the paps which thou hast sucked.

x. But he said, Yea rather, blessed are they that hear the word of God, and keep it.

4-2. Jesus' true family; Visit of his mother and brother.

a. While he yet talked to the people, behold his mother and his brethren came, and, stood without, desiring to speak with him, and could not come at him for the press, sent unto him, calling him.

b. And the multitude sat about him, and, then one said unto him, Behold, thy mother and thy brethren stand without, desiring to speak with thee.

c. But he answered and said unto him that told him, saying, Who is my mother, and who are my brethren?

d. And he looked around about on them which sat about him, and he stretched forth his hand toward his disciples, and said, Behold my mother and my brethren!

e. For whosoever shall hear and do the will of my Father which is in heaven, the same is my brother, and my sister, and mother.

4-3. The parable of the sower.

a. And it came to pass afterward, that he went throughout every city and village, preaching and showing the glad tidings of the kingdom of God: and the twelve were with him.

b. And certain women, which had been healed of evil spirits and infirmities, Mary called Magdalene, out of whom went seven devils, And Joanna the wife of Chuza Herod's steward, and Susanna, and many others, which ministered unto him of their substance.

c. The same day went Jesus out of the house and sat by the sea side and he began again to teach.

d. And great multitudes were gathered together, and were come to him out of every city, so that he went into a ship, and sat in the sea; and the whole multitude stood on the shore.

e. And he taught many things unto them in parables, and said unto them in his doctrine.

f. **Hearken; behold, a sower went forth to sow. And when he sowed, some seeds fell by the way side; and it was trodden down, and the fowls came and devoured them up.**

g. **Some fell upon stony places, where they had not much earth: and forthwith they sprung up, because they had no deepness of earth. And when the sun was up, they were scorched; and because they had no root, they withered away, because it lacked moisture.**

h. **And some fell among thorns, and the thorns grew up, and choked it, and it yielded no fruit.**

i. **But other fell into good ground, and brought forth fruit, some an hundredfold, some sixty fold, some thirty fold.**

j. And when he had said these things, he cried, **he that hath ears to hear, let him hear.**

k. And when he was alone the disciples came, and said unto him, Why speakest thou unto them in parables? What might this parable be?

l. He answered and said unto them, **Because it is given unto you to know the mysteries of the kingdom of heaven, but to others in parables.**

m. **For whosoever hath, to him shall be given, and he shall have more abundance: but whosoever hath not, from him shall be taken away even that he hath.**

n. **Therefore speak I to them in parables: That seeing they may see, and not perceive; and hearing they may hear, and not understand; lest at any time they should be converted, and their sins should be forgiven them.**

o. And he said unto them, **know ye not this parable? And how then will ye know all parables?**

p. **And in them is fulfilled the prophecy of Esaias, which saith, By hearing ye shall hear, and shall not understand; and seeing ye shall see, and shall not perceive:** (Fulfilled Prophecy: *"And he said, Go, and tell this people, Hear ye indeed, but understand not; and see ye indeed, but perceive not."* Isaiah 6:9).

q. **For this people's heart is waxed gross, and their ears are dull of hearing, and their eyes they have closed; lest at any time they should see with their eyes, and hear with their ears, and should understand with their heart, and should be converted, and I should heal them.**

r. **But blessed are your eyes, for they see: and your ears, for they hear. For verily I say unto you, That many prophets and righteous men have desired to see those things which ye see, and have not seen them; and to hear those things which ye hear, and have not heard them.**

s. Hear ye therefore the parable of the sower. Now the parable is this: The seed is the word of God. Those by the way side are they that heareth the word of the kingdom, and understand it not, then Satan come immediately, and taketh away the word that was sown in their hearts, lest they should believe and be saved.

t. But he that received the seed into stony places, the same is he that heareth the word, and immediately receive it with gladness; Yet hath he not root in himself, which for a while believe, and so endure but for a time: afterwards, when affliction or persecution ariseth for the word's sake, by and by he is offended, and in time of temptation fall away.

u. He also that received seed among the thorns is he that heareth the word; go forth and are choked with cares and riches and pleasures of this world and he becometh unfruitful, and bring no fruit to perfection.

v. But he that received seed into the good ground is he that heareth the word, and understand it and keep it. Which also beareth fruit, and bringeth forth fruit with patience, some thirtyfold, some sixty, and some an hundred.

w. No man, when he hath lighted a candle, covereth it with a vessel, or putteth it under a bushel, or under a bed; but setteth it on a candlestick, that they which enter in may see the light.

x. For nothing is secret, that shall not be made manifest, neither any thing hid, that shall not be known and come abroad. If any man have ears to hear, let him hear.

y. And he said unto them, Take heed what ye hear: with what measure ye mete, it shall be measured to you: and unto you that hear shall more be given.

z. For he that hath, to him shall be given: and he that hath not, from him shall be taken, even that which he hath.

4-4. The parables about the Kingdom.

a. And he said, So is the kingdom of God, as if a man should cast seed into the ground; And should sleep, and rise night and day, and the seed should spring and grow up, he knoweth not how.

b. For the earth bringeth forth fruit of herself; first the blade, then the ear, after that the full corn in the ear.

c. But when the fruit is brought forth, immediately he putteth in the sickle, because the harvest is come.

d. Another parable put he forth unto them, saying, The kingdom of heaven is likened unto a man which sowed good seed in his field: But while men slept, his enemy came and sowed tares among the wheat, and went his way.

e. But when the blade was sprung up, and brought forth fruit, then appeared the tares also.

f. So the servants of the householder came and said unto him, Sir, didst not thou sow good seed in thy field? From whence then hath it tares?

g. He said unto them, An enemy hath done this.

h. The servants said unto him, wilt thou then that we go and gather them up?

i. But he said, Nay; lest while ye gather up the tares, ye root up also the wheat with them.

j. Let both grow together until the harvest: and in the time of harvest I will say to the reapers, Gather ye together first the tares, and bind them in bundles to burn them: but gather the wheat into my barn.

k. Another parable put he forth unto them, saying, **Whereunto shall we liken the kingdom of God? or with what comparison shall we compare it? The kingdom of heaven is like to a grain of mustard seed, which a man took, and sowed in his field:**

l. **Which indeed is the least of all seeds: but when it is grown, it is the greatest among herbs, and shooteth out great branches; and becometh a great tree, so that the birds of the air come under the shadow of it, and lodge in the branches thereof.**

m. And again he said, **whereunto shall I liken the kingdom of God.** Another parable spake he unto them; **The kingdom of heaven is like unto leaven, which a woman took, and hid in three measures of meal, till the whole was leavened.**

n. All these things spake Jesus unto the multitude in parables, as they were able to hear it; and without a parable spake he not unto them: That it might be fulfilled which was spoken by the prophet saying, I will open my mouth in parables; I will utter things which have been kept secret from the foundation of the world. (Fulfilled Prophecy: *"Then said I, Ah Lord GOD! they say of me, Doth he not speak parables?"* Ezekiel 20:49). And when they were alone, he expounded all things to his disciples.

4-5. The parables of the sower and tares explained.

a. Then Jesus sent the multitude away, and went into the house: and his disciples came unto him, saying, Declare unto us the parable of the tares of the field.

b. He answered and said unto them, **He that soweth the good seed is the Son of man.**

c. **The field is the world; the good seed are the children of the kingdom; but the tares are the children of the wicked one.**

d. The enemy that sowed them is the devil; the harvest is the end of the world; and the reapers are the angel.

e. As therefore the tares are gathered and burned in the fire; so shall it be in the end of this world.

f. The Son of man shall send forth his angels, and they shall gather out of his kingdom all things that offend, and them which do iniquity; And shall cast them into a furnace of fire: there shall be wailing and gnashing of teeth.

g. Then shall the righteous shine forth as the sun in the kingdom of their Father. Who hath ears to hear, let him hear.

4-6. Further parables of the kingdom.

a. Again, the kingdom of heaven is like unto treasure hid in a field; the which when a man hath found, he hideth, and for joy thereof goeth and selleth all that he hath, and buyeth that field.

b. Again, the kingdom is like unto a merchant man, seeking goodly pearls: Who, when he had found one pearl of great price, went and sold all that he had, and bought it.

c. Again, the kingdom of heaven is like unto a net, that was cast into the sea, and gathered of every kind: Which, when it was full, they drew to shore, and sat down, and gathered the good into vessels, but cast the bad away.

d. So shall it be at the end of the world: the angels shall come forth, and sever the wicked from among the just.

e. And shall cast them into the furnace of fire: there shall be wailing and gnashing of teeth.

f. Jesus saith unto them, **Have ye understood all these things?** They say unto him, Yea, Lord.

g. Then said he unto them, **Therefore every scribe which is instructed unto the kingdom of heaven is like unto a man that is an householder, which bringeth forth out of his treasure things new and old.**

4-7. Jesus second rejection at Nazareth.

a. And it came to pass, that when Jesus had finished these parables, he departed thence into his own country; and his disciples follow him.

b. And when the sabbath was come, he began to teach in the synagogue: and many hearing him were astonished, saying, From whence hath this man these things?

c. And what wisdom is this which is given unto him, that even such mighty works are wrought by his hands?

d. Is not this the carpenter's son? Is not his mother called Mary? And his brethren, James, and Joses, and Simon, and Judas? And his sisters, are they not all with us? Whence then hath this man all these things? And they were offended in him.

e. But Jesus said unto them, **A prophet is not without honour, but in his own country, and among his own kin and in his own house.**

f. And he could there do no mighty works, because of their unbelief, save that he laid his hands upon a few sick folk, and healed them.

g. And he marvelled because of their unbelief. And he went round about the villages, teaching.

4-8. The centurion servant healed.

    a. Now when he had ended all his sayings in the audience of the people, he entered into Capernaum.

    b. And a certain centurion's servant, who was dear unto him, was sick, and ready to die.

    c. And when he heard of Jesus, he sent unto him the elders of the Jews, beseeching him that he would come and heal his servant.

    d. And when they came to Jesus, they besought him instantly, saying, that he was worthy for whom he should do this: For he loveth our nation, and he hath built us a synagogue. Then Jesus went with them.

    e. And when he was now not far from the house, the centurion sent friends to him, saying unto him, Lord, trouble not thyself: for I am not worthy that thou shouldest enter under my roof.

    f. There came unto him a centurion, beseeching him, Wherefore neither thought I myself worthy to come unto thee: And saying, Lord, my servant lieth at home sick of the palsy, grievously tormented.

    g. And Jesus saith unto him, **I will come and heal him.**

    h. The centurion answered and said, Lord, I am not worthy that thou shouldest come under my roof: but speak the word only, and my servant shall be healed.

    i. For I also am a man set under authority, having soldiers under me, and I say unto this man, Go, and he goeth; and to another, Come, and he cometh; and to my servant, Do this, and he doeth it.

    j. When Jesus heard these things, he marvelled at him, and turned him about, and said unto the people that followed him, **Verily I say unto you, I have not found so great faith, no, not in Israel.**

k. **And I say unto you, that many shall sit down with Abraham, and Isaac, and Jacob, in the kingdom of heaven. But the children of the kingdom shall be cast out into outer darkness: there shall be weeping and gnashing of teeth.**

l. And Jesus saith unto the centurion, **Go thy way; and as thou hast believed, so be it done unto thee.**

m. And his servant was healed in the selfsame hour.

n. And they that were sent, returning to the house, found the servant whole that had been sick.

4-9. The raising of the widow's son at Nain.

a. And it came to pass the day after, that he went into a city called Nain; and many of his disciples went with him, and much people.

b. Now when he came nigh to the gate of the city, behold, there was a dead man carried out, the only son of his mother, and she was a widow: and much people of the city was with her.

c. And when the Lord saw her, he had compassion on her, and said unto her, **Weep not.**

d. And he came and touched the bier (*a wooden frame which a coffin is carried on*): and they that bare him stood still.

e. And he said, **Young man, I say unto thee, Arise.**

f. And he that was dead sat up, and began to speak.

g. And he delivered him to his mother.

h. And there came a fear on all: and they glorified God, saying, That a great prophet is risen up among us; and, That God has visited his people.

i. And this rumor of him went forth throughout all Judaea, and throughout all the region round about.

4-10. Tribute to John the Baptist.

a. And the disciples of John showed him of all things, the works of Christ.

b. And John calling unto him two of his disciples sent them to Jesus, saying, Art thou he that should come? or do we look for another?

c. When the men were come unto him, they said, John the Baptist, hath sent us unto thee, saying, Art thou he that should come? or look we for another?

d. And in that same hour he cured many of their infirmities and plagues, and of evil spirits; and unto many that were blind he gave sight.

e. Then Jesus answering said unto them, **Go your way again, and tell John what things ye have seen and heard; how that the blind receive their sight, the lame walk, the lepers are cleansed, the deaf hear, the dead are raised up, and the poor have the gospel preached to them.**

f. **And blessed is he, whosoever shall not be offended in me.**

g. And when the messengers of John were departed, he began to speak unto the people concerning John, **What went ye out into the wilderness for to see?**

h. **A reed shaken with the wind? But what ye went out for to see? A man clothed in soft raiment? behold, they that wear soft clothing are in kings' houses.**

i. **Behold, they which are gorgeously apparelled, and live delicately, are in kings' courts.**

j. **But what went ye out for to see? A prophet? Yea, I say unto you, and much more than a prophet.**

k. **For this is he, of whom it is written, Behold, I send my messenger before thy face, which shall prepare the way before thee.**

l. Verily I say unto you, Among those that are born of women there is not risen a greater prophet than John the Baptist: but he that is least in the kingdom of God is greater than he.

m. And from the days of John the Baptist until now the kingdom of heaven suffered violence, and the violent take it by force.

n. For all the prophets and the law prophesied until John.

o. And if ye will receive it, this is Elias, which was for to come.

p. He that hath ears to hear, let him hear.

q. And all the people that heard him, and the publicans, justified God, being baptized with the baptism of John.

r. But the Pharisees and lawyers rejected the counsel of God against themselves, being not baptized of him.

s. And the Lord said, Whereunto then shall I liken the men of this generation? And to what are they like?

t. They are like unto children sitting in the marketplace, and calling one to another, and saying, We have piped unto you, and ye have not danced; we have mourned to you, and ye have not wept.

u. For John the Baptist came neither eating bread nor drinking wine; and ye say, He hath a devil.

v. The Son of man is come eating and drinking; and ye say, Behold a gluttonous man, and a winebibber, a friend of publicans and sinners! But wisdom is justified of all her children.

4-11. Jesus forgives a sinful woman.

a. And one of the Pharisees desired him that he would eat with him. And he went into the Pharisee's house, and sat down to meat.

b. And, behold, a woman in the city, which was a sinner, when she knew that Jesus sat at meat in the Pharisee's house, brought an alabaster box of ointment, And stood at his feet behind him weeping, and began to wash his feet with tears and did wipe them with the hairs of her head, and kissed his feet, and anointed them with the ointment.

c. Now when the Pharisee which had bidden him saw it, he spake within himself, saying, this man, if he were a prophet, would have known who and what manner of woman this is that toucheth him: for she is a sinner.

d. And Jesus answering said unto him, **Simon, I have somewhat to say unto thee.**

e. And he saith, Master, say on. **There was a certain creditor which had two debtors: the one owed five hundred pence, and the other fifty. And when they had nothing to pay, he frankly forgave them both. Tell me therefore, which of them will love him most?**

f. Simon answered and said, I suppose that he, to whom he forgave most.

g. And he said unto him, **Thou hast rightly judged.**

h. And he turned to the woman, and said unto Simon, **Seest thou this woman? I entered into thine house, thou gavest me no water for my feet: but she hath washed my feet with tears, and wiped them with the hairs of her head.**

i. **Thou gavest me no kiss: but this woman since the time I came in hath not ceased to kiss my feet.**

j. **My head with oil thou didst not anoint: but this woman hath anointed my feet with ointment.**

k. **Wherefore I say unto thee, Her sins, which are many, are forgiven; for she loved much: but to whom little is forgiven, the same loveth little.**

l. And he said unto her, **Thy sins are forgiven.**

m. And they that sat at meat with him began to say within themselves, Who is this that forgiveth sins also?

n. And he said to the woman, **Thy faith hath saved thee; go in peace.**

4-12. The storm stilled.

a. And the same day, when the even was come, he saith unto them, **Let us pass over unto the other side.**

b. And when he was entered into a ship, his disciples followed him.

c. And when they had sent away the multitude, they took him even as he was in the ship. And there were also with him other little ships.

d. And he said unto them, **Let us go over unto the other side of the Lake.**

e. And they launched forth. But as they sailed he fell asleep.

f. And, behold, there arose a great storm of wind on the lake, and the waves beat into the ship, so that it was filled with water, and they were in jeopardy.

g. And he was in the hinder (*at the back*) part of the ship, asleep on a pillow: and his disciples came to him, and awoke him, and say unto him, Master, carest thou not that we perish? Lord, save us: we perish, Master, master, we perish.

h. And he arose, and rebuked the wind, and said unto the sea, **Peace, be still.**

i. And the wind and the raging of the water ceased, and there was a great calm.

j. And he said unto them, **Why are ye so fearful? Where is your faith? how is it that you have no faith? O ye of little faith?**

k. And they feared exceedingly, and they marvelled, saying one to another, What manner of man is this, that even the winds, and the sea obey him?

4-13. Legion of devils cast out (swine).

a. And they came over unto the other side of the sea, into the country of the Gadarenes', which is over against Galilee.

b. And when he was come out of the ship to land, immediately there met him out of the city a certain man, with an unclean spirit, possessed with devils, coming out of the tombs, exceeding fierce, so that no man might pass by that way, which had devils long time, and wore no clothes, neither abode in any house. (Controversy: Matthew 8:28 *said there were two men*; Mark 5:2 *said there was one man*; Luke 8:27 *said there was one man; I went with the majority here*).

c. Who had his dwelling among the tombs; and no man could bind him, no, not the chains: Because that he had been often bound with fetters (*Chain or shackle to somebody's feet or ankle*) and chains, and the chains had been plucked asunder by him, and the fetters broken in pieces: neither could any man tame him.

d. And always, night and day, he was in the mountains, and in the tombs, crying, and cutting himself with stones.

e. But when he saw Jesus afar off, he ran and fell down before him and worshipped him. And cried out with a loud voice, and said, What have I to do with thee, Jesus, thou Son of the most high God?

f. I adjure thee by God, that thou torment me not, art thou come to torment us before the time. For he said unto him, **Come out of the man, thou unclean spirit.**

g. (For he had commanded the unclean spirit to come out of the man. For oftentimes it had caught him: and he was kept bound with chains and in fetters; and he brake the bands, and was driven of the devil into the wilderness.)

h. And Jesus asked him, saying, **What is thy name?**

i. And he answered, saying, My name is Legion: for we are many.

j. And they besought him much that he would not send them away out of the country into the deep.

k. Now there was there nigh unto the mountains a good way off from them a great herd of many swine feeding on the mountain.

l. And all the devils besought him, saying, if thou cast us out, suffer us to go away into the herd of swine, that we may enter into them.

m. And forth with he suffered them. Jesus gave them leave and said unto them, **go.**

n. And the unclean spirits went out of the man, and entered into the swine: and, behold, the whole herd of swine ran violently down a steep place into the lake, (they were about two thousand;) and perished in the waters.

o. When they that fed the swine saw what was done, they fled, and went their ways into the city, and told everything in the city, and in the country; what was befallen to the possessed of the devils.

p. And they went out to see what it was that was done.

q. And, behold, the whole city came out to meet Jesus and see him that was possessed with the devil, and had the legion, and found the man, out of whom the devils was departed sitting at the feet of Jesus, and clothed, and in his right mind: and they were afraid.

r. They also which saw it told them by what means he that was possessed of the devils was healed, and also concerning the swine.

s. Then the whole multitude of the country of the Gadarenes' round about besought him to depart out of their coasts; for they were taken with great fear: and he went up into the ship, and returned back again.

t. And when he was come into the ship, the man that had been possessed with the devil prayed him that he might be with him.

u. Howbeit Jesus suffered him not, but saith unto him, **Return to thine own house, Go home to thy friends, and tell them how great things the Lord hath done for thee, and hath had compassion on thee.**

v. And he departed, and began to publish throughout the whole city in Decapolis how great things Jesus had done for him: and all men did marvel.

4-14. The plaque woman; Jairus daughter raised.

a. And when Jesus was passed over again by ship unto the other side, much people gathered unto him: and he was nigh unto the sea, the people gladly received him: for they were all waiting for him.

b. While he spake these things unto them, behold, there came one of the rulers of the synagogue, Jairus by name; and when he saw him, he fell down at Jesus feet, and worshipped him, and besought him greatly that he would come into his house:

c. Saying, My little daughter lieth at the point of death: I pray thee, come and lay thy hands on her, that she may be healed; and she shall live. For he had only one daughter, about twelve years of age, and she lay a dying. But as he won't the people thronged him.

d. And Jesus arose, and followed him, and so did his disciples; and much people followed him, and thronged him.

e. And, behold, a certain woman, which was diseased with an issue of blood twelve years.

f. And had suffered many things of many physicians, and had spent all that she had upon physicians, and was nothing bettered or healed of any, but rather grew worse.

g. When she had heard of Jesus, came in the press behind him, and touched the border hem of his garment. For she said within herself, If I may but touch his garment, I shall be whole.

h. And immediately the fountain of her blood was dried up; and she felt in her body that she was healed of the plague.

i. And Jesus, immediately knowing in himself that virtue had gone out of him, turned him about in the press, and said, **Who touched my clothes?**

j. When all denied, Peter and his disciples said unto him, Master Thou seest the multitude thronging thee, and press thee and sayest thou, Who touched me?

k. And Jesus said, **Somebody hath touched me: for I perceive that virtue is gone out of me.**

l. And he looked round about to see her that had done this thing.

m. And when the woman saw that she was not hid, she came fearing and trembling, knowing what was done in her, came and falling down before him, she declared unto him before all the people for what cause she had touched him, and how she was healed immediately.

n. And he said unto her, **Daughter, be of good comfort, thy faith hath made thee whole; go in peace, and be whole of thy plaque.**

o. And the woman was made whole from that hour.

p. While he yet spake, there cometh one from the ruler of the synagogue's house, saying to him, Thy daughter is dead; troublest not the Master any further?

q. As soon as Jesus heard the word that was spoken, he saith unto the ruler of the synagogue, **Fear not, Be not afraid, only believe, and she shall be made whole.**

r. And he suffered no man to follow him, save Peter, and James, and John the brother of James. And the father and the mother of the maiden.

s. And when Jesus came into house of the ruler of the synagogue, and seeth the tumult, and the minstrels (*medieval traveling musician*) and them that wept and bewailed her greatly.

t. And when he was come in, he saith unto them, **Give place, Why make ye this ado** (*excited activity or bother*), **and weep? Weep not, The damsel is not dead, but sleepeth.**

u. And they laughed him to scorn, knowing that she was dead.

v. But when he had put them all out, he taketh the father and the mother of the damsel, and them that were with him, and entereth in where the damsel was lying.

w. And he took the damsel by the hand, and said unto her, **Talitha cumi; which is, being interpreted, Damsel, I say unto thee, arise.**

x. And her spirit came again; And straightway the damsel arose, and walked. And her parents were astonished with a great astonishment.

y.   And he charged them straightly that no man should know what was done; and he commanded to give her meat to eat.

z.   And the fame hereof went abroad into all that land.

4-15. Two blind men; A dumb demoniac healed.

a.   And when Jesus departed thence, two blind men followed him, crying, and saying, Thou son of David, have mercy on us.

b.   And when he was come into the house, the blind men came to him: and Jesus saith unto them, **Believe ye that I am able to do this?**

c.   They said unto him, Yea, Lord. Then touched he their eyes, saying, **According to your faith be it unto you.**

d.   And their eyes were opened; and Jesus straightly charged them, saying, **See that no man know it.**

e.   But they, when they were departed, spread abroad his fame in all that country.

f.   As they went out, behold, they brought to him a dumb man possessed with a devil.

g.   And when the devil was cast out, the dumb spake: and the multitudes marvelled, saying, It was never so seen in Israel.

h.   But the Pharisees said, He casteth out devils through the prince of the devils.

4-16. Second Galilean tour; the need for labourers.

a.   And Jesus went about all the cities and villages, teaching in their synagogues, and preaching the gospel of the kingdom, and healing every sickness and every disease among the people.

b. But when he saw the multitudes, he was moved with compassion on them, because they fainted, and were scattered abroad, as sheep having no shepherd.

c. Then saith he unto his disciples, **The harvest truly is plenteous, but the labourers are few; Pray ye therefore the Lord of the harvest, that he will send forth labourers into his harvest.**

4-17. The mission of the twelve.

a. Then he called his twelve disciples together, and gave them power and authority over all devils, and to cure diseases.

b. These twelve Jesus sent forth by two and two, and commanded them, saying, **Go not into the way of the Gentiles, and into any city of the Samaritans enter ye not: But go rather to the lost sheep of the house of Israel.**

c. **And as ye go, preach, saying, The kingdom of God is at hand. Heal the sick, cleanse the lepers, raise the dead, cast out devils: freely ye have received, freely give.**

d. And he said unto them, **Take nothing for your journey, neither staves** (*a stick, pole, or rod that is carried in hand for support in walking or climbing*) **no scrip, no bread, no money in their purse, neither shoes: for the workman is worthy of his meat** (Controversy: Matthew 10:10 *said nor yet staves* (not at this time); Mark 6:8 *said save a staff only*; Luke 9:3 *said neither staves; I went with the majority of no staves*).

e. **Provide neither gold, nor silver, nor brass in your purses. But be shod** (*shoed*) **with sandals; and neither have two coats apiece.**

f. And into whatever city or town ye shall enter, inquire who in it is worthy; and there abide till ye go thence.

g. And when ye come into an house, salute it. And whatsoever house ye enter into, there abide till ye depart from that place.

h. And if the house be worthy, let your peace come upon it: but if it be not worthy, let your peace return to you.

i. And whosoever shall not receive you, nor hear your words, when ye depart out of that house or city, shake off the dust under your feet for a testimony against them.

j. Verily I say unto you, It shall be more tolerable for the land of Sodom and Gomorrah in the day of judgment, than for that city.

k. Behold, I send you forth as sheep in the midst of wolves: be ye therefore wise as serpents, and harmless as doves.

l. But beware of men: for they will deliver you up to the councils, and they will scourge you in their synagogues.

m. And ye shall be brought before governors and kings for my sake, for a testimony against them and the Gentiles.

n. But when they deliver you up, take no thought how or what ye shall speak: For it shall be given you in that hour what ye shall speak. For it is not ye that speak, but the Spirit of your Father which speaketh in you.

o. And the brother shall deliver up the brother to death, and the father the child: and the children shall rise up against their parents, and cause them to be put to death.

p. And ye shall be hated of all men for my name's sake: but he that endureth to the end shall be saved.

q. But when they persecute you in this city, flee ye into another: for verily I say unto you, Ye shall not have gone over the cities of Israel, till the Son of man be come.

r. The disciple is not above his master, nor the servant above his lord. It is enough for the disciple that he be as his master, and the servant as his lord.

s. If they have called the master of the house Beelzebub, how much more shall they call them of his household?

t. Fear them not therefore: for there is nothing covered, that shall not be revealed; and hid, that shall not be known. What I tell you in darkness, that speak ye in light: and what ye hear in the ear, that preach ye upon the housetops.

u. And fear not them which kill the body, but are not able to kill the soul: but rather fear him which is able to destroy both soul and body in hell.

v. Are not two sparrows sold for a farthing? and one of them shall not fall on the ground without your Father. But the very hairs of your head are all numbered. Fear ye not therefore, ye are of more value than many sparrows.

w. Whosoever therefore shall confess me before men, him will I confess also before my Father which is in heaven. But whosoever shall deny me before men, him will I also deny before my Father which is in heaven.

x. Think not that I am come to send peace on earth: I came not to send peace, but a sword.

y. For I am come to set a man at variance against his father, and the daughter against her mother, and the daughter-in-law against her mother-in-law.

z. And a man's foe shall be they of his own household.

aa. He that loveth father or mother more than me is not worthy of me: and he that loveth son or daughter more than me is not worthy of me.

bb. And he that taketh not his cross, and followed after me, is not worthy of me.

cc. He that findeth his life shall lose it: and he that loseth his life for my sake shall find it.

dd. He that receiveth you receiveth me, and he that receiveth me, receive him that sent me.

ee. He that receiveth a prophet in the name of a prophet shall receive a prophet's reward; and he that receiveth a righteous man in the name of a righteous man shall receive a righteous man's reward.

ff. And whosoever shall give to drink unto one of these little ones a cup of cold water only in the name of a disciple, verily I say unto you, he shall in no wise lose his reward.

gg. And it came to pass, when Jesus had made an end of commanding his twelve disciples, he departed thence to teach and to preach in their cities.

hh. And they departed, and went through the towns, preaching the gospel that men should repent, and healing everywhere.

ii. And they cast out many devils, and anointed with oil many that were sick, and healed them.

4-18. The Judgment of the unrepentant.

a. Then began he to unbraid the cities wherein most of his mighty works were done, because they repented not: **Woe unto thee, Chorazin! woe unto thee, Bethsaida! for if the mighty works, which were done in you, had been done in Tyre and Sidon, they would have repented long ago in sackcloth and ashes.**

b. **But I say unto you, It shall be more tolerable for Tyre and Sidon at the day of judgment, than for you.**

c. **And thou, Capernaum, which are exalted unto heaven, shalt be brought down to hell: for if the mighty works, which have been done in thee, had been done in Sodom, it would have remained until this day.**

d. **But I say unto you, That it shall be more tolerable for the land of Sodom in the day of judgment, than for thee.**

4-19. Jesus reveals the Father.

a. In that hour Jesus rejoiced in spirit, and said, **I thank thee, O Father, Lord of heaven and earth, because thou hast hid these things from the wise and prudent, and hast revealed them unto babes. Even so, Father: for so it seemed good in thy sight.**

b. **All things are delivered to me of my Father: and no man knoweth the Son, but the Father; neither knoweth any man the Father, save the Son and he to whomsoever the Son will reveal him.**

c. **Come unto me, all ye that labour and are heavy laden, and I will give you rest.**

d. **Take my yoke upon you, and learn of me; for I am meek and lowly in heart: and ye shall find rest unto your souls. For my yoke is easy, and my burden is light.**

The Combined Gospel of Jesus Christ

Chapter Five
Closing Galilean Ministry

5-1. Death of John the Baptist.

a. And when a convenient day was come, that Herod on his birthday made a supper to his lords, high captains, and chief estates of Galilee.

b. But when Herod's birthday was kept, the daughter of the said Herodias came in, and danced, and pleased Herod and them that sat with him, the king said unto the damsel, Ask of me whatsoever thou wilt, and I will give it thee.

c. Whereupon he promised with an oath to give her whatsoever she would ask. And he sware unto her, whatsoever thou shalt ask of me, I will give it thee, unto the half of my kingdom.

d. And she went forth, and said unto her mother, What shall I ask? And she said, The head of John the Baptist.

e. And she, being before instructed of her mother, came in straightway with haste unto the king, and asked, saying, I will that thou give me by and by in a charger the head of John the Baptist's.

f. And the king was exceeding sorry: nevertheless for his oath's sake, and for their sakes which sat with him at meat, he would not reject her; he commanded it to be given her.

g. And immediately the king sent an executioner, and commanded his head to be brought: and he went and beheaded him in the prison.

h. And his head was brought in a charger, and given to the damsel: and the damsel gave it to her mother.

i. And when his disciples heard of it, they came, and took up his corpse, and buried it in a tomb. And went and told Jesus.

5-2. Jesus fame is heard of by King Herod.

a. At that time, King Herod the tetrarch heard of all that was done by the fame of Jesus; (for his name was spread abroad:) and he was perplexed, because that it was said of some, that John was risen from the dead.

b. But when Herod heard thereof, he said unto his servants, This is John the Baptist, he is risen from the dead; and therefore mighty works do show forth themselves in him.

c. Others said, That it is Elias. And others said, that one of the old prophets was risen again.

d. And Herod said, John have I beheaded, but who is this, of whom I hear such things? And he desired to see him.

5-3. The five thousand fed.

a. When Jesus heard of it (*John the Baptist death*), and the apostles when they were returned, gathered themselves together unto Jesus, and told him all things, both what they had done, and what they had taught.

b. And he said unto them, **Come ye yourselves apart into a desert place belonging to the city called Bethsaida, and rest a while:** for there were many coming and going, and they had no leisure so much as to eat.

c. And they departed into a desert place by ship privately over the sea of Galilee, which is the sea of Tiberias.

d.   And when the people had heard thereof, a great multitude followed him, because they saw his miracles which he did on them that were diseased.

e. And the people saw them departing, and many knew him, they followed him on foot and ran out of all cities, and outwent them, and came together unto him.

f. And Jesus, when he came out *(of the ship)*, he went up into a mountain, and there he sat with his disciples.

g. And the Passover, a feast of the Jews, was nigh.

h. When Jesus then went forth, and lifted up his eyes, and saw a great multitude come unto him, and was moved with compassion toward them, because they were as sheep not having a shepherd: and he began to teach them many things of the kingdom of God, and he healed their sick.

i. And when the day was now far spent and it was evening, his disciples came unto him, and said, This is a desert place, and now the time is far passed.

j. Send the multitude away, that they may go into the towns and country round about, and into the villages, and lodge, and buy themselves bread and victuals: for we are here in a desert place; for they have nothing to eat.

k. He saith unto Philip, **They need not depart; Give ye them to eat.** And this he said to prove him: for he himself knew what he would do.

l. Philip answered him, Whence shall we buy bread, that these may eat? Shall we go and buy two hundred pennyworth of bread is not sufficient for them, and buy meat for all this peoples and give them a little to eat?

m. He saith unto them, **How many loaves have ye? go and see.**

n. One of his disciple, Andrew, Simon Peter's brother, saith unto him. There is a lad here, which hath five barley loaves, and two small fishes: but what are they among so many?

o. Jesus said, **bring them hither to me.**

p. And he commanded his disciples to make the multitude sit down by fifties in a company upon the green grass. Now there was much grass in the place. And they did so, and made them all sit down.

q. And they sat down in ranks, by hundreds, and by fifties.

r. Then Jesus took the five loaves, and the two fishes, he looked up to heaven, and blessed them and when he had given thanks, and brake the loaves, and gave them to his disciples to set before the multitude; and the two fishes divided he among them all, and the disciples to the multitude.

s. And they did all eat, and were all filled, he said unto his disciples, **Gather up the fragments that remained, that nothing be lost.**

t. Therefore they gathered them together, and filled twelve baskets with the fragments of the five barley loaves, and of the fishes which remained over and above unto them that had eaten.

u. And they that did eat of the loaves were about five thousand men, beside women and children.

v. Then those men, when they had seen the miracle that Jesus did, said, This is of a truth that prophet that should come into the world.

5-4. Jesus walks on the sea.

a. When Jesus therefore perceived that they would come and take him by force, to make him a king.

b. And straightway he constrained his disciples to get into the ship, and to go before him to the other side unto Bethsaida, while he sent the multitudes away.

c. And when he had sent the multitudes away, he departed again up into a mountain apart to pray.

d. And when even was now come, his disciples went down unto the sea, And entered into a ship, and went over the sea toward Capernaum.

e. And it was now dark, and Jesus was not come to them. The ship was in the midst of the sea, and he alone on the land.

f. And the sea arose by reason of a great wind that blew.

g. And he saw them toiling in rowing, tossed with waves: for the wind was contrary unto them: and in the fourth watch of the night he cometh unto them, walking upon the sea, and would have passed by them.

h. But when the disciples had rowed about five and twenty or thirty furlongs, they saw Jesus walking upon the sea, and drawing nigh unto the ship: they supposed it had been a spirit and they were afraid, and cried out: It is a spirit; and they cried for fear. For they all saw him, and were troubled.

i. And immediately he talked with them, and saith unto them, **Be of good cheer: it is I; be not afraid.**

j. And Peter answered him and said, Lord, if it be thou, bid me come unto thee on the water. And he said, **Come**.

k. And when Peter was come down out of the ship, he walked on the water, to go to Jesus.

l. But when he saw the wind boisterous, he was afraid; and beginning to sink, he cried, saying, Lord, save me.

m. And immediately Jesus stretched forth his hand, and caught him, and said unto him, **O thou of little faith, wherefore didst thou doubt?**

n. And when they were come into the ship; they willingly received him into the ship, and the wind ceased: and they were sore amazed in themselves beyond measure, and wondered.

o. Then they that were in the ship came and worshipped him, saying, Of a truth thou art the Son of God.

p. For they considered not the miracle of the loaves: for their heart was hardened.

q. And immediately the ship had passed over, they came into the land of Gennesaret, and drew to the shore.

r. And when they were come out of the ship, straightway the men of that place had knowledge of him.

s. And ran and sent out into that whole region round about, and began to carry about in beds those that were sick, and all that were diseased, where they heard he was.

t. And whithersoever he entered, into the villages, or cities, or country, they laid the sick in the streets, and besought him that they might touch if it were but the border of his garment: and as many as touched him were made perfectly whole.

5-5. Jesus the bread of life.

a. The day following, when the people which stood on the other side of the sea saw that there was none other boat there, save that one whereinto his disciples were entered, and that Jesus went not with his disciples into the boat, but that his disciples were gone away alone; (Howbeit there came other boats from Tiberias nigh unto the place where they did eat bread, after that the Lord had given thanks:).

b. When the people therefore saw that Jesus was not there, neither his disciples, they also took shipping, and came to Capernaum, seeking for Jesus.

c. And when they had found him on the other side of the sea, they said unto him, Rabbi, when camest thou hither?

d. Jesus answered them and said, **Verily, verily, I say unto you, Ye seek me, not because ye saw the miracles, but because ye did eat of the loaves, and were filled. Labour not for the meat which perisheth, but for that meat which endureath unto everlasting life, which the Son of man shall give unto you: for him hath God the Father sealed.**

e. Then said they unto him, What shall we do, that we might work the works of God?

f. Jesus answered and said unto them, **This is the work of God, that ye believe on him whom he hath sent.**

g. They said therefore unto him, What sign showest thou then, that we may see, and believe thee? what dost thou work? Our fathers did eat manna in the desert; as it is written, He gave them bread from heaven to eat.

h. Then Jesus said unto them, **Verily, verily, I say unto you, Moses gave you not that bread from heaven; but my Father giveth you the true bread from heaven. For the bread of God is he which cometh down from heaven, and giveth life unto the world.**

i. Then said they unto him, Lord, evermore give us this bread. And Jesus said unto them, **I am the bread of life: he that cometh to me shall never hunger; and he that believeth on me shall never thirst.**

j. But I said unto you, That ye also have seen me, and believe not.

k. All that the Father giveth me shall come to me; and him that cometh to me I will in no wise cast out. For I came down from heaven, not to do mine own will, but the will of him that sent me.

l. And this is the Father's will which hath sent me, that of all which he hath given me I should lose nothing, but should raise it up again at the last day.

m. And this is the will of him that sent me, that every one which seeth the Son, and believeth on him, may have everlasting life: and I will raise him up at the last day.

n. The Jews then murmured at him, because he said, I am the bread which came down from heaven.

o. And they said, Is not this Jesus, the son of Joseph, whose father and mother we know? How is it then that he saith, I came down from heaven?

p. Jesus therefore answered and said unto them, **Murmur not among yourselves. No man can come to me, except the Father which hath sent me draw him:** and I will raise him up at the last day.

q. It is written in the prophets, And they shall be all taught of God. Every man therefore that hath heard, and hath learned of the Father, cometh unto me. Not that any man hath seen the Father, save he which is of God, he hath seen the Father.

r. Verily, verily, I say unto you, He that believeth on me hath everlasting life. I am the bread of life. Your fathers did eat manna in the wilderness, and are dead.

s. This is the bread which cometh down from heaven, that a man may eat thereof, and not die. I am the living bread which came down from heaven: if any man eat of this bread, he shall live for ever: and the bread that I will give is my flesh, which I will give for the life of the world.

t. The Jews therefore strove among themselves, saying, How can this man give us his flesh to eat?

u. Then Jesus said unto them, **Verily, verily, I say unto you, Except ye eat the flesh of the Son of man, and drink his blood, ye have no life in you.**

v. **Whoso eateth my flesh, and drinketh my blood, hath eternal life; and I will raise him up at the last day.**

w. **For my flesh is meat indeed, and my blood is drink indeed. He that eateth my flesh, and drinketh my blood, dwelleth in me, and I in him.**

x. **As the living Father hath sent me, and I live by the Father: so he that eateth me, even he shall live by me.**

y. **This is that bread which came down from heaven: not as your fathers did eat manna, and are dead: he that eateth of this bread shall live for ever.**

z. **These things said he in the synagogue, as he taught in Capernaum.**

5-6. The questioning disciples.

a. Many therefore of his disciples, when they had heard this, said, This is an hard saying; who can hear it?

b. When Jesus knew in himself that his disciples murmured at it, he said unto them, **Doth this offend you?**

c. **What and if ye shall see the Son of man ascend up where he was before?**

d. **It is the spirit that quickeneth; the flesh profiteth nothing: the words that I speak unto you, they are spirit, and they are life.**

e. **But there are some of you that believe not.**

f. For Jesus knew from the beginning who they were that believed not, and who should betray him.

g. And he said, **Therefore said I unto you, that no man can come unto me, except it were given unto him of my Father.**

h. From that time many of his disciples went back, and walked no more with him.

i. Then said Jesus unto the twelve, **Will ye also go away?**

j. Then Simon Peter answered him, Lord, to whom shall we go? Thou hast the words of eternal life.

k. And we believe and are sure that thou art that Christ, the Son of the living God.

l. Jesus answered them, **Have not I chosen you twelve, and one of you is a devil?**

m. He spake of Judas Iscariot the son of Simon: for he it was that should betray him, being one of the twelve.

5-7. Jesus at the feast of tabernacles.

a. After these things Jesus walked in Galilee: for he would not walk in Jewry, because the Jews sought to kill him.

b. Now the Jews' feast of tabernacles was at hand. His brethren therefore said unto him, Depart hence, and go into Judaea, that thy disciples also may see the works that thou doest.

c. For there is no man that doeth any thing in secret, and he himself seeketh to be known openly. If thou do these things, show thyself to the world. For neither did his brethren believe in him.

d. Then Jesus said unto them, **My time is not yet come: but your time is always ready. The world cannot hate you; but me it hateth, because I testify of it, that the works thereof are evil.**

e. **Go ye up unto this feast: I go not up yet unto this feast; for my time is not yet full come.**

f. When he had said these words unto them, he abode still in Galilee.

g. But when his brethren were gone up, then went he also up unto the feast, not openly, but as it were in secret.

h. Then the Jews sought him at the feast, and said, Where is he?

i. And there was much murmuring among the people concerning him: for some said, He is a good man: others said, Nay; but he deceiveth the people.

j. Howbeit no man spake openly of him for fear of the Jews.

5-8. What defiles a man.

a. Then came together unto him the Pharisees, and certain of the scribes, which came from Jerusalem.

b. And when they saw some of his disciples eat bread with defiled, that is to say, with unwashen, hands, they found fault.

c. For the Pharisees, and all the Jews, except they wash their hands oft, eat not, holding the tradition of the elders.

d. And when they come from the market, except they wash, they eat not.

e. And many other things there be, which they have received to hold, as the washing of cups, and pots, brasen vessels, and of tables.

f. Then the Pharisees and the scribes asked him, Why do thy disciples transgress the tradition of the elders? for they wash not their hands when they eat bread.

g. He answered and said unto them, **Why do ye also**

transgress the commandment of God by your tradition.

h. Well hath Esaias prophesied of you hypocrites, as it is written, This people draweth nigh unto me with their mouth, and honoureth me with their lips; but their heart is far from me.

i. Howbeit in vain do they worship me, teaching for doctrines the commandments of men.

j. For laying aside the commandment of God, ye hold the tradition of men, as the washing of pots and cups: and many other such like things ye do.

k. And he said unto them, full well ye reject the commandment of God, that ye may keep your own tradition.

l. For Moses said, God commanded, saying, Honour thy father and thy mother; and, Whoso curseth father or mother, let him die the death.

m. But ye say, If a man shall say to his father or mother, It is Corban, that is to say, a gift, by whatsoever thou mightest be profited by me; And honour not his father or mother, he shall be free.

n. And ye suffer him no more to do aught for his father or his mother. Making the word of God of none effect through your tradition, which ye have delivered: and many such like things do ye.

o. And when he had called all the people unto him, he said unto them, Hearken unto me every one of you, and understand: There is nothing which goeth into the mouth defileth a man; but that which cometh out of the mouth, this defileth a man.

p. If a man hath ears to hear, let him hear.

q. And when he was entered into the house from the people, then came his disciples, and said unto him, Knowest thou that the Pharisees were offended, after they heard this saying?

r. But he answered and said, **Every plant, which my heavenly Father hath not planted, shall be rooted up.**

s. **Let them alone: they be blind leaders of the blind. And if the blind lead the blind, both shall fall into the ditch.**

t. Then answered Peter and said unto him, Declare unto us this parable.

u. And he saith unto them, **Are ye so without understanding also? Do ye not perceive, that whatsoever thing from without entereth into the man, it cannot defile him.**

v. **Because it entereth not into his heart, but into the belly, and goeth out into the draught, purging all meats?**

w. And he said, **those things which proceed out of the mouth come forth from the heart; and they defile the man.**

x. **For from within, out of the heart of men, proceed evil thoughts, adulteries, fornications, murders, thefts, covetousness, wickedness, deceit, lasciviousness, an evil eye, blasphemy, pride, foolishness: all these evil things come from within, and defile the man: but to eat with unwashen hands defileth not a man.**

5-9. The faith of a Canaanite (Greek) woman.

a. Then from thence Jesus arose, and went into the coasts of Tyre and Sidon, and entered into an house, and would have no man know it: but he could not be hid.

b. And, behold, a Greek woman of Canaan, a Syrophenician by nation came out of the same coasts, whose young daughter had an unclean spirit, heard of him, and came and fell at his feet: and cried unto him, saying, Have mercy on me, O Lord, thou son of David; my daughter is grievously vexed with a devil, and she besought him that he would cast forth the devil out of her daughter.

c. But he answered her not a word.

d. And his disciples came and besought him, saying, Send her away; for she crieth after us.

e. But he answered and said, **I am not sent but unto the lost sheep of the house of Israel.**

f. Then came she and worshipped him, saying, Lord, help me.

g. But Jesus answered and said unto her, **Let the children first be filled, for it is not meet to take the children's bread, and to cast it unto the dogs.**

h. And she answered and said unto him, Yes, Lord: yet the dogs under the table eat of the children's crumbs which fall from their masters' table.

i. Then Jesus answered and said unto her, **O woman, great is thy faith: For this saying go thy way; be it unto thee even as thou wilt; the devil is gone out of thy daughter.**

j. And her daughter was made whole from that very hour. And when she was come to her house, she found the devil gone out, and her daughter laid upon the bed.

5-10. The deaf mute healed.

a. And again, Jesus departed from the coasts of Tyre and Sidon, he came nigh unto the sea of Galilee, through the midst of the coasts of Decapolis; and went up into a mountain, and sat down there.

b. And great multitudes came unto him, having with them those that were lame, blind, dumb, maimed, and many others, and cast them down at Jesus' feet; and he healed them:

c. And they bring unto him one that was deaf, and had an impediment in his speech; and they beseech him to put his hand upon him.

d. And he took him aside from the multitude, and put his fingers unto his ears, and he spit, and touched his tongue;

e. And looking up to heaven, he sighed, and saith unto him, **Ephphatha, that is, be opened.**

f. And straightway his ears were opened, and the string of his tongue was loosed, and he spake plain.

g. And he charged them that they should tell no man: but the more he charged them, so much the more a great deal they published it; And were beyond measure astonished;

h. Insomuch that the multitude wondered, when they saw the dumb to speak, the maimed to be whole, the lame to walk, and the blind to see, saying, He hath done all things well: he maketh both the deaf to hear, and the dumb to speak: and they glorified the God of Israel.

5-11. The four thousand fed.

a. In those days the multitude being very great, and having nothing to eat.

b. Then Jesus called his disciples unto him, and said unto them, **I have compassion on the multitude, because they continue with me now three days, and have nothing to eat: and I will not send them away fasting to their own houses, lest they faint in the way, for divers of them came from afar.**

c. And his disciples say unto him, Whence should we have so much bread in the wilderness, as to fill so great a multitude?

d. And Jesus saith unto them, **How many loaves have ye?**

e. And they said, Seven, and a few little fishes.

f. And he commanded the multitude to sit down on the ground.

g. And he took the seven loaves and the fishes, and gave thanks, and brake them, and gave to his disciples, and the disciples to the multitude.

h. And they did all eat, and were filled: and they took up of the broken meat that was left seven baskets full.

i. And they that did eat were four thousand men, beside women and children.

j. And he sent away the multitude, and straightway he entered into a ship with his disciples, and came into the parts of Dalmanutha, into the coasts of Magdala.

5-12. The Pharisees ask for a sign.

a. The Pharisees also with the Sadducees came forth, and began to question with him, and tempting desired him that he would show them a sign from heaven.

b. And he sighed deeply in his spirit. He answered and said unto them, **Why doth this generation seek after a sign? verily I say unto you, There shall no sign be given unto this generation.**

c. **When it is evening, ye say, It will be fair weather: for the sky is red. And in the morning, It will be foul weather to day: for the sky is red and lowering.**

d. **O ye hypocrites, ye can discern the face of the sky; but can ye not discern the signs of the times?**

e. **A wicked and adulterous generation seeketh after a sign; and there shall no sign be given unto it, but the sign of the prophet Jonas.**

f. And he left them and entering into the ship again departed to the other side.

g. And when his disciples were come to the other

side, they had forgotten to take bread. Neither had they in the ship with them more than one loaf.

h. Then Jesus said unto them, **take heed and beware of the leaven of the Pharisees and of the Sadducees and of Herod.**

i. And they reasoned among themselves, saying, It is because we have taken no bread.

j. Which when Jesus perceived, he said unto them, **O ye of little faith, why reason ye among yourselves, because ye have brought no bread? have ye your heart yet hardened.**

k. **Having eyes, see ye not? and having ears, hear ye not? and do ye not remember? Do ye not yet understand, neither remember the five loaves of the five thousand, and how many baskets full of fragments ye took up?**

l. They say unto him, Twelve.

m. **Neither the seven loaves of the four thousand, and how many baskets full of fragments ye took up?**

n. And they said, Seven.

o. **How is it that ye do not understand that I spake it not to you concerning bread, that ye should beware of the leaven of the Pharisees and of the Sadducees?**

p. Then understood they how that he bade them not beware of the leaven of bread, but of the doctrine of the Pharisees and of the Sadducees.

5-13. A blind man healed.

a. And he cometh to Bethsaida; and they bring a blind man unto him, and besought him to touch him.

b. And he took the blind man by the hand, and led him out of the town; and when he had spit on his eyes, and put his hands upon him, he asked him if he saw aught.

c. And he looked up, and said, I see men as trees, walking.

d. After that he put his hands again upon his eyes, and made him look up: and he was restored, and saw every man clearly.

e. And he sent him away to his house, saying, **Neither go into the town, nor tell it to any in the town.**

5-14. Peter's confession of faith.

a. And Jesus went out, and his disciples, into the towns of Caesarea Philippi, and it came to pass, as he was alone praying, his disciples were with him: and he asked his disciples, saying, **Whom do the people say that I the Son of man, am?**

b. And they answered, Some say that thou art John the Baptist: some say, Elias; and others, Jeremias, or one of the old prophets is risen again.

c. And he saith unto them, **But whom say ye that I am?**

d. And Simon Peter answered and said, Thou art the Christ, the Son of the living God.

e. And Jesus answered and said unto him, **Blessed art thou, Simon Barjona: for flesh and blood hath not revealed it unto thee, but my Father which is in heaven.**

f. And I say also unto thee, **That thou art Peter, and upon this rock I will build my church; and the gates of hell shall not prevail against it.**

g. **And I will give unto thee the keys of the kingdom of heaven: and whatsoever thou shalt bound on earth shall be bound in heaven: and whatsoever thou shalt loose on earth shall be loosed in heaven.**

h. Then he straitly charged and commanded he his disciples that they should tell no man that he was Jesus the Christ.

5-15. Jesus foretells his death and resurrection.

a. From that time forth began Jesus to teach his disciples, saying, **The Son of man must go into Jerusalem, and suffer many things, and be rejected of the elders and chief priests and scribes, and be killed, and be raised again the third day.**

b. And he spake that saying openly.

c. Then Peter took him, and began to rebuke him, saying, Be it far from thee, Lord: this shall not be unto thee.

d. But when he turned about and looked on his disciples, he rebuked Peter, and said unto Peter, **Get thee behind me, Satan: thou art an offence unto me: for thou savourest not the things that be of God, but those that be of men.**

e. And when he had called the people unto him with his disciples also, he said unto them, **Whosoever will come after me, let him deny himself, and take up his cross daily, and follow me.**

f. **For whosoever will save his life shall lose it: and whosoever will lose his life for my sake and the gospel's, the same shall save it.**

g. **For what shall it profit a man, if he shall gain the whole world, and lose his own soul? or be cast away? or what shall a man give in exchange for his soul?**

h. **Whosoever therefore shall be ashamed of me and of my words in this adulterous and sinful generation: of him also shall the Son of man be ashamed, when he cometh in the glory of his Father with the holy angels; and then he shall reward every man according to his works.**

i. **Verily I say unto you of a truth, There be some standing here, which shall not taste of death, till they see the Son of man coming in his kingdom with power.**

5-16. The transfiguration.

a. And after six days Jesus taketh with him Peter, James, and John his brother, and leadeth them up into an high mountain apart by themselves to pray, (Controversy: Matthew 17:1 and Mark 9:2 *says six days;* Luke 9:28 *says about eight days. I went with six days*).

b. And as he prayed, the fashion of his countenance was altered, and he was transfigured before them: and his face did shine as the sun.

c. And his raiment became shinning and glistering, exceeding white as snow; so as no fuller on earth can white them.

d. And, behold, there appeared unto them Moses and Elias talking with Jesus.

e. Who appeared in glory, and spake of his decease which he should accomplish at Jerusalem.

f. But Peter and they that were with him were heavy with sleep: and when they were awake, they saw his glory, and the two men that stood with him.

g. Then answered Peter, and said unto Jesus, Master, it is good for us to be here: if thou wilt, let us make here three tabernacles; one for thee, and one for Moses, and one for Elias: not knowing what he said; for they were sore afraid.

h. While he yet spake, behold, a bright cloud overshadowed them: and they feared as they entered into the cloud, and behold a voice out of the cloud, which said, ***This is my beloved Son, in whom I am well pleased; hear ye him.***

i. And when the disciples heard it, they fell on their face, and were sore afraid.

j. And it came to pass, when the voice was past, as they departed from him, Jesus was found alone.

k. And Jesus came and touched them, and said, **Arise, and be not afraid.**

l. And suddenly when they had lifted up their eyes, looked round about, they saw no man any more, save Jesus only with themselves.

m. And as they came down from the mountain, Jesus charged them, saying, **Tell the vision to no man, until the Son of man be risen again from the dead.**

n. And they kept that saying with themselves, and told no man in those days any of those things which they had seen, questioning one with another what the rising from the dead should mean.

o. And his disciples asked him, saying, Why then say the scribes that Elias must first come?

p. And Jesus answered and said unto them, **Elias truly shall first come, and restore all things; and how it is written of the Son of man, that he must suffer many things, and be set at nought.**

q. **But I say unto you, That Elias is come already, and they knew him not, but have done unto him whatsoever they listed, as it is written of him. Likewise shall also the Son of man suffer of them.**

r. Then the disciples understood that he spake unto them of John the Baptist.

5-17. A demoniac boy healed.

a. And it came to pass, that on the next day, when he came to his disciples, he saw a great multitude about them, and the scribes questioning with them.

b. When they were come down from the hill, much people met him.

c. And straightway all the people, when they beheld him, were greatly amazed, and running to him saluted him.

d. And he asked the scribes, **What question ye with them?**

e. And when they were come to the multitude, there came to him a certain man, kneeling down to him, and cried out saying, Master, I beseech thee.

f. Lord, have mercy and look upon my son: for he is mine only child: for he is a lunatic, and sore vexed: for ofttimes he falleth into the fire, and oft into the water. He hath a dumb spirit.

g. And, lo, a spirit taketh him, and he suddenly crieth out; and it teareth him: and he foamed, and gnasheth with his teeth, and pineth away: and bruising him hardly departed from him.

h. And I brought him to thy disciples, that they should cast him out, and they could not cure him.

i. Then Jesus answered and said, **O faithless and perverse generation, how long shall I be with you. How long shall I suffer you? Bring thy son hither to me.**

j. And they brought him unto him: And as he was yet a coming, and when he saw him, the devil threw him down, and straightway the spirit tare him; and he fell on the ground, and wallowed foaming.

k. And he asked his father, **How long is it ago since this came unto him?**

l. And he said, Of a child. And ofttimes it hath cast him into the fire, and into the waters, to destroy him: but if thou canst do anything, have compassion on us, and help us.

m. Jesus said unto him, **If thou canst believe, all things are possible to him that believeth.**

n. And straightway the father of the child cried out, and said with tears, Lord, I believe; help thou mine unbelief.

o. When Jesus saw that the people came running together, he rebuked the foul spirit, saying unto him, **Thou dumb and deaf spirit, I charge thee, come out of him, and enter no more unto him.**

p. And the spirit cried, and rent him sore, and came out of him: and he was as one dead; insomuch that many said, He is dead.

q. But Jesus took him by the hand, and lifted him up; and he arose; and delivered him again to his father: and the child was cured from that very hour.

r. And they were all amazed at the mighty power of God. But while they wondered every one at all things which Jesus did *(Jesus and his disciples go into a house).*

s. And when he was come into the house, his disciples asked him privately, Why could not we cast him out?

t. And Jesus said unto them, **because of your unbelief: for verily I say unto you, If ye have faith as a grain of a mustard seed, ye shall say unto this mountain, Remove hence to yonder place; and it shall remove; and nothing shall be impossible to you. Howbeit this kind goeth not out but by prayer and fasting.**

5-18. Jesus tells his disciples about his death and resurrection.

a. And they departed thence, and passed through Galilee; and while they abode in Galilee, he would not that any man should know it.

b. Jesus taught his disciples, and said unto them.

c. **Let these sayings sink down into your ears: for the Son of man shall be betrayed into the hands of men.**

d. **And they shall kill him, and after that he is killed, the third day he shall be raised again.**

e. And they were exceeding sorry.

f. But they understood not this saying, and it was hid from them, that they perceive it not: and they feared to ask him of that saying.

5-19. The money in the fish's mouth.
a. And when they were come to Capernaum, they that received tribute money came to Peter, and said, Doth not your master pay tribute? He saith, Yes.

b. And when he (*Peter*) was come into the house, Jesus prevented him, saying, **What thinkest thou, Simon? Of whom do the kings of the earth take custom or tribute? Of their own children, or of strangers?**

c. Peter saith unto him, Of strangers. Jesus saith unto him, **Then are the children free. Nothwithstanding, lest we should offend them, go thou to the sea, and cast an hook, and take up the fish that first cometh up; and when thou hast opened his mouth, thou shalt find a piece of money: that take, and give unto them for me and thee.**

The Combined Gospel of Jesus Christ

Chapter Six
Jesus heals the man born blind

6-1. Jesus teach in the temple.

a. Now about the midst of the feast Jesus went up into the temple, and taught.

b. And the Jews marvelled, saying, How knoweth this man letters, having never learned?

c. Jesus answered them, and said, **My doctrine is not mine, but his that sent me. If any man will do this will, he shall know of the doctrine, whether it be of God, or whether I speak of myself.**

d. **He that speaketh of himself seeketh his own glory: but he that seeketh his glory that sent him, the same is true, and no unrighteousness is in him.**

e. **Did not Moses give you the law, and yet none of you keepeth the law? Why go ye about to kill me?**

f. The people answered and said, Thou hast a devil: who goeth about to kill thee?

g. Jesus answered and said unto them, **I have done one work, and ye all marvel. Moses therefore gave unto you circumcision; (not because it is of Moses, but of the fathers;) and ye on the sabbath day circumcise a man.**

h. **If a man on the sabbath day receive circumcision, that the law of Moses should not be broken; are ye angry at me, because I have made a man every whit whole on the sabbath day?**

i. **Judge not according to the appearance, but judge righteous judgment.**

j. Then said some of them of Jerusalem, Is not this he, whom they seek to kill? But, lo, he speaketh boldly, and they say nothing unto him.

k. Do the rulers know indeed that this is the very Christ? Howbeit we know this man whence he is: but when Christ cometh, no man knoweth whence he is.

l. Then cried Jesus in the temple as he taught, saying, **ye both know me, and ye know whence I am: and I am not come of myself, but he that sent me is true, whom ye know not. But I know him: for I am from him, and he hath sent me.**

m. Then they sought to take him: but no man laid hands on him, because his hour was not yet come.

n. And many of the people believed on him, and said, When Christ cometh, will he do more miracles than these which this man hath done?

o. The Pharisees heard that the people murmured such things concerning him; and the Pharisees and the chief priests sent officers to take him.

p. Then said Jesus unto them, **Yet a little while am I with you, and then I go unto him that sent me. Ye shall seek me, and shall not find me: and where I am, thither ye cannot come.**

q. Then said the Jews among themselves, Whither will he go, that we shall not find him? will he go unto the dispersed among the Gentiles, and teach the Gentiles?

r. What manner of saying is this that he said, Ye shall seek me, and shall not find me: and where I am, thither ye cannot come?

6-2. The last day of the feast.

a. In the last day, that great day of the feast, Jesus stood and cried, saying, **If any man thirst, let him come unto me, and drink.**

b. **He that believeth on me, as the scripture hath said, out of his belly shall flow rivers of living water.** (But this spake he of the Spirit, which they that believe on him should receive: for the Holy Ghost was not yet given; because that Jesus was not yet glorified.)

c. Many of the people therefore, when they heard this saying, said, Of a truth this is the Prophet.

d. Others said, This is the Christ, But some said, Shall Christ come out of Galilee? Hath not the scripture said, That Christ cometh of the seed of David, and out of the town of Bethlehem, where David was?

e. So there was a division among the people because of him?

f. And some of them would have taken him; but no man laid hands on him.

g. Then came the officers to the chief priests and Pharisees; and they said unto them, Why have ye not brought him?

h. The officers answered, Never man spake like this man.

i. Then answered them the Pharisee, Are ye also deceived? Have any of the rulers or of the Pharisees believed on him? But this people who knoweth not the law are cursed.

j. Nicodemius saith unto them, (he that came to Jesus by night, being one of them,). Doth our law judge any man, before it hear him, and know what he doeth?

k. They answered and said unto him, Art thou also of Galilee? Search, and look: for out of Galilee ariseth no prophet.

l. And every man went unto his own house.

6-3. The woman caught in adultery.

a. Jesus went unto the mount of Olives.

b. And early in the morning he came again into the temple, and all the people came unto him; and he sat down, and taught them.

c. And the scribes and Pharisees brought unto him a woman taken in adultery; and when they had set her in the midst.

d. They say unto him, Master, this woman was taken in adultery, in the very act. Now Moses in the law commanded us, that such should be stoned: but what sayest thou? This they said, tempting him, that they might have to accuse him.

e. But Jesus stooped down, and with his finger wrote on the ground, as though he heard them not.

f. So when they continued asking him, he lifted up himself, and said unto them, **He that is without sin among you, let him first cast a stone at her.**

g. And again he stopped down, and wrote on the ground. And they which heard it, being convicted by their own conscience, went out one by one, beginning at the eldest, even unto the last: and Jesus was left alone, and the woman standing in the midst.

h. When Jesus had lifted up himself, and saw none but the woman, he said unto her, **Woman, where are those thine accusers? Hath no man condemned thee?**

i. She said, No man, Lord. And Jesus said unto her, **Neither do I condemn thee: go, and sin no more.**

6-4. Jesus the light of the world.

a. Then spake Jesus again unto them, saying, **I am the light of the world: he that followed me shall not walk in darkness, but shall have the light of life.**

b. The Pharisees therefore said unto him, Thou bearest record of thyself; thy record is not true.

c. Jesus answered and said unto them, **Though I bear record of myself, yet my record is true: for I know whence I came, and whither I go; but ye cannot tell whence I come, and whither I go.**

d. **Ye judge after the flesh; I judge no man. And yet if I judge, my judgment is true: for I am not alone, but I and the Father that sent me.**

e. **It is also written in your law, that the testimony of two men is true. I am one that bear witness of myself, and the Father that sent me beareth witness of me.**

f. Then said they unto him, Where is thy Father?

g. Jesus answered, **Ye neither know me, nor my Father: if ye had known me, ye should have known my Father also.**

h. These words spake Jesus in the treasury, as he taught in the temple: and no man laid hands on him; for his hours was not yet come.

6-5. **Jesus warns against unbelief.**

a. Then said Jesus again unto them, **I go my way, and ye shall seek me, and shall die in your sins: whither I go, ye cannot come.**

b. Then said the Jews, Will he kill himself? because he saith, Whither I go, ye cannot come.

c. And he said unto them, **Ye are from beneath; I am from above: ye are of this world; I am not of this world.**

d. **I said therefore unto you, that ye shall die in your sins: for if ye believe not that I am he, ye shall die in your sins.**

e. Then said they unto him, Who art thou?

f. And Jesus saith unto them, **Even the same that said unto you from the beginning. I have many things to say and to judge of you: but he that sent me is true; and I speak to the world those things which I have heard of him.**

g. They understood not that he spake to them of the Father.

h. Then said Jesus unto them, **When ye have lifted up the Son of man, then shall ye know that I am he, and that I do nothing of myself; but as my Father hath taught me, I speak these things.**

i. **And he that sent me is with me: the Father hath not left me alone; for I do always those things that please him.**

j. As he spake these words, many believed on him.

6-6. The true children of Abraham.

a. Then said Jesus to those Jews which believed on him, **If ye continue in my word, then are ye my disciples indeed. And ye shall know the truth, and the truth shall make you free.**

b. They answered him, We be Abraham's seed, and were never in bondage to any man: how sayest thou, Ye shall be made free?

c. Jesus answered them, **Verily, verily, I say unto you, Whosoever committeth sin is the servant of sin. And the servant abideth not in the house for ever: but the Son abideth ever.**

d. **If the Son therefore shall make you free, ye shall be free indeed. I know that ye are Abraham's seed; but ye seek to kill me, because my word hath no place in you.**

e. **I speak that which I have seen with my Father: and ye do that which ye have seen with your father.**

f. They answered and said unto him, Abraham is our father.

g. Jesus saith unto them, **If ye were Abraham's children, ye would do the works of Abraham.**

h. **But now ye seek to kill me, a man that hath told you the truth, which I have heard of God: this did not Abraham. Ye do the deeds of your father.**

i. Then said they to him, We be not born of fornication; we have one Father, even God.

j. Jesus said unto them, **If God were your Father, ye would love me: for I proceeded forth and came from God; neither came I of myself, but he sent me.**

k. **Why do ye not understand my speech? even because ye cannot hear my word.**

l. **Ye are of your father the devil, and the lusts of your father ye will do. He was a murderer from the beginning, and abode not in the truth, because there is no truth in him.**

m. **When he speaketh a lie, he speaketh of his own: for he is a liar, and the father of it.**

n. **And because I tell you the truth, ye believe me not. Which of you convinceth me of sin?**

o. **And if I say the truth, why do ye not believe me. He that is of God heareth God's words: ye therefore hear them not, because ye are not of God.**

6-7. Jews say Jesus hast a devil.

a. Then answered the Jews, and said unto him, Say we not well that thou art a Samaritan, and hast a devil?

b. Jesus answered, **I have not a devil; but I honour my Father, and ye do dishonour me. And I seek not mine own glory: there is one that seeketh and judgeth.**

c. **Verily, verily, I say unto you, If a man keep my saying, he shall never see death.**

d. Then said the Jews unto him, Now we know that thou hast a devil. Abraham is dead, and the prophets; and thou sayest, If a man keep my saying, he shall never taste of death.

e. Art thou greater than our father Abraham, which is dead? And the prophets are dead: whom makest thou thyself?

f. Jesus answered, **If I honour myself, my honour is nothing: it is my Father that honoureth me; of whom ye say, that he is your God.**

g. **Yet ye have not known him; but I know him: and if I should say, I know him not, I shall be a liar like unto you: but I know him, and keep his saying.**

h. **Your father Abraham rejoiced to see my day: and he saw it, and was glad.**

i. Then said the Jews unto him, Thou art not yet fifty years old, and hast thou seen Abraham?

j. Jesus said unto them, **Verily, verily, I say unto you, Before Abraham was, I am.**

k. Then took they up stones to cast at him: but Jesus hid himself, and went out of the temple, going through the midst of them, and so passed by.

6-8. Jesus heals the man born blind.

a. And as Jesus passed by, he saw a man which was blind from his birth.

b. And his disciples asked him, saying, Master, who did sin, this man, or his parents, that he was born blind?

c. Jesus answered, **Neither hath this man sinned, nor his parents: but that the works of God should be made manifest in him.**

d. **I must work the works of him that sent me, while it is day: the night cometh, when no man can work. As long as I am in the world, I am the light of the** world.

e. **When he had thus spoken, he spat on the ground, and made clay of the spittle, and he anointed the eyes of the blind man with the clay.**

f. **And said unto him, Go, wash in the pool of Siloam,** (which is by interpretation, Sent.) He went his way therefore, and washed, and came seeing.

g. The neighbours therefore, and they which before had seen him that he was blind, said, Is not this he that sat and begged?

h. Some said, This is he: others said, He is like him: but he said, I am he. Therefore said they unto him, How were thine eyes opened?

i. He answered and said, A man that is called Jesus made clay, and anointed mine eyes, and said unto me, Go to the pool of Siloam, and wash: and I went and washed, and I received sight.

j. Then said they unto him, Where is he? He said, I knew not.

6-9. Pharisees question the healed man.

a. They brought to the Pharisees him that aforetime was blind.

b. And it was the sabbath day when Jesus made the clay, and opened his eyes.

c. Then again the Pharisees also asked him how he had received his sight. He said unto them, He put clay upon mine eyes, and I washed, and do see.

d. Therefore said some of the Pharisees, This man is not of God, because he keepeth not the sabbath day.

e. Others said, How can a man that is a sinner do such miracles? And there was division among them.

f. They say unto the blind man again, What sayest thou of him, that he had opened thine eyes? He said, He is a prophet.

g. But the Jews did not believe concerning him, that he had been blind, and received his sight, until they called the parents of him that had received his sight.

h. And they asked them, saying, Is this your son, who ye say was born blind? how then doth he now see?

i. His parents answered them and said, We know that this is our son, and that he was born blind: But by what means he now seeth, we know not; or who hath opened his eyes, we know not: he is of age; ask him: he shall speak for himself.

j. These words spake his parents, because they feared the Jews: for the Jews had agreed already, that if any man did confess that he was Christ, he should be put out of the synagogue. Therefore said his parents, He is of age; ask him.

k. Then again called they the man that was blind, and said unto him, Give God the praise: we know that this man is a sinner.

l. He answered and said, Whether he be a sinner or no, I know not: one thing I know, that, whereas I was blind, now I see.

m. Then said they to him again, What did he to thee? how opened he thine eyes?

n. He answered them, I have told you already, and ye did not hear: wherefore would ye hear it again? Will ye also be his disciples?

o. Then they revived him, and said, Thou art his disciple; but we are Moses' disciples. We know that God spake unto Moses: as for this fellow, we know not from whence he is.

p. The man answered and said unto them, Why herein is a marvellous thing, that ye know not from whence he is, and yet he hath opened mine eyes.

q. Now we know that God heareth not sinners, but if any man be a worshipper of God, and doeth his will, him he heareth.

r. Since the world began was it not heard that any man opened the eyes of one that was born blind. If this man were not of God, he could do nothing.

s. They answered and said unto him, Thou wast altogether born in sins, and dost thou teach us? And they cast him out.

6-10. Jesus talks to the healed man.

a. Jesus heard that they had cast him out; and when he had found him, he said unto him, **Dost thou believe on the Son of God?**

b. He answered and said, Who is he, Lord, that I might believe on him?

c. And Jesus said unto him, **Thou hast both seen him, and it is he that talked with thee.**

d. And he said, Lord, I believe. And he worshipped him.

e. And Jesus said, **For judgment I am come into this world, that they which see not might see; and that they which see might be made blind.**

f. And some of the Pharisees which were with him heard these words, and said unto him, Are we blind also.

g. Jesus said unto them, **If ye were blind, ye should have no sin: but now ye say, We see; therefore your sin remaineth.**

6-11. The parable of the shepherd.

a. Verily, verily I say unto you, He that entereth not by the door into the sheepfold, but climbed up some other way, the same is a thief and a robber.

b. But he that entereth in by the door is the shepherd of the sheep. To him the porter openeth; and the sheep hear his voice: and he calleth his own sheep by name, and leadeth them out.

c. And when he putteth forth his own sheep, he goeth before them, and the sheep follow him: for they know his voice.

d. And a stranger will they not follow, but will flee from him: for they know not the voice of strangers.

e. This parable spake Jesus unto them: but they understood not what things they were which he spake unto them.

f. Then said Jesus unto them again, **Verily, verily, I say unto you, I am the door of the sheep. All that ever came before me are thieves and robbers: but the sheep did not hear them.**

g. I am the door: by me if any man enter in, he shall be saved, and shall go in and out, and find pasture.

h. The thief cometh not, but for to steal, and to kill, and to destroy: I am come that they might have life, and that they might have it more abundantly.

i. I am the good shepherd: the good shepherd giveth his life for the sheep.

j. But he that is an hireling, and not the shepherd, whose own the sheep are not, seeth the wolf coming, and leaveth the sheep, and fleeth: and the wolf catcheth them, and scattered the sheep.

k. The hireling fleeth, because he is an hireling, and careth not for the sheep.

l. I am the good shepherd, and know my sheep, and am known of mine. As the Father knoweth me, even so know I the Father: and I lay down my life for the sheep.

m. And other sheep I have, which are not of this fold: them also I must bring, and they shall hear my voice; and there shall be one fold, and one shepherd.

n. Therefore doth my Father love me, because I lay down my life, that I might take it again. No man taketh it from me, but I lay it down of myself.

o. I have power to lay it down, and I have power to take it again. This commandment have I received of my Father.

p. There was a division therefore again among the Jews for these sayings.

q. And many of them said, He hath a devil, and is mad; why hear ye him?

r. Others said, These are not the words of him that hath a devil. Can a devil open the eyes of the blind?

6-12. The Jews try to arrest Jesus.

a. And it was at Jerusalem the feast of the dedication, and it was winter.

b. And Jesus walked in the temple in Solomon's porch.

c. Then came the Jews round about him, and said unto him, How long dost thou make us to doubt? If thou be the Christ, tell us plainly.

d. Jesus answered them, **I told you, and ye believed not: the works that I do in my Father's name, they bear witness of me.**

e. **But ye believe not, because ye are not of my sheep, as I said unto you. My sheep hear my voice, and I know them, and they follow me: And I give unto them** eternal life; and they shall never perish, neither shall any man pluck them out of my hand.

f. **My Father, which gave them me, is greater than all; and no man is able to pluck them out of my Father's hand. I and my Father are one.**

g. Then the Jews took up stones again to stone him.

h. Jesus answered them, **Many good works have I shown you from my Father; for which of these works do ye stone me?**

i. The Jews answered him, saying, For a good work we stone thee not; but for blasphemy; and because that thou, being a man, makest thyself God.

j. Jesus answered them, **Is it not written in your law, I said, Ye are gods?**

k. **If he called them gods, unto whom the word of God came, and the scripture cannot be broken; Say ye of him, whom the Father hath sanctified, and sent into the world, Thou blasphemest; because I said, I am the Son of God?**

l. **If I do not the works of my Father, believe me not. But if I do, though ye believe not me, believe the works: that ye may know, and believe, that the Father is in me, and I in him.**

m. Therefore they sought again to take him: but he escaped out of their hand.

n. And went away again beyond Jordan into the place where John at first baptized; and there he abode.

o. And many resorted unto him, and said, John did no miracle: but all things that John spake of this man were true. And many believed on him there.

6-13. The greatest in the kingdom.

a. Then there arose a reasoning among them, which of them should be greatest.

b. And he came to Capernaum, at the same time came the disciples unto Jesus: and being in the house he asked them, **What was it that ye disputed among yourselves by the way?**

c. But they held their peace: for by the way they had disputed among themselves, who should be the greatest in the kingdom of heaven?

d. And he sat down, and called the twelve, and saith unto them, **If any man desire to be first, the same shall be last of all, and servant of all.**

e. And Jesus, perceiving the thought of their heart called a little child unto him, and set him, by him, in the midst of them; and when he had taken him in his arms, he said unto them. (Controversy: Matthew 18:1 *said the disciples ask Jesus who would be the greatest in the Kingdom of Heaven;* Mark 9:34 *said they held their peace;* Luke 9:47 *said Jesus perceive their thoughts, I used Mark and Luke accounts*).

f. **Whosoever shall receive one of such little child in my name, receiveth me: and whosoever shall receive me, receiveth not me, but him that sent me: for he that is least among you all, the same shall be great.**

g. And said, **Verily I say unto you, Except ye be converted, and become as little children, ye shall not enter into the kingdom of heaven.**

h. **Whosoever therefore shall humble himself as this little child, the same is the greatest in the kingdom of heaven.**

i. **But whoso shall offend one of these little ones which believe in me, it were better for him that a milestone were hanged about his neck, and that he was drowned in the depth of the sea.**

j. **Woe unto the world because of offences! For it must needs be that offences come; but woe to that man by whom the offence cometh!**

k. Wherefore if thy hand or thy foot offend thee, cut them off, and cast them from thee: it is better for thee to enter into life halt or maimed, rather than having two hands or two feet to be cast into everlasting fire that never shall be quenched *(to be extinguished or put out)*. Where their worm dieth not, and the fire is not quenched.

l. And if thine eye offend thee, pluck it out, and cast it from thee: it is better for thee to enter into the kingdom of God with one eye, rather than having two eyes to be cast into hell fire: Where their worm dieth not, and the fire is not quenched.

m. Take heed that ye despise not one of these little ones; for I say unto you, That in heaven their angels do always behold the face of my Father which is in heaven.

n. For every one shall be salted with fire, and every sacrifice shall be salted with salt. Salt is good: but if the salt has lost his saltness, wherewith will ye season it? Have salt in yourselves, and have peace one with another.

o. And John answered and said, Master, we saw one casting out devils in thy name; and we forbad him, because he followeth not with us.

p. And Jesus said unto him, **Forbid him not: for there is no man which shall do a miracle in my name, that can lightly speak evil of me: for he that is not against us is for us.**

q. For whosoever shall give you a cup of water to drink in my name, because ye belong to Christ, verily I say unto you, he shall not lose his reward.

6-14. James and John rebuked.

a. And it came to pass, when the time was come that he should be received up, he steadfastly set his face to go to Jerusalem.

b. And sent messengers before his face: and they went, and entered into a village of the Samaritans, to make ready for him.

c. And they did not receive him, because his face was as though he would go to Jerusalem.

d. And when his disciples James and John saw this, they said, Lord, wilt thou that we command fire to come down from heaven, and consume them, even as Elias did?

e. But he turned, and rebuked them, and said, **Ye know not what manner of spirit ye are of. For the Son of man is not come to destroy men's live, but to save them.**

f. And they went to another village.

6-15. Teaching about discipleship.

a. Now when Jesus saw great multitudes about him, he gave commandment to depart unto the other side.

b. And it came to pass, that, as they went in the way, a certain scribe came, and said unto him, Master, I will follow thee whithersoever thou goest.

c. And Jesus saith unto him, **The foxes have holes, and the birds of the air have nests; but the Son of man hath not where to lay his head.**

d. And he said unto another, **Follow me.**

e. And another of his disciples said unto him, Lord, suffer me first to go and bury my father.

f. But Jesus saith unto him, **Follow me; and let the dead bury their dead; but go thou and preach the kingdom of God.**

g. And another also said, Lord, I will follow thee; but let me first go bid them farewell, which are at home at my house.

h. And Jesus said unto him, **No man, having put his hand to the plough, and looking back, is fit for the kingdom of God.**

6-16. The mission of the seventy.

a. After these things the Lord appointed other seventy also, and sent them two and two before his face into every city and place, whither he himself would come.

b. Therefore said he unto them, **The harvest truly is great, but the labourers are few: pray ye therefore the Lord of the harvest, that he would send forth labourers into his harvest.**

c. **Go your ways: behold, I send you forth as lambs among wolves. Carry neither purse, nor scrip, nor shoes: and salute no man by the way.**

d. **And into whatsoever house ye enter, first say, Peace be to this house. And if the son of peace be there, your peace shall rest upon it: if not, it shall turn to you again.**

e. **And in the same house remain, eating and drinking such things as they give: for the labourer is worthy of his hire. Go not from house to house.**

f. **And into whatsoever city ye enter, and they receive you, eat such things as are set before you. And heal the sick that are therein, and say unto them, The kingdom of God is come nigh unto you.**

g. But into whatsoever city ye enter, and they receive you not, go your ways out into the streets of the same, and say, Even the very dust of your city, which cleaveth on us, we do wipe off against you: notwithstanding be ye sure of this, that the kingdom of God is come nigh unto you.

h. But I say unto you, that it shall be more tolerable in that day for Sodom, than for that city.

i. Woe unto thee, Chorazin! Woe unto thee, Bethsaida! For if the mighty works had been done in Tyre and Sidon, which have been done in you, they had a great while ago repented, sitting in sackcloth and ashes.

j. But it shall be more tolerable for Tyre and Sidon at the judgment, than for you.

k. And thou, Capernaum, which are exalted to heaven, shalt be thrust down to hell.

l. He that heareth you heareth me; and he that despiseth you despiseth me; and he that despsieth me despiseth him that sent me.

m. And the seventy returned again with joy, saying, Lord, even the devils are subject unto us through thy name.

n. And he said unto them, **I beheld Satan as lightning fall from heaven. Behold, I give unto you power to tread on serpents and scorpions, and over all the power of the enemy: and nothing shall by any means hurt you.**

o. Notwithstanding in this rejoice not, that the spirits are subject unto you; but rather rejoice, because your names are written in heaven.

p. And he turned him unto his disciples, and said privately, **Blessed are the eyes which see the things that ye see: For I tell you, that many prophets and kings have desired to see those things which ye see, and have not seen them; and to hear those things which ye hear, and have not heard them.**

6-17. The parable of the good Samaritan.

a. And, behold, a certain lawyer stood up, and tempted him, saying, Master, what shall I do to inherit eternal life?

b. He said unto him, **What is written in the law? how readest thou?**

c. And he answering said, Thou shalt love the Lord thy God with all thy heart, and with all thy soul, and with all thy strength, and with all thy mind; and thy neighbour as thyself.

d. And he said unto him, **Thou hast answered right: this do, and thou shalt live.**

e. But he, willingly to justify himself, said unto Jesus, And who is my neighbour?

f. And Jesus answering said, **A certain man went down from Jerusalem to Jericho, and fell among thieves, which stripped him of his raiment, and wounded him, and departed, leaving him half dead.**

g. **And by chance there came down a certain priest that way: and when he saw him, he passed by on the other side.**

h. **And likewise a Levite, when he was at the place, came and looked on him, and passed by on the other side.**

i. But a certain Samaritan, as he journeyed, came where he was: and when he saw him, he had compassion on him, And went to him, and bound up his wounds, pouring in oil and wine, and set him on his own beast, and brought him to an inn, and took care of him.

j. And on the morrow when he departed, he took out two pence, and gave them to the host, and said unto him, Take care of him; and whatsoever thou spendest more, when I come again, I will repay thee.

k. Which now of these three, thinkest thou, was neighbour unto him that fell among the thieves?

l. And he said, He that showed mercy on him. Then said Jesus unto him, Go, and do thou likewise.

6-18. The parable of the lost sheep.

a. Then drew near unto him all the publicans and sinners for to hear him. And the Pharisees and scribes murmured, saying, This man receiveth sinners, and eateth with them.

b. And he spake this parable unto them, saying. For the Son of man is come to save that which was lost. How think ye? If a man have an hundred sheep, and one of them be gone astray, doth he not leave the ninety and nine in the wilderness, and goeth into the mountains, and seeketh that which is gone astray, until he find it.

c. And if so be, that he find it, verily I say unto you, he layeth it on his shoulders, and rejoiceth more of that sheep, than of the ninety and nine which went not astray.

d. And when he cometh home, he calleth together his friends and neighbours, saying unto them, Rejoice with me; for I have found my sheep which was lost.

e. Even so it is not the will of your Father which is in heaven, that one of these little ones should perish.

f. I say unto you, that likewise joy shall be in heaven over one sinner that repenteth, more than over ninety and nine just persons, which need no repentance.

6-19. Sin and forgiveness.

a. Moreover if thy brother shall trespass against thee, go and tell him his fault between thee and him alone: if he shall hear thee, thou hast gained thy brother.

b. But if he will not hear thee, then take with thee one or two more, that in the mouth of two or three witnesses every word may be established.

c. And if he shall neglect to hear them, tell it unto the church: but if he neglect to hear the church, let him be unto thee as an heathen man and a publican.

d. Verily I say unto you, Whatsoever ye shall bind on earth shall be bound in heaven: and whatsoever ye shall loose on earth shall be loosed in heaven.

e. Again I say unto you, That if two of you shall agree on earth as touching any thing that they shall ask, it shall be done for them of my Father which is in heaven.

f. For where two or three or gathered together in my name, there am I in the midst of them.

g. Then came Peter to him, and said, Lord, how oft shall my brother sin against me, and I forgive him? till seven times?

h. Jesus saith unto him, I say not unto thee, Until seven times: but, Until seventy times seven.

6-20. The parable of the unforgiving servant.

a. Therefore is the kingdom of heaven likened unto a certain king, which would take account of his servants.

b. And when he had begun to reckon, one was brought unto him, which owed him ten thousand talents.

c. But forasmuch as he had not to pay, his lord commanded him to be sold, and his wife, and children, and all that he had, and payment to be made.

d. The servant therefore fell down, and worshipped him, saying, Lord, have patience with me, and I will pay thee all.

e. Then the lord of that servant was move with compassion, and loosed him, and forgave him the debt.

f. But the same servant went out, and found one of his fellowservants, which owed him an hundred pence: and he laid hands on him, and took him by the throat, saying, Pay me that thou owest.

g. And his fellow servant fell down at his feet, and besought him, saying, Have patience with me, and I will pay thee all. And he would not: but went and cast him into prison, till he should pay him the debt.

h. So when his fellowservants saw what was done, they were very sorry, and came and told unto their lord all that was done.

i. Then his lord, after that he had called him, said unto him, O thou wicked servant, I forgave thee all that debt, because thou desiredst me.

j. Shouldest not thou also have had compassion on thy fellow servant, even as I had pity on thee?

k. And his lord was wroth, and delivered him to the tormentors, till he should pay all that was due unto him.

l. So likewise shall my heavenly Father do also unto you, if ye from your hearts forgive not every one his brother their trespasses.

6-21. Marriage and divorce.

a. And it came to pass, that when Jesus had finished these sayings; And he arose from thence and departed from Galilee, and cometh into the coasts of Judaea by the farther side of Jordan: and great multitudes resort unto him again; and he healed them there; and, as he was won't, he taught them again.

b. And the Pharisees also came to him, tempting him and asked him, Is it lawful for a man to put away his wife for every cause?

c. And he answered and said unto them, **What did Moses command you?** And they said, Moses suffered to write a bill of divorcement, and to put her away.

d. And Jesus answered and said unto them, **Moses wrote you this precept, because of the hardness of your hearts suffered you to put away your wives: but from the beginning it was not so.**

e. **Have ye not read, that from the beginning of creation, God made them male and female. For this cause shall a man leave his father and mother, and cleave to his wife; And they twain shall be one flesh: wherefore they are no more twain, but one flesh.**

f. **What therefore God had joined together, let no man put asunder.**

g. **And I say unto you, Whosoever shall put away his wife, except it be for fornication, and shall marry another, committeth adultery: and whoso marrieth her which is put away doth commit adultery.**

h. And in the house his disciples asked him again of the same matter.

i. And he saith unto them, **Whosoever shall put away his wife, and marry another, committeth adultery against her.**

j. **And if a woman shall put away her husband, and be married to another, she committeh adultery.**

k. His disciples say unto him, If the case of the man be so with his wife, it is not good to marry.

l. But he said unto them, **All men cannot receive this saying, save they to whom it is given.**

m. **For there are some eunuchs** (*a man that have his testicles removed or an ineffectual man*), **which were so born from their mother's womb: and there are some eunuchs, which were made eunuchs of men: and there be eunuchs, which have made themselves eunuchs for the kingdom of heaven's sake.**

n. **He that is able to receive it, let him receive it.**

6-22. Jesus bless the little children.

a. Then were there brought unto him little children, also infants, that he should touch them, and pray; but when his disciples saw it, they rebuked those that brought them.

b. But when Jesus saw it, he was much displeased, and called them (*disciples*) unto him, and said, **Suffer little children to come unto me, and forbid them not: for such is the kingdom of God.**

c. **Verily I say unto you, Whosoever shall not receive the kingdom of God as a little child, he shall not enter therein.**

d. And he took them up in his arms, put his hands upon them, and blessed them, and departed thence.

6-23. The rich young ruler.

a. And when he was gone forth into the way, there came one running, and kneeled to him, and asked him, Good Master, what good thing shall I do, that I may inherit eternal life?

b. And he said unto him, **Why callest thou me good? there is none good but one, that is, God: but if thou wilt enter into life, keep the commandments.**

c. He saith unto him, Which? Jesus said, **Thou knowest the commandments, Thou shalt do no murder, Thou shalt not commit adultery, Thou shalt not steal, Thou shalt not bear false witness.**

d. **Honour thy father and thy mother, Defraud not: and, Thou shalt love thy neighbour as thyself.**

e. The young man saith unto him, All these things have I kept from my youth up: what lack I yet.

f. Then Jesus beholding *(to see or observe)* him, loved him, and said unto him, **One thing thou lackest, If thou wilt be perfect, go and sell that thou hast, and give to the poor, and thou shalt have treasure in heaven: and come, take up the cross, and follow me.**

g. But when the young man heard that saying, he went away sorrowful: for he was very rich.

h. And when Jesus saw that he was very sorrowful, he looked round about, Then said Jesus unto his disciples, **Verily I say unto you, That a rich man shall hardly enter into the kingdom of heaven.**

i. And the disciples were astonished at his words. But Jesus answered again, and saith unto them, **Children, how hard is it for them that trust in riches to enter into the kingdom of God.**

j. **And again I say unto you, It is easier for a camel to go through the eye of a needle, than for a rich man to enter into the kingdom of God.**

k. When his disciples heard it, they were exceedingly amazed and astonished out of measure, saying among themselves, Who then can be saved?

l. But Jesus beheld them, and said unto them, **With men this is impossible; but not with God, for with God all things are possible.**

m. Then answered Peter and said unto him, Behold, we have forsaken all, and followed thee; what shall we have therefore?

n. And Jesus said unto them, **Verily I say unto you, That ye which have followed me, in the regeneration when the Son of man shall sit in the throne of his glory, ye also shall sit upon twelve thrones, judging the twelve tribes of Israel.**

o. **And every one that hath forsaken houses, or brethren, or sisters, or fathers, or mother, or wife, or children, or lands, for my name's sake and the gospel's, shall receive an hundredfold now in this time, houses, and brethren, and sisters, and mothers, and children, and lands, with persecutions; and in the world to come live everlasting.**

p. **But many that are first shall be last; and the last shall be first.**

6-24. The parable of the vineyard workers.

a. **For the kingdom of heaven is like unto a man that is an householder, which went out early in the morning** (zero hour = 6:00 AM?) **to hire laborers into his vineyard. And when he had agreed with the laborers for a penny a day, he sent them into his vineyard.**

b. **And he went out about the third hour** (9:00 AM), **and saw others standing idle in the marketplace, And said unto them; Go ye also into the vineyard, and** whatsoever is right I will give you. And they went their way.

    c. **Again he went out about the sixth** *(12:00 AM)* **and ninth hour** *(3:00 PM)*, **and did likewise.**

    d. **And about the eleventh hour** *(5:00 PM)* **he went out, and found others standing idle, and saith unto them, why stand ye here all the day idle? They say unto him, Because no man hath hired us. He saith unto them, Go ye also into the vineyard; and whatsoever is right, that shall ye receive.**

    e. **So when even was come** (6:01 PM; Evening 6:01 – 9:00 PM), **the lord of the vineyard saith unto his steward, Call the laborers, and give them their hire, beginning from the last unto the first.**

    f. **And when they came that were hired about the eleventh hour, they received every man a penny.**

    g. **But when the first came, they supposed that they should have received more; and they likewise received every man a penny.**

    h. **And when they had received it, they murmured against the goodman of the house,**

    i. **Saying, These last have wrought but one hour, and thou hast made them equal unto us, which have borne the burden and heat of the day.**

    j. **But he answered one of them, and said, Friend, I do thee no wrong: didst not thou agree with me for a penny? Take that thine is, and go thy way: I will give unto this last, even as unto thee.**

    k. **Is it not lawful for me to do what I will with my own? Is thine eye evil, because I am good.**

    l. **So the last shall be first, and the first last: for many be called, but few chosen.**

The Combined Gospel of Jesus Christ

Chapter Seven
Jesus raises Lazarus from the dead

7-1. Good gifts.

a. Ask, and it shall be given you; seek, and ye shall find; knock, and it shall be opened unto you: For every one that asketh receiveth; and he that seeketh findeth; and to him that knocketh it shall be opened.

b. Or what man is there of you, whom if his son ask bread, will he give him a stone? Or if he ask a fish, will he give him a serpent?

c. If ye then, being evil, know how to give good gifts unto your children, how much more shall your Father which is in heaven give good things to them that ask him?

d. Therefore all things whatsoever ye would that men should do to you, do ye even so to them: for this is the law and the prophets.

7-2. The strait and wide gates.

a. And he went through the cities and villages, teaching, and journeying toward Jerusalem. Then said one unto him, Lord, are there few that be saved?

b. And he said unto them. **Strive to enter ye in at the strait gate: for many, I say unto you, will seek to enter in, and shall not be able. For wide is the gate, and broad is the way, that leadeth to destruction, and many there be which go in thereat.**

c. **Because strait is the gate, and narrow is the way, which leadeth unto life, and few there be that find it.**

d. **When once the master of the house is risen up,**

and hath shut to the door, and ye begin to stand without, and to knock at the door, saying, Lord, Lord, open unto us; and he shall answer and say unto you, I know you not whence ye are.

e. Then shall ye begin to say, We have eaten and drunk in thy presence, and thou has taught in our streets. But he shall say, I tell you, I know you not whence ye are; depart from me, all ye workers of iniquity.

f. There shall be weeping and gnashing of teeth, when ye shall see Abraham, and Isaac, and Jacob, and all the prophets, in the kingdom of God, and you yourselves thrust out.

g. And they shall come from the east, and from the west, and from the north, and from the south, and shall sit down in the kingdom of God.

h. And, behold, there are last which shall be first, and there are first which shall be last.

7-3. The test of false prophets.

a. Beware of false prophets, which come to you in sheep's clothing, but inwardly they are ravening wolves. Ye shall know them by their fruits. Do men gather grapes of thorns, or figs of thistles?

b. For of thorns men do not gather grapes or figs, nor of a bramble bush gather they grapes, or figs of thistles.

c. Even so every good tree bringeth forth good fruit; but a corrupt tree bringeth forth evil fruit. A good tree cannot bring forth evil fruit, neither can a corrupt tree bring forth good fruit.

d. Every tree that bringeth not forth good fruit is hewn down, and cast into the fire. Wherefore by their fruits ye shall know them.

e. A good man out of the good treasure of his heart bringeth forth that which is good; and an evil man out of the evil treasure of his heart bringeth forth that which is evil: for of the abundance of the heart his mouth speaketh.

f. Not every one that saith unto me, Lord, Lord, shall enter into the kingdom of heaven; but he that doeth the will of my Father which is in heaven.

g. Many will say to me in that day, Lord, Lord, have we not prophesied in thy name? and in thy name have cast out devils? and in thy name done many wonderful works?

h. And then will I profess unto them, I never knew you: depart from me, ye that work iniquity.

7-4. Jesus visits Mary and Martha.

a. Now it came to pass, as they went, that he entered into a certain village: and a certain woman named Martha received him into her house.

b. And she had a sister called Mary, which also sat at Jesus' feet, and heard his word.

c. But Martha was cumbered about much serving, and came to him, and said, Lord, dost thou not care that my sister hath left me to serve alone? bid her therefore that she help me.

d. And Jesus answered and said unto her, **Martha, Martha, thou art careful and troubled about many things: But one thing is needful: and Mary hath chosen that good part, which shall not be taken away from her.**

7-5. The Lord's prayer.

a. And it came to pass, that, as he was praying in a certain place, when he ceased, one of his disciples said unto him, Lord, teach us to pray, as John also taught his disciples.

b. And he said unto them, **when thou prayest, thou shalt not be as the hypocrites are: for they love to pray standing in the synagogues and in the corners of the streets, that they may be seen of men.** Verily I say unto you, They have their reward.

c. But thou, when thou prayest, enter into thy closet, and when thou hast shut thy door, pray to thy Father which is in secret; and thy Father which seeth in secret shall reward thee openly.

d. But when ye pray, use not vain repetitions, as the heathen do: for they think that they shall be heard for their much speaking. Be not ye therefore like unto them: for your Father knoweth what things ye have need of, before you ask him.

e. After this manner therefore pray ye: Our Father which art in heaven, Hallowed be thy name. Thy kingdom come. Thy will be done in earth, as it is in heaven. Give us this day our daily bread. And forgive us our debts, as we forgive our debtors. And lead us not into temptation, but deliver us from evil: For thine is the kingdom, and the power, and the glory, for ever. Amen.

f. For if ye forgive men their trespasses, your heavenly Father will also forgive you: But if ye forgive not men their trespasses, neither will your Father forgive your trespasses.

g. Moreover when ye fast, be not, as the hypocrites, of a sad countenance: for they disfigure their faces, that they may appear unto men to fast. Verily I say unto you, They have their reward.

h. But thou, when thou fastest, anoint thine head, and wash thy face. That thou appear not unto men to fast, but unto thy Father which is in secret: and thy Father, which seeth in secret, shall reward thee openly.

7-6. The golden rule.

a. And he said unto them, **Which of you shall have a friend, and shall go unto him at midnight, and say unto him, Friend, lend me three loaves; For a friend of mine in his journey is come to me, and I have nothing to set before him?**

b. **And he from within shall answer and say, Trouble me not: the door is now shut, and my children are with me in bed; I cannot rise and give thee.**

c. **I say unto you, Though he will not rise and give him, because he is his friend, yet because of his importunity** *(persistent demands)* **he will rise and give him as many as he needeth.**

d. **And I say unto you, Ask, and it shall be given you; seek, and ye shall find; knock, and it shall be opened unto you.**

e. **For every one that asketh receiveth; and he that seeketh findeth; and to him that knocketh it shall be opened.**

f. **If a son shall ask bread of any of you that is a father, will he give him a stone? Or if he ask a fish, will he for a fish give him a serpent? Or if he shall ask an egg, will he offer him a scorpion?**

g. **If ye then, being evil, know how to give good gifts unto your children: how much more shall your heavenly Father give the Holy Spirit to them that ask him?**

7-7. Warning against seeking signs.

a. And when the people were gathered thick together. Then certain of the scribes and of the Pharisees answered, saying, Master, we would see a sign from thee.

b. But he answered and said unto them, **An evil and adulterous generation seeketh after a sign; and there shall no sign be given to it, but the sign of the prophet Jonas: For as Jonas was a sign unto the Ninevites, so shall also the Son of man be to this generation.**

c. **For as Jonas was three days and three nights in the whale's belly; so shall the son of man be three days and three nights in the heart of the earth.**

d. **The men of Nineveh shall rise in judgment with this generation, and shall condemn it: because they repented at the preaching of Jonas; and, behold, a greater than Jonas is here.**

e. **The queen of the south shall rise up in the judgment with this generation, and shall condemn it: for she came from the uttermost parts of the earth to hear the wisdom of Solomon; and, behold, a greater than Solomon is here.**

f. **When the unclean spirit is gone out of a man, he walketh through dry places, seeking rest, and findeth none. Then he saith, I will return into my house from whence I came out; and when he is come, he findeth it empty, swept, and garnished.**

g. **Then goeth he, and taketh with himself seven other spirits more wicked than himself, and they enter in and dwell there: and the last state of that man is worse than the first. Even so shall it be also unto this wicked generation.**

7-8. The parable of the candle.

a. **Lay not up for yourselves treasure upon earth, where moth and rust doth corrupt, and where thieves break through and steal:**

b. But lay up for yourselves treasures in heaven, where neither moth nor rust doth corrupt, and where thieves do not break through nor steal: For where your treasure is, there will your heart be also.

c. No man, when he hath lighted a candle, putteth it in a secret place, neither under a bushel, but on a candlestick, that they which come in may see the light.

d. The light of the body is the eye: if therefore thine eye be single, thy whole body shall be full of light.

e. But if thine eye be evil, thy whole body shall be full of darkness. If therefore the light that is in thee be darkness, how great is that darkness! Take heed therefore that the light which is in thee be not darkness.

f. If thy whole body therefore be full of light, having no part dark, the whole shall be full of light, as when the bright shining of a candle doth give thee light.

g. No man can serve two masters: for either he will hate the one, and love the other; or else he will hold to the one, and despise the other. Ye cannot serve God and mammon.

7-9. The warning against Pharisaism.

a. And as he spake, a certain Pharisee besought him to dine with him: and he went in, and sat down to meat. And when the Pharisee saw it, he marvelled that he had not first washed before dinner.

b. And the Lord said unto him, **Now do ye Pharisees make clean the outside of the cup and the platter; but your inward part is full of ravening and wickedness.**

c. Ye fools, did not he that made that which is without make that which is within also? But rather give alms of such things as ye have; and, behold, all things are clean unto you.

d. But woe unto you, Pharisees! For ye tithe mint and rue and all manner of herbs, and pass over judgment and the love of God: these ought ye to have done, and not to leave the other undone.

e. Woe unto you, Pharisees! For ye love the uppermost seats in the synagogues, and greetings in the markets.

f. Woe unto you, scribes and Pharisees, hypocrites! for ye are as graves which appear not, and the men that walk over them are not aware of them.

g. Then answered one of the lawyers, and said unto him, Master, thus saying thou reproachest us also.

h. And he said, Woe unto ye also, ye lawyers! for ye lade men with burdens grievous to be borne, and ye yourselves touch not the burdens with one of your fingers.

i. Woe unto you! for ye build the sepulchres (*graves or tombs*) of the prophets, and your fathers killed them. Truly ye bear witness that ye allow the deeds of your fathers: for they indeed killed them, and ye build their sepulchres.

j. Therefore also said the wisdom of God, I will send them prophets and apostles, and some of them they shall slay and persecute: That the blood of all the prophets, which was shed from the foundation of the world, may be required of this generation;

k. From the blood of Abel unto the blood of Zacharias, which perished between the altar and the temple: verily I say unto you, It shall be required of this generation.

l. Woe unto you, lawyers! for ye have taken away the key of knowledge: ye entered not in yourselves, and them that were entering in ye hindered.

m. And as he said these things unto them, the scribes and the Pharisees began to urge him vehemently, and to provoke him to speak of many things: Laying wait for him, and seeking to catch something out of his mouth, that they might accuse him.

7-10. The value of life.

a. In the mean time, when there were gathered together an innumerable multitude of people, insomuch that they trode one upon another, he began to say to his disciples first of all, **Beware ye of the leaven of the Pharisees, which is hypocrisy.**

b. **For there is nothing covered, that shall not be revealed; neither hid, that shall not be known.**

c. **Therefore whatseover ye have spoken in darkness shall be heard in the light; and that which ye have spoken in the ear in closets shall be proclaimed upon the housetops.**

d. **And I say unto you my friends, Be not afraid of them which kill the body, and after that have no more that they can do.**

e. **But I will forewarn you whom ye shall fear: Fear him, which after he hath killed hath power to cast into hell; yea, I say unto you, Fear him.**

f. **Are not five sparrows sold for two farthings, and not one of them is forgotten before God.**

g. **But even the very hairs of your head are all numbered. Fear not therefore: ye are of more value than many sparrows.**

h. **Also I say unto you, Whosoever shall confess me before men, him shall the Son of man also confess before the angels of God. But he that denieth me before men, shall be denied before the angels of God.**

i. And whosoever shall speak a word against the Son of man, it shall be forgiven him: but unto him that blasphemeth against the Holy Ghost it shall not be forgiven.

j. And when they bring you into the synagogues, and unto the magistrates, and powers, take ye no thought how or what thing ye shall answer, or what ye shall say: For the Holy Ghost shall teach you in the same hour what ye ought to say.

7-11. The parable of the rich fool.

a. And one of the company said unto him, Master, speak to my brother, that he divide the inheritance with me.

b. And he said unto him, **Man, who made me a judge or a divider over you?**

c. And he said unto them, **Take heed, and beware of covetousness: for a man's life consisteth not in the abundance of the things which he possesseth.**

d. And he spake a parable unto them, saying, **The ground of a certain rich man brought forth plentifully: And he thought within himself, saying, What shall I do, because I have no room where to bestow my fruits?**

e. **And he said, This will I do: I will pull down my barns, and build greater; and there will I bestow all my fruits and my goods.**

f. **And I will say to my soul, Soul, thou hast much goods laid up for many years; take thine ease, eat, drink, and be merry.**

g. **But God said unto him, Thou fool, this night thy soul shall be required of thee: then whose shall those things be, which thou hast provided?**

h. **So is he that layeth up treasure for himself, and is not rich toward God.**

7-12. Seek God's kingdom first.

   a. And he said to his disciples, **Therefore I say unto you, Take no thought for your life, what ye shall eat, or what ye shall drink; nor yet for your body, what ye shall put on. The life is more than meat, and the body is more than raiment?**

   b. **Consider the ravens: for they sow not, neither do they reap, nor gather into barns nor storehouses; yet your heavenly Father feedeth them. Are ye not much better than the fowls?**

   c. **Which of you by taking thought can add one cubit unto his stature? If ye then be not able to do that thing which is least, why take ye thought for the rest.**

   d. **And why take ye thought for raiment? consider the lilies of the field, how they grow: they toil not, neither do they spin: And yet I say unto you, That even Solomon in all his glory was not arrayed like one of these.**

   e. **Wherefore, if God so clothe the grass of the field, which to day is, and to morrow is cast into the oven, shall he not much more clothe you, O ye of little faith?**

   f. **Therefore take no thought, saying, what shall we eat? Or, What shall we drink? Or, Wherewithal shall we be clothed? neither be ye of doubtful mind.**

   g. **For all these things do the nations of the world seek after: for your heavenly Father knoweth that ye have need of all these things.**

   h. **But seek ye first the kingdom of God, and his righteousness; and all these things shall be added unto you. Fear not, little flock; for it is your Father's good pleasure to give you the kingdom.**

i. Sell that ye have, and give alms; provide yourselves bags which wax not old, a treasure in the heavens that faileth not, where no thief approacheth, neither moth corrupted.

j. For where your treasure is, there will your heart be also. Take therefore no thought for the morrow: for the morrow shall take thought for the things of itself. Sufficient unto the day is the evil thereof.

7-13. The parables of the watching servants.

a. Take ye heed, watch and pray: for ye know not when the time is. Let your loins be girded about, and your lights burning; For the son of man is a man taking a far journey, who left his house, and gave authority to his servants, and to every man his work, and commanded the porter to watch.

b. And ye yourselves like unto men that wait for their lord, when he will return from the wedding; that when he cometh and knocketh, they may open until him immediately.

c. Watch ye therefore: for ye know not when the master of the house cometh, at even, or at midnight, or at the cockcrowing, or in the morning: Lest coming suddenly he find you sleeping.

d. Blessed are those servants, whom the lord when he cometh shall find watching: verily I say unto you, that he shall gird himself, and make them to sit down to meat, and will come forth and serve them.

e. And if he shall come in the second watch, or come in the third watch, and find them so, blessed are those servants.

f. And what I say unto you I say unto all, Watch.

g. And this know, that if the goodman of the house had known what hour the thief would come, he would have watched, and not have suffered his house to be broken through.

h. **Be ye therefore ready also: for the Son of man cometh at an hour when ye think not.**

i. Then Peter said unto him, Lord speakest thou this parable unto us, or even to all?

j. And the Lord said, **Who then is that faithful and wise servant, whom his lord shall make ruler over his household, to give them their portion of meat in due season?**

k. **Blessed is that servant, whom his lord when he cometh shall find so doing.**

l. **Of a truth I say unto you, that he will make him ruler over all that he hath.**

m. **But and if that evil servant say in his heart, My lord delayed his coming; and shall begin to beat the menservants and maidens, and to eat and drink with the drunken, and to be drunken;**

n. **The lord of that servant will come in a day when he looketh not for him, at an hour when he is not aware of, and will cut him asunder, and will appoint him his portion with the unbelievers: there shall be weeping and gnashing of teeth.**

o. **And that servant, which knew his lord's will, and prepared not himself, neither did according to his will, shall be beaten with many stripes. But he that knew not, and did commit things worthy of stripes, shall be beaten with few stripes.**

p. **For unto whomsoever much is given, of him shall much be required: and to whom men have committed much, of him they will ask the more.**

7-14. Jesus the divider.

    a. I am come to send fire on the earth; and what will I, if it be already kindled. But I have a baptism to be baptized with; and how am I straitened till it be accomplished.

    b. Suppose ye that I am come to give peace on earth? I tell you, Nay; but rather division: For from henceforth there shall be five in one house divided, three against two, and two against three.

    c. The father shall be divided against the son, and the son against the father; the mother against the daughter, and the daughter against the mother; the mother in law against her daughter in law, and the daughter in law against her mother in law.

7-15. Discerning the time.

    a. And he said also to the people, When ye see a cloud rise out of the west, straightway ye say, There cometh a shower; and so it is. And when ye see the south wind blow, ye say, There will be heat; and it cometh to pass.

    b. Ye hypocrites, ye can discern the face of the sky and of the earth; but how is it that ye do not discern this time? Yea, and why even of yourselves judge ye not what is right?

    c. When thou goest with thine adversary to the magistrate, as thou art in the way, give diligence that thou mayest be delivered from him; lest he hale thee to the judge, and the judge deliver thee to the officer, and the officer cast thee into prison.

    d. I tell thee, thou shalt not depart thence, till thou hast paid the very last mite *(small amount).*

7-16. The parable of the fruitless fig tree.

a. There were present at that season some that told him of the Galilaeans, whose blood Pilate had mingled with their sacrifices.

b. And Jesus answering said unto them, **Suppose ye that these Galilaeans were sinners above all the Galilaeans, because they suffered such things? I tell you, Nay: but, except ye repent, ye shall all likewise perish.**

c. **Or those eighteen, upon whom the tower in Siloam fell, and slew them, think ye that they were sinners above all men that dwelt in Jerusalem? I tell you, Nay: but, except ye repent, ye shall all likewise perish.**

d. He spake also this parable; **A certain man had a fig tree planted in his vineyard; and he came and sought fruit thereon, and found none.**

e. **Then said he unto the dresser of his vineyard, Behold, these three years I come seeking fruit on this fig tree, and find none: cut it down; why cumbereth** (burden) **it the ground?**

f. **And he answering said unto him, Lord, let it alone this year also, till I shall dig about it, and dung** (to cover with manure) **it. And if it bear fruit, well: and if not, then after that thou shalt cut it down.**

7-17. A woman healed on the Sabbath.

a. And he was teaching in one of the synagogues on the sabbath. And, behold, there was a woman which had a spirit of infirmity eighteen years, and was bowed together, and could in now wise lift up herself.

b. And when Jesus saw her, he called her to him, and said unto her, **Woman, thou art loosed from thine infirmity. And he laid his hands on her: and immediately she was made straight, and glorified God.**

c. And the ruler of the synagogue answered with indignation, because that Jesus had healed on the sabbath day, and said unto the people, There are six days in which men ought to work: in them therefore come and be healed, and not on the sabbath day.

d. The Lord then answered him, and said, **Thou hypocrite, doth not each one of you on the sabbath loose his ox or his ass from the stall, and lead him away to watering?**

e. **And ought not this woman, being a daughter of Abraham, whom Satan hath bound, lo, these eighteen years, be loosed from this bound on the sabbath day?**

f. And when he had said these things, all his adversaries were ashamed: and all the people rejoiced for all the glorious things that were done by him.

7-18. Jesus hears of Lazarus' death.

a. Now a certain man was sick, named Lazarus, of Bethany, the town of Mary and her sister Martha. (It was that Mary which anointed the Lord with ointment, and wiped his feet with her hair, whose brother Lazarus was sick).

b. Therefore his sisters sent unto him, saying, Lord, behold, he whom thou lovest is sick.

c. When Jesus heard that, he said, **This sickness is not unto death, but for the glory of God, that the Son of God might be glorified thereby.**

d. Now Jesus loved Martha, and her sister, and Lazarus. When he had heard therefore that he was sick, he abode two days still in the same place where he was.

e. Then after that saith he to his disciples, **Let us go into Judaea again.** His disciples say unto him, Master, the Jews of late sought to stone thee; and goest thou thither again?

f. Jesus answered, **Are there not twelve hours in the day? If any man walk in the day, he stumbleth not, because he seeth the light of this world.**

g. **But if a man walk in the night, he stumbleth, because there is no light in him.**

h. These things said he: and after that he saith unto them, **Our friends Lazarus sleepeth; but I go, that I may awake him out of sleep.**

i. Then said his disciples, Lord, if he sleep, he shall do well. Howbeit Jesus spake of his death: but they thought that he had spoken of taking of rest in sleep.

j. Then said Jesus unto them plainly, **Lazarus is dead. And I am glad for your sakes that I was not there, to the intent ye may believe; nevertheless let us go into him.**

k. Then said Thomas, which is called Didymus, unto his fellow disciples, Let us also go, that we may die with him.

7-19. Jesus visit Lazarus tomb.

a. Then when Jesus came, he found that he had lain in the grave four days already.

b. Now Bethany was nigh unto Jerusalem, about fifteen furlongs off: And many of the Jews came to Martha and Mary, to comfort them concerning their brother.

c. Then Martha, as soon as she heard that Jesus was coming, went and met him: but Mary sat still in the house.

d. Then said Martha unto Jesus, Lord, if thou hadst been here, my brother had not died. But I know, that even, now, whatsoever thou wilt ask of God, God will give it thee.

e. Jesus saith unto her, **Thy brother shall rise again.** Martha saith unto him, I know that he shall rise again in the resurrection at the last day.

f. Jesus saith unto her, **I am the resurrection, and the life: he that believeth in me, though he were dead, yet shall he live. And whosoever liveth and believeth in me shall never die. Believest thou this?**

g. She saith unto him, Yea, Lord: I believe that thou art the Christ, the Son of God, which should come into the world.

h. And when she had so said, she went her way, and called Mary her sister secretly, saying, The Master is come, and calleth for thee.

i. As soon as she heard that, she arose quickly, and came unto him. Now Jesus was not yet come into the town, but was in that place where Martha met him.

j. The Jews then which were with her in the house, and comforted her, when they saw Mary, that she rose up hastily and went out, followed her, saying, She goeth unto the grave to weep there.

k. Then when Mary was come where Jesus was, and saw him, she fell down at his feet, saying unto him, Lord, if thou hadst been here, my brother had not died.

l. When Jesus therefore saw her weeping, and the Jews also weeping which came with her, he groaned in the spirit, and was troubled.

m. And said, **Where have ye laid him?** They said unto him, Lord, come and see. Jesus wept.

n. Then said the Jews, Behold how he loved him! And some of them said, Could not this man, which opened the eyes of the blind, have caused that even this man should not have died?

7-20. Jesus raises Lazarus from the dead.

a. Jesus therefore again groaning in himself cometh to the grave. It was a cave, and a stone lay upon it.

b. Jesus said, **Take ye away the stone.** Martha, the sister of him that was dead, saith unto him, Lord, by this time he stinketh: for he hath been dead four days.

c. Jesus saith unto her, **Said I not unto thee, that, if thou wouldest believe, thou shouldest see the glory of God?**

d. Then they took away the stone from the place where the dead was laid.

e. And Jesus lifted up his eyes, and said, **Father, I thank thee that thou hast heard me. And I knew that thou hearest me always: but because of the people which stand by I said it, that they may believe that thou has sent me.**

f. And when he thus had spoken, he cried with a loud voice, **Lazarus, come forth.**

g. And he that was dead came forth, bound hand and foot with graveclothes: and his face was bound about with a napkin. Jesus saith unto them, **Loose him, and let him go.**

7-21. Caiaphas prophesied of Jesus death.

a. Then many of the Jews which came to Mary, and had seen the things which Jesus did, believed on him. But some of them went their ways to the Pharisees, and told them what things Jesus had done.

b. Then gathered the chief priests and the Pharisees a council, and said, What do we? For this man doeth many miracles.

c. If we left him thus alone, all men will believe on him: and the Romans shall come and take away both of our place and nation.

d. And one of them, named Caiaphas, being the high priest that same year, said unto them, Ye know nothing at all, Nor consider that it is expedient for us, that one man should die for the people, and that the whole nation perish not.

e. And this spake he not of himself: but being high priest that year, he prophesied that Jesus should die for the nation; And not for that nation only, but that also he should gather together in one the children of God that were scattered abroad.

f. Then from that day forth they took counsel together for to put him to death.

g. Jesus therefore walked no more openly among the Jews; but went thence unto a country near to the wilderness, into a city called Ephraim, and there continued with the disciples.

h. And the Jews' Passover was nigh at hand: and many went out of the country up to Jerusalem before the passover, to purify themselves.

i. Then sought they for Jesus, and spake among themselves, as they stood in the temple, What think ye, that he will not come to the feast?

j. Now both the chief priests and the Pharisees had given a commandment, that, if any man knew where he were, he should show it, that they might take him.

7-22. The lament over Jerusalem.

a. The same day there came certain of the Pharisees, saying unto him, Get thee out, and depart hence: for Herod will kill thee.

b. And he said unto them, **Go ye, and tell that fox, Behold, I cast out devils, and I do cures today and to morrow, and the third day I shall be perfected.**

c. **Nevertheless I must walk to day, and to morrow, and the day following: for it cannot be that a prophet perish out of Jerusalem.**

d. **O Jerusalem, Jerusalem, which killest the prophets, and stonest them that are sent unto thee; how often would I have gathered thy children together, as a hen doth gather her brood under her wings, and ye would not!**

e. **Behold, your house is left unto you desolate: and verily I say unto you, Ye shall not see me, until the time come when ye shall say, Blessed is he that cometh in the name of the Lord.**

7-23. Jesus heals man on the Sabbath.

a. And it came to pass, as he went into the house of one of the chief Pharisees to eat bread on the sabbath day, that they watched him.

b. And, behold, there was a certain man before him which had the dropsy (*edema-excess fluid buildup*).

c. And Jesus answering spake unto the lawyers and Pharisees, saying, **Is it lawful to heal on the sabbath day?** And they held their peace. And he took him, and healed him, and let him go.

d. And answered them, saying, **Which of you shall have an ass or an ox fallen into a pit, and will not straightway pull him out on the sabbath day.** And they could not answer him again to these things.

7-24. The parable of the wedding guest.

a. And he put forth a parable to those which were bidden, when he marked how they chose out the chief rooms; saying unto them.

b. **When thou art bidden of any man to a wedding, sit not down in the highest room; lest a more honorable man than thou be bidden of him; And he that bade thee and him come and say to thee, Give this man place; and thou begin with shame to take the lowest room.**

c. **But when thou art bidden, go and sit down in the lowest room; that when he that bade thee cometh, he may say unto thee, Friend, go up higher: then shalt thou have worship in the presence of them that sit at meat with thee.**

d. **For whosoever exalteth himself shall be abased; and he that humbleth himself shall be exalted.**

e. Then said he also to him that bade him, **When thou makest a dinner or a supper, call not thy friends, nor thy brethren, neither thy kinsmen, nor thy rich neighbours; lest they also bid thee again, and a recompence** (*pay or reward somebody*) **be made thee.**

f. **But when thou makest a feast, call the poor, the maimed, the lame, the blind: And thou shalt be blessed; for they cannot recompense thee: for thou shalt be recompensed at the resurrection of the just.**

7-25. The parable of the great supper.

a. And when one of them that sat at meat with him heard these things, he said unto him, Blessed is he that shall eat bread in the kingdom of God.

b. Then said he unto him, **A certain man made a great supper, and bade many: And sent his servant at supper time to say to them that were bidden, Come; for all things are now ready. And they all with one consent began to make excuse.**

c. **The first said unto him, I have bought a piece of ground, and I must needs go and see it: I pray thee have me excused.**

d. **And another said, I have bought five yoke of oxen, and I go to prove them: I pray thee have me excused.**

e. **And another said, I have married a wife, and therefore I cannot come. So that servant came, and showed his lord these things.**

f. **Then the master of the house being angry said to his servant, Go out quickly into the streets and lanes of the city, and bring in hither the poor, and the maimed, and the halt, and the blind.**

g. **And the servant said, Lord, it is done as thou has commanded, and yet there is room.**

h. **And the lord said unto the servant, Go out unto the highways and hedges, and compel them to come in, that my house may be filled.**

i. **For I say unto you, That none of those men which were bidden shall taste of my supper.**

Chapter Eight
The Parable of the Lost Son

8-1. Jesus sought by the Greeks.

a. And there were certain Greeks among them that came up to worship at the feast. The same came therefore to Philip, which was of Bethsaida of Galilee, and desired him, saying, Sir, we would see Jesus.

b. Philip cometh and telleth Andrew: and again Andrew and Philip tell Jesus. And Jesus answered them, saying, **The hour is come, that the Son of man should be glorified.**

c. **Verily, verily, I say unto you, Except a corn of wheat fall into the ground and die, it abideth alone: but if it die, it bringeth forth much fruit.**

d. **He that loveth his life shall lose it; and he that hateth his life in this world shall keep it unto life eternal.**

e. **If any man serve me, let him follow me; and where I am, there shall also my servant be: if any man serve me, him will my Father honour.**

f. **Now is my soul troubled; and what shall I say? Father, save me from this hour: but for this cause came I unto this hour.**

g. **Father, glorify thy name.** Then came there a voice from heaven, saying, *I have both glorified it, and will glorify it again. 16*

h. The people therefore, that stood by, and heard it, said that it thundered: others said, An angel spake to him. Jesus answered and said, **This voice came not because of me, but for your sakes.**

i. Now is the judgment of this world: now shall the prince of this world be cast out.

j. **And I, if I be lifted up from the earth, will draw all men unto me. This he said, signifying what death he should die.**

k. The people answered him, We have heard out of the law that Christ abideth for ever: and how sayest thou, The son of man must be lifted up? Who is this Son of man?

l. Then Jesus said unto them, **Yet a little while is the light with you. Walk while ye have the light, lest darkness come upon you: for he that walketh in darkness knoweth not whither he goeth.**

m. **While ye have light, believe in the light, that ye may be the children of the light.** These things spake Jesus, and departed, and did hide himself from them.

8-2. The non-believers.

a. But though he had done so many miracles before them, yet they believed not on him: That the saying of Esaias the prophet might be fulfilled, which he spake, Lord, who hath believed our report? And to whom hath the arm of the Lord been revealed? (Fulfilled Prophecy: *"WHO hath believed our report? And to whom is the LORD revealed? For he shall grow up before him as a tender plant, and as a root out of a dry ground: he hath no form nor comeliness; and when we shall see him, there is no beauty that we should desire him. He is despised and rejected of men; a man of sorrows, and acquainted with grief: and we hid as it were our faces from him; he was despised, and we esteemed him not."* Isaiah 53:1-3).

b.   Therefore they could not believe, because that Esaias said again.   He hath blinded their eyes, and hardened their heart; that they should not see with their eyes, nor understand with their heart, and be converted, and I should heal them.   These things said Esaias, when he saw his glory, and spake of him. (Prophecy fulfilled: *"Make the heart of this people fat, and make their ears heavy, and shut their eyes; lest they see with their eyes, and hear with their ears, and understand with their heart, and convert, and be healed."* Isaiah 6:10).

c.   Nevertheless among the chief rulers also many believed on him; but because of the Pharisees they did not confess him, lest they should be put out of the synagogue. For they loved the praise of men more than the praise of God.

8-3. A summary of Jesus claims.

a.   Jesus cried and said, **He that believeth on me, believeth not on me, but on him that sent me.   And he that seeth me seeth him that sent me.**

b.   **I am come a light into the world, that whosoever believeth on me should not abide in darkness.**

c.   **And if any man hear my words, and believe not, I judge him not: for I came not to judge the world but to save the world.**

d.   **He that rejected me, and receiveth not my words, hath one that judgeth him: the word that I have spoken, the same shall judge him in the last day.**

e.   **For I have not spoken of myself; but the Father which sent me, he gave me a commandment, what I should say, and what I should speak.**

f.   **And I know that his commandment is life everlasting: whatsoever I speak therefore, even as the Father said unto me, so I speak.**

8-4. The cost of discipleship.

a. And there went great multitudes with him: and he turned, and said unto them. **If any man come to me, and hate not his father, and mother, and wife, and children, and brethren, and sisters, yes, and his own life also, he cannot be my disciple.**

b. **And whosoever doth not bear his cross, and come after me, cannot be my disciple. For which of you, intending to build a tower, sitteth not down first, and counteth the cost, whether he have sufficient to finish it?**

c. **Lest haply, after he hath laid the foundation, and is not able to finish it, all that behold it begin to mock him. Saying, this man began to build, and was not able to finish.**

d. **Or what king, going to make war against another king, sitteth not down first, and consulteth whether he be able with ten thousand to meet him that cometh against him with twenty thousand?**

e. **Or else, while the other is yet a great way off, he sendeth an ambassage** (*a diplomatic official*)**, and desireth conditions of peace.**

f. **So likewise, whosoever he be of you that forsaketh not all that he hath, he cannot be my disciple.**

g. **Salt is good: but if the salt have lost his savour, wherewith shall it be seasoned? It is neither fit for the land, nor yet for the dunghill; but men cast it out. He that hath ears to hear, let him hear.**

8-5. The lost piece of silver.

a. **Either what woman having ten pieces of silver, if she lose one piece, doth not light a candle, and sweep the house, and seek diligently till she find it?**

b. And when she hath found it, she calleth her friends and her neighbors together, saying, Rejoice with me; for I have found the piece which I had lost.

c. Likewise, I say unto you, there is joy in the presence of the angels of God over one sinner that repenteth.

8-6. The parable of the lost son.

a. And he said, A certain man had two sons: And the younger of them said to his father, Father, give me the portion of goods that falleth to me. And he divided unto them his living.

b. And not many days after the younger son gathered all together, and took his journey into a far country, and there wasted his substance with riotous living. And when he had spent all, there arose a mighty famine in that land; and he began to be in want.

c. And he went and joined himself to a citizen of that country; and he sent him into his fields to feed swine. And he would fain have filled his belly with the husks that the swine did eat: and no man gave unto him.

d. And when he came to himself, he said, How many hired servants of my father's have bread enough and to spare, and I perish with hunger.

e. I will arise and go to my father, and will say unto him, Father, I have sinned against heaven, and before thee. And am no more worthy to be called thy son: make me as one of thy hired servants.

f. And he arose, and came to his father. But when he was yet a great way off, his father saw him, and had compassion, and ran, and fell on his neck, and kissed him.

g. And the son said unto him, Father, I have sinned against heaven, and in thy sight, and am no more worthy to be called thy son.

h. But the father said to his servants, Bring forth the best robe, and put it on him; and put a ring on his hand, and shoes on his feet.

i. And bring hither the fatted calf, and kill it; and let us eat, and be merry. For this my son was dead, and is alive again; he was lost, and is found. And they began to be merry.

j. Now his elder son was in the field: and as he came and drew nigh to the house, he heard music and dancing.

k. And he called one of the servants, and asked what these things meant.

l. And he said unto him, thy brother is come; and thy father hath killed the fatted calf, because he hath received him safe and sound.

m. And he was angry, and would not go in: therefore came his father out, and entreated him.

n. And he answering said to his father, Lo, these many years do I serve thee, neither transgressed I at any time thy commandment: and yet thou never gavest me a kid, that I might make merry with my friends:

o. But as soon as this thy son was come, which hath devoured thy living with harlots, thou hast killed for him the fatted calf.

p. And he said unto him, Son, thou art ever with me, and all that I have is thine. It was meet that we should make merry, and be glad: for this thy brother was dead, and is alive again; and was lost, and is found.

8-7. The parable of the unrighteous steward.

a. And he said also unto his disciples, **There was a certain rich man, which had a steward; and the same was accused unto him that he had wasted his goods.**

b. **And he called him, and said unto him, How is it that I hear this of thee? give an account of thy stewardship** (*property manager*); **for thy mayest be no longer steward.**

c. **Then the steward said within himself, What shall I do? for my lord taketh away from me the stewardship: I cannot dig; to beg I am ashamed. I am resolved what to do, that, when I am put out of the stewardship, they may receive me into their houses.**

d. **So he called every one of his lord's debtors unto him, and said unto the first, How much owest thou unto my lord? And he said, An hundred measures of oil. And he said unto him, Take thy bill, and sit down quickly, and write fifty.**

e. **Then said he to another, And how much owest thou? And he said, An hundred measures of wheat. And he said unto him, Take thy bill, and write fourscore.**

f. **And the lord commended the unjust steward, because he had done wisely: for the children of this world are in their generation wiser than the children of light.**

g. **And I say unto you, Make to yourselves friends of the mammon of unrighteousness; that, when ye fail, they may receive you into everlasting habitations.**

h. **He that is faithful in that which is least is faithful also in much: and he that is unjust in the least is unjust also in much. If therefore ye have not been faithful in the unrighteous mammon, who will commit to your trust the true riches?**

i. And if ye have not been faithful in that which is another man's, who shall give you that which is your own?

j. No servant can serve two masters: for either he will hate the one, and love the other; or else he will hold to the one, and despise the other. Ye cannot serve God and mammon.

k. And the Pharisees also, who were covetous, heard all these things: and they derided him. And he said unto them, Ye are they which justify yourselves before men; but God knoweth your hearts: for that which is highly esteemed among men is abomination in the sight of God.

l. The law and the prophets were until John: since that time the kingdom of God is preached, and every man presseth unto it. And it is easier for heaven and earth to pass, than one title of the law to fail.

8-8. The rich man and Lazarus.

a. There was a certain rich man, which was clothed in purple and fine linen, and fared sumptuously every day: And there was a certain beggar named Lazarus, which was laid at his gate, full of sores, And desiring to be fed with the crumbs which fell from the rich man's table: moreover the dogs came and licked his sores.

b. And it came to pass, that the beggar died, and was carried by the angels into Abraham's bosom: the rich man also died, and was buried; And in hell he lift up his eyes, being in torments, and seeth Abraham afar off, and Lazarus in his bosom.

c. And he cried and said, Father Abraham, have mercy on me, and send Lazarus, that he may dip the tip of his finger in water, and cool my tongue; for I am tormented in this flame.

d. But Abraham said, Son, remember that thou in thy lifetime receivedst thy good things, and likewise Lazarus evil things: but now he is comforted, and thou art tormented.

e. And beside all this, between us and you there is a great gulf fixed: so that they which would pass from hence to you cannot; neither can they pass to us, that would come from thence.

f. Then he said, I pray thee therefore, father, that thou wouldest send him to my father's house: For I have five brethren; that he may testify unto them, lest they also come into this place of torment.

g. Abraham saith unto him, They have Moses and the prophets; let them hear them.

h. And he said, Nay, father Abraham: but if one went unto them from the dead, they will repent.

i. And he said unto him, If they hear not Moses and the prophets, neither will they be persuaded, though one rose from the dead.

8-9. Faith and forgiveness.

a. Then said he unto the disciples, **It is impossible but that offences will come: but woe unto him, through whom they come! It were better for him that a milestone were hanged about his neck, and he cast into the sea, than that he should offend one of these little ones.**

b. **Take heed to yourselves: If thy brother trespass against thee, rebuke him; and if he repent, forgive him. And if he trespass against thee seven times in a day, and seven times in a day turn again to thee, saying, I repent; thou shalt forgive him.**

c. And the apostles said unto the Lord, Increase our faith. And the Lord said, **If ye had faith as a grain of a mustard seed, ye might say unto this sycamine tree, Be thou plucked up by the root, and be thou planted in the sea; and it should obey you.**

d. **But which of you, having a servant plowing or feeding cattle, will say unto him by and by, when he is come from the field, Go and sit down to meat?**

e. **And will not rather say unto him, Make ready wherewith I may sup, and gird thyself, and serve me, till I have eaten and drunken; and afterward thou shalt eat and drink?**

f. **Doth he thank that servant because he did the things that were commanded him? I trow** (*to think that something is the case*) **not.**

g. **So likewise ye, when ye shall have done all those things which are commanded you, say, We are unprofitable servants: we have done that which was our duty to do.**

8-10. The healing of the ten lepers.

a. And it came to pass, as he went to Jerusalem, that he passed through the midst of Samaria and Galilee. And as he entered into a certain village, there met him ten men that were lepers, which stood afar off.

b. And they lifted up their voices, and said, Jesus, Master, have mercy on us.

c. And when he saw them, he said unto them, **Go show yourselves unto the priests.**

d. And it came to pass, that, as they went, they were cleansed.

e. And one of them, when he saw that he was healed, turned back, and with a loud voice glorified God.

f. And fell down on his face at his feet, giving him thanks: and he was a Samaritan.

g. And Jesus answering said, **Were there not ten cleansed? but where are the nine?**

h. There are not found that returned to give glory to God, save this stranger.

i. And he said unto him, **Arise, go thy way: thy faith hath made thee whole.**

8-11. The coming of the kingdom.

a. And when he was demanded of the Pharisees, when the kingdom of God should come, he answered them and said, **The kingdom of God cometh not with observation: Neither shall they say, Lo here! Or, lo there! For, behold, the kingdom of God is within you.**

b. And he said unto the disciples, **The days will come, when ye shall desire to see one of the days of the Son of man, and ye shall not see it. And they shall say to you, See here; or, see there: go not after them, nor follow them.**

c. **For as the lightning, that lighteneth out of the one part under heaven, shineth unto the other part under heaven; so shall also the Son of man be in his day. But first must he suffer many things, and be rejected of this generation.**

d. **And as it was in the days of Noe, so shall it be also in the days of the Son of man. They did eat, they drank, they married wives, they were given in marriage, until the day that Noe entered into the ark, and the flood came, and destroyed them all.**

e. Likewise also as it was in the days of Lot; they did eat, they drank, they bought, they sold, they planted, they builded; But the same day that Lot went out of Sodom it rained fire and brimstone from heaven, and destroyed them all.

f. Even thus shall it be in the day when the Son of man is revealed. In that day he which shall be upon the housetop, and his stuff in the house, let him not come down to take it away: and he that is In the field, let him likewise not return back. Remember Lot's wife.

g. Whosoever shall seek to save his life shall lose it; and whosoever shall lose his life shall preserve it. I tell you, in that night there shall be two men in one bed; the one shall be taken, and the other shall be left.

h. Two women shall be grinding together; the one shall be taken, and the other left. Two men shall be in the field; the one shall be taken, and the other left.

i. And they answered and said unto him, Where, Lord? And he said unto them, **Wheresoever the body is, thither will the eagles be gathered together.**

8-12. The parable of the judge and the widow.

a. And he spake a parable unto them to this end, that men ought always to pray, and not to faint; Saying, There was in a city a judge, which feared not God, neither regarded man: And there was a widow in that city; and she came unto him, saying, Avenge me of mine adversary.

b. And he would not for a while: but afterward he said within himself, Though I fear not God, nor regard man; Yet because this widow troubleth me, I will avenge her, lest by her continual coming she weary me.

c. And the Lord said, **Hear what the unjust judge saith. And shall not God avenge his own elect, which cry day and night unto him, though he bear long with them?**

d. **I tell you that he will avenge them speedily. Nevertheless when the Son of man cometh, shall he find faith on the earth?**

8-13. The parable of the Pharisee and the publican.

a. And he spake this parable unto certain which trusted in themselves that they were righteous, and despised others: **Two men went up into the temple to pray; the one a Pharisee** (*someone who is self-righteous or hypocritical*)**, and the other a publican.**

b. **The Pharisee stood and prayed thus with himself, God, I thank thee, that I am not as other men are, extortioners, unjust, adulterers, or even as this publican. I fast twice in the week, I give tithes of all that I possess.**

c. **And the publican, standing afar off, would not lift up so much as his eyes unto heaven, but smote upon his breast, saying, God be merciful to me a sinner.**

d. **I tell you, this man went down to his house justified rather than the other: for every one that exalted himself shall be abased; and he that humbleth himself shall be exalted.**

8-14. Jesus again foretell his death.

a. And they were in the way going up to Jerusalem; and Jesus went before them: and they were amazed; and as they followed, they were afraid.

b. And Jesus going up to Jerusalem took the twelve disciples apart in the way, and said unto them.

c. **Behold, we go up to Jerusalem; and all things that are written by the prophets concerning the Son of man shall be accomplished; And the Son of man shall be betrayed and delivered unto the chief priests and unto the scribes, and they shall condemn him to death.**

d. **And he shall be delivered unto the Gentiles to be mocked, spitefully entreated and to scourge, and spitted on, and to crucify him: and the third day he shall rise again.**

e. And they understood none of these things: and this saying was hid from them, neither knew they the things which were spoken.

8-15. The ambition of James and John.

a. Then came to him the mother of Zebedee's children with her sons James and John, worshipping him, and desiring a certain thing of him.

b. And he said unto her, **What wilt thou?** She saith unto him, Grant that these my two sons may sit, the one on the right hand, and the other on the left, in thy kingdom. (Controversy: Mark 10:35-37 *said the disciples asked Jesus, but* Matthew 20:20-21 *says the mother asked. I went with Matthew's account, I believe their Mother requested it).*

c. But Jesus answered and said, **Ye know not what ye ask. Are ye able to drink of the cup that I shall drink of, and to be baptized with the baptism that I am baptized with?**

d. They say unto him, We are able.

e. And he saith unto them, **Ye shall drink indeed of my cup, and be baptized with the baptism that I am baptized with** (*James was the first of the twelve disciples to be a martyr by the sword. John died of natural causes after being spared an attempt on his life by a chalice of poison*): **but to sit** on my right hand, and on my left, is not mine to give, but it shall be given to them for whom it is prepared of my Father.

f. And when the ten heard it, they were moved with indignation against the two brethren, James and John.

g. But Jesus called them to him, and said, **Ye know that they which are accounted to rule over the Gentiles exercise lordship over them; and their great ones exercise authority upon them.**

h. **But it shall not be so among you: but whosoever will be great among you, let him be your minister. And whosoever will be the chiefest, shall be servant of all.**

i. **Even as the Son of man came not to be ministered unto, but to minister, and to give his life a ransom for many.**

8-16. Bartimaeus receive his sight.

a. And they came to Jericho: and as he went out of Jericho with his disciples and a great number of people, blind Bartimaeus, the son of Timaeus, sat by the highway side begging (Controversy: Matthew 20:29-34 *said there were two*, Mark 10:46-52 *and* Luke 18:35-43 *said there was only one. I will go with the majority, because Mark named him).*

b. And hearing the multitude pass by, he asked what it meant.

c. And they told him that Jesus of Nazareth passeth by.

d. And when he heard that it was Jesus of Nazareth, he began to cry out, and say, Jesus, thou son of David, have mercy on me.

e. And many charged him that he should hold his peace: but he cried the more a great deal, Thou son of David, have mercy on me.

f. And Jesus stood still, and commanded him to be brought unto him.

g. And they call the blind man, saying unto him, Be of good comfort, rise; he calleth thee.

h. And he, casting away his garment, rose, and came to Jesus: and when he was come near, he asked him, **What wilt thou that I should do unto thee?**

i. The blind man said unto him, Lord, that I might receive my sight.

j. And Jesus said unto him, **Receive thy sight: Go thy way; thy faith hath made thee whole.**

k. And immediately he received his sight, and followed Jesus, glorifying God: and all the people, when they saw it, gave praise unto God.

8-17. The conversion of Zacchaeus.

a. And Jesus entered and passed through Jericho.

b. And, behold, there was a man named Zacchaeus, which was the chief among the publicans, and he was rich.

c. And he sought to see Jesus who he was; and could not for the press, because he was little of stature.

d. And he ran before, and climbed up into a sycamore tree to see him: for he was to pass that way.

e. And when Jesus came to the place, he looked up, and saw him, and said unto him, **Zacchaeus, make haste, and come down; for to day I must abide at thy house.**

f. And he made haste, and came down, and received him joyfully. And when they saw it, they all murmured, saying, That he was gone to be guest with a man that is a sinner.

g. And Zacchaeus stood, and said unto the Lord; Behold, Lord, the half of my goods I give to the poor; and if I have taken any thing from any man by false accusation, I restore him fourfold.

h. And Jesus said unto him, **This day is salvation come to this house, forasmuch as he also is a son of Abraham. For the son of man is come to seek and to save that which was lost.**

8-18. The parable of the pounds.

a. And as they heard these things, he added and spake a parable, because he was nigh to Jerusalem, and because they thought that the kingdom of God should immediately appear.

b. He said therefore, **A certain nobleman went into a far country to receive for himself a kingdom, and to return.**

c. **And he called his ten servants, and delivered them ten pounds, and said unto them, Occupy till I come. But his citizens hated him, and sent a message after him, saying, We will not have this man to reign over us.**

d. **And it came to pass, that when he was returned, having received the kingdom, then he commanded these servants to be called unto him, to whom he had given the money, that he might know how much every man had gained by trading.**

e. **Then came the first, saying, Lord, thy pound hath gained ten pounds. And he said unto him, Well, thou good servant: because thou has been faithful in a very little, have thou authority over ten cities.**

f. **And the second came, saying, Lord, thy pound hath gained five pounds. And he said likewise to him, Be thou also over five cities.**

g. And another came, saying, Lord, behold here is thy pound, which I have kept laid up in a napkin: For I feared thee, because thou art an austere (*grimly unsmiling, humorless*) man: thou takest up that thou layedst not down, and reapest that thou didst not sow.

h. And he saith unto him, Out of thine own mouth will I judge thee, thou wicked servant. Thou knewest that I was an austere man, taking up that I laid not down, and reaping that I did not sow.

i. Wherefore then gavest not thou my money into the bank, that at my coming I might have required mine own with usury?

j. And he said unto them that stood by, Take from him the pound, and give it to him that hath ten pounds. (And they said unto him, Lord, he hath ten pounds.).

k. For I say unto you, That unto every one which hath shall be given; and from him that hath not, even that he hath shall be taken away from him.

l. But those mine enemies, which would not that I should reign over them, bring hither, and slay them before me.

The Combined Gospel of Jesus Christ

Chapter Nine
Prophecy of Jerusalem destruction (A.D. 70); and signs of the end of the world

9-1. The triumphal entry to Jerusalem.

a. On the next day much people that were come to the feast, when they heard that Jesus was coming to Jerusalem, took branches of palm trees, and went forth to meet him, and cried, Hosanna: Blessed is the King of Israel that cometh in the name of the Lord.

b. And when he had thus spoken, he went before, ascending up to Jerusalem.

c. And when they came nigh unto Jerusalem, unto Bethphage and Bethany, at the mount of Olives, he sendeth forth two of his disciples, saying unto them, **Go your way into the village over against you: and as soon as ye be entered into it, ye shall find an ass** (*donkey-long ears*) **tied, and a colt** (*a young uncastrated male donkey under four years old*) **with her: whereon yet never man sat; loose him, and bring him unto me.** (Controversy: Matthew 21:2, *says there were an ass and a colt loosed and brought to Jesus*; Mark 11:2, Luke 19:30, *and* John 12:14-15, *says there was only one ass colt; I decided to go with the majority*).

d. **And if any man say unto you, Why do ye loose him? thus shall ye say unto him, because the Lord hath need of him; and straightway he will send him hither.**

e. All this was done, that it might be fulfilled which was spoken by the prophet, saying, Tell ye the daughter of Zion, fear not, Behold, thy King cometh unto thee, meek, and sitting on an ass's colt. (Fulfilled Prophecy: *"Rejoice greatly, O daughter of Zion; shout, O daughter of Jerusalem: behold, thy King cometh unto thee: he is just, and having salvation; lowly, and riding upon an ass, and upon a colt the foal of an ass."* Zechariah 9:9).

f. And the disciples went their way, and did as Jesus commanded them, and found the colt tied by the door without in a place where two ways met; and they loose him.

g. And as they were loosing the colt, the owners thereof that stood there said unto them, Why loose ye the colt? And they said, The Lord hath need of him. And they let them go.

h. And they brought the colt to Jesus, and cast their garments upon the colt, and they set Jesus thereon; as it is written.

i. And as he went, they spread their clothes in the way. These things understood not his disciples at the first: but when Jesus was glorified, then remembered they that these things were written of him, and that they had done these things unto him.

j. The people therefore that was with him, when he called Lazarus out of his grave, and raised him from the dead, bare record. For this cause the people also met him, for that they heard that he had done this miracle.

k. And when he was come nigh, even now at the descent of the mount of Olives, the whole multitude of the disciples began to rejoice and praise God with a loud voice for all the mighty works that they had seen; Saying, Blessed be the King that cometh in the name of the Lord: peace in heaven, and glory in the highest.

l. The Pharisees therefore said among themselves, Perceive ye how ye prevail nothing? Behold, the world is gone after him. And some of the Pharisees from among the multitude said unto him, Master, rebuke thy disciples.

m. And he answered and said unto them, **I tell you that, if these should hold their peace, the stones would immediately cry out.**

n. And when he was come near, he beheld the city, and wept over it, Saying, **If thou hadst known, even thou, at least in this thy day, the things which belong unto thy peace! but now they are hid from thine eyes.**

o. **For the days shall come upon thee, that thine enemies shall cast a trench about thee, and compass thee round, and keep thee in on every side.**

p. **And shall lay thee even with the ground, and thy children within thee; and they shall not leave in thee one stone upon another; because thou knewest not the time of thy visitation** (*Jesus speaking in prophecy of AD 70, when the Romans attacked and destroyed the city*).

q. And a very great multitude spread their garments in the way: others cut down branches from the trees, and strawed them in the way.

r. And the multitudes that went before, and that followed, cried, saying, Hosanna to the son of David: Blessed is he that cometh in the name of the Lord:

s. Blessed be the kingdom of our father David, that cometh in the name of the Lord:

t. Blessed be the kingdom of our father David, that cometh in the name of the Lord: Hosanna in the highest.

u. And when he was come into Jerusalem, and into the temple: all the city was moved, saying, Who is this?

v. And the multitude said, This is Jesus the prophet of Nazareth of Galilee, and when he had looked around about upon all things, and now the eventide was come, he went out unto Bethany with the twelve.

9-2. The cursed fig tree.

a. Now in the morning, when they were come from Bethany, as he returned into the city, he hungered.

b. And when he saw a fig tree afar off having leaves, and when he came to it, and found nothing thereon, but leaves only, for the time of figs was not yet; and Jesus answered and said unto it, **Let no fruit grow on thee henceforward for ever.**

c. And his disciples heard it; And presently the fig tree withered away. And when the disciples saw it, they marvelled, saying, How soon is the fig tree withered away!

d. Jesus answered and said unto them, **Verily I say unto you, If ye have faith, and doubt not, ye shall not only do this which is done to the fig tree, but also if ye shall say unto this mountain, Be thou removed, and be cast into the sea; it shall be done.**

e. **And all things, whatsoever ye shall ask in prayer, believing, ye shall receive.**

9-3. The second cleansing of the temple.

a. And they come to Jerusalem: and Jesus went into the temple of God, and began to cast out all them that sold and bought in the temple, and overthrew the tables of the moneychangers, and the seats of them that sold doves;

b. And would not suffer that any man should carry any vessel through the temple.

c. And he taught, saying unto them, **Is it not written, my house shall be called of all nations the house of prayer? but ye have made it a den of thieves.**

d. And the scribes and chief priests and the chief of the people heard it, and sought how they might destroy him: for they feared him, because all the people was astonished at his doctrine.

    e. And could not find what they might do: for all the people were very attentive to hear him.

    f. And he taught daily in the temple. And the blind and the lame came to him in the temple; and he healed them.

    g. And when the chief priests and scribes saw the wonderful things that he did, and the children crying in the temple, and saying, Hosanna to the son of David; they were so displeased,

    h. And said unto him, Hearest thou what these say? And Jesus saith unto them, **Yea; have ye never read, Out of the mouth of babes and sucklings thou hast perfected praise?**

    i. And when even was come, he left them, and went out of the city into Bethany; and he lodged there.

9-4. The power of faith.

    a. And in the morning, as they passed by, they saw the fig tree dried up from the roots. And Peter calling to remembrance saith unto him, Master, behold, the fig tree which thou cursedst is withered away.

    b. And Jesus answering saith unto them, **Have faith in God. For verily I say unto you, That whosoever shall say unto this mountain, Be thou removed, and be thou cast into the sea; and shall not doubt in his heart, but shall believe that those things which he saith shall come to pass; he shall have whatsoever he saith.**

    c. **Therefore I say unto you, What things soever ye desire, when ye pray, believe that ye receive them, and ye shall have them.**

    d. **And when ye stand praying, forgive, if ye have aught against any: that your Father also which is in heaven may forgive you your trespasses. But if ye do** not forgive, neither will your Father which is in heaven forgive your trespasses.

9-5. Jesus authority challenged.

a. And they come again to Jerusalem; And it came to pass, that on one of those days, as he taught the people in the temple, and preached the gospel, the chief priests and the scribes came upon him with the elders of the people, as he was walking in the temple.

b. And spake unto him, saying, Tell us, by what authority doest thou do these things? Or who is he that gave thee this authority?

c. And Jesus answered and said unto them, **I will also ask you one thing; which if ye tell me, I in like wise will tell you by what authority I do these things. The baptism of John, whence was it from heaven, or of men? answer me.**

d. And they reasoned with themselves, saying, If we shall say, From heaven; he will say, Why did ye not then believe him? But if we shall say, Of men; we fear all the people will stone us: for they be persuaded that John was a prophet indeed. And they answered Jesus, and said, We cannot tell .

e. And Jesus said unto them, **Neither do I tell you by what authority I do these things.**

9-6. The parable of the two sons.

a. **But what think ye? A certain man had two sons; and he came to the first, and said, Son, go work to day in my vineyard. He answered and said, I will not: but afterward he repented, and went.**

b. **And he came to the second, and said likewise. And he answered and said, I go, sir: and went not. Whether of them twain did the will of his father? They** say unto him, The first.

c. Jesus saith unto them, **Verily I say unto you, That the publicans and the harlots go into the kingdom of God before you.**

d. **For John came unto you in the way of righteousness, and ye believed him not: but the publicans and the harlots believed him: and ye, when ye had seen it, repented not afterward, that ye might believe him.**

9-7. The parable of the husbandman.

a. **Hear another parable: There was a certain householder, which planted a vineyard, and hedged it round about, and digged a place for the winefat, and built a tower, and let it out to husbandmen, and went into a far country for a long time.**

b. **And at the time of the season when the fruit drew near, he sent to the husbandmen a servant, that he might receive from the husbandmen, the fruit of the vineyard: but the husbandman caught him, and beat him, and sent him away empty.**

c. **And again he sent unto them another servant: and they beat him also, and at him they cast stones, and wounded him in the head, and entreated him shamefully, and sent him away empty.**

d. **And again he sent a third: and him they killed, and cast him out, and many others more than the first: and they did unto them likewise; beating some, and killing some.**

e. **Then said the lord of the vineyard, what shall I do? having yet therefore one son, his well beloved, he sent him also last unto them, saying, They will reverence my son when they see him.**

f. **But when the husbandmen saw him, they**

reasoned among themselves, This is the heir; come, let us kill him, and the inheritance shall be our's.

g. And they caught him and killed him, and cast him out of the vineyard. When the lord therefore of the vineyard cometh, what will he do unto those husbandmen?

h. They say unto him, He will miserably destroy those wicked men, and will let out his vineyard unto other husbandmen, which shall render him the fruits in their seasons. And when they heard it, they said, God forbid.

i. Jesus beheld them, and said, **Did ye never read in the scriptures, The stone which the builders rejected, the same is become the head of the corner: this is the Lord's doing, and it is marvelous in our eyes?**

j. **Therefore say I unto you, The kingdom of God shall be taken from you, and given to a nation bringing forth the fruits thereof.**

k. **And whosoever shall fall on this stone shall be broken: but on whomsoever it shall fall, it will grind him to powder.**

l. And when the chief priests and Pharisees had heard his parables, for they knew he had spoken the parable against them.

m. But when they sought to lay hands on him the same hour, they feared the multitude, because they took him for a prophet: and they left him, and went their way.

9-8. The Parable of the king son's marriage.

a. And Jesus answered and spake unto them again by parables, and said, **the kingdom of heaven is like unto a certain king, which made a marriage for his son, and sent forth his servants to call them that were bidden to the wedding: and they would not come.**

b. Again, he sent forth other servants, saying, tell them which are bidden, Behold, I have prepared my dinner: my oxen and my fatlings are killed, and all things are ready: come unto the marriage.

c. But they made light of it, and went their ways, one to his farm, another to his merchandise: And the remnant took his servants, and entreated them spitefully, and slew them.

d. But when the king heard thereof, he was wroth: and he sent forth his armies, and destroyed those murderers, and burned up their city.

e. Then saith he to his servants, The wedding is ready, but they which were bidden were not worthy. Go ye therefore into the highways, and as many as ye shall find, bid to the marriage.

f. So those servants went out into the highways, and gathered together all as many as they found, both bad and good: and the wedding was furnished with guests.

g. And when the king came in to see the guests, he saw there a man which had not on a wedding garment: And he saith unto him, Friend, how camest thou in hither not having a wedding garment? And he was speechless.

h. Then said the king to the servants, Bind him hand and foot, and take him away, and cast him into outer darkness; there shall be weeping and gnashing of teeth. For many are called, but few are chosen.

9-9. Tribute money to Caesar.

a. Then went the Pharisees, and took counsel how they might entangle him in his talk.

b. And they watched him, and sent forth spies, which should feign themselves just men, that they might take hold of his words, that so they might deliver him unto the power and authority of the governor.

c. And they sent out unto him their disciples with the Herodians, saying, Master, we know that thou art true, and teachest the way of God in truth, neither carest thou for any man: for thou regardest not the person of men.

d. Tell us therefore, What thinkest thou? Is it lawful to give tribute unto Caesar, or not? Shall we give, or shall we not give? But Jesus perceived their craftiness and wickedness, and said unto them, **Why tempt ye me, ye hypocrites? bring me a penny that I may see it.**

e. And they brought unto him a penny. And he saith unto them, **Whose is this image and superscription?** And they said unto him, Caesar's.

f. Then saith Jesus unto them, **Render therefore unto Caesar the things which are Caesar's; and unto God the things that are God's.**

g. When they had heard these words, they marvelled at his answer, and held their peace and left him, and went their way.

9-10. Sadducees and the resurrection.

a. The same day came to him certain of the Sadducees, which deny that there is any resurrection: and they asked him, saying, Master, Moses wrote unto us, If any man's brother die, having a wife, and he die without children, that his brother should take his wife, and raise up seed to his brother.

b. There were therefore seven brethren: and the first took a wife, and died without children. And the second took her to wife, and he died childless. And the third took her, and in like manner the seven also: and they left no children, and died. Last of all the woman died also.

c. In the resurrection therefore, when they shall rise, whose wife shall she be of the seven? For they all had her to wife.

d. And Jesus answering said unto them, **Ye do err, not knowing the scriptures, nor the power of God. The children of this world marry, and are given in marriage: But they which shall be accounted worthy to obtain that world, and the resurrection from the dead; when they shall rise from the dead, they neither marry, nor are given in marriage:**

e. **Neither can they die any more: for they are equal unto the angels of God in heaven; and are the children of God, being the children of the resurrection.**

f. **And as touching the resurrection of the dead, that they rise: have ye not read in the book of Moses, how in the bush God spake unto him, saying, I am the God of Abraham, and the God of Isaac, and the God of Jacob?**

g. **For he is not a God of the dead, but of the living: for all live unto him. Ye therefore do greatly err.** And when the multitude heard this, they were astonished at his doctrine.

h. Then certain of the scribes answering said, Master, thou hast well said. And after that they durst not ask him any question at all.

9-11. The first and great commandment.

a. But when the Pharisees had heard that he had put the Sadducees to silence, they were gathered together.

b. Then one of the scribes came, which was a lawyer, and having heard them reasoning together, and perceiving that he had answered them well, asked him a question, tempting him, and saying, Master which is the first and great commandment of all in the law?

c. Jesus answered him, **The first of all the commandments is, Hear, O Israel; The Lord our God is one Lord, Thou shalt love the Lord thy God with all thy heart, and with all thy soul, and with all thy mind, and with all thy strength. This is the first and great commandment.**

d. **And the second is like unto it, Thou shalt love thy neighbor as thyself: There is none other commandment greater than these.**

e. **On these two commandments hang all the law and the prophets.**

f. And the scribe said unto him, Well, Master, thou hast said the truth: for there is one God; and there is none other but he: And to love him with all the heart, and with all the understanding, and with all the soul, and with all the strength, and to love his neighbor as himself, is more than all whole burnt offerings and sacrifices.

g. And when Jesus saw that he answered discreetly, he said unto him, **Thou art not far from the kingdom of God.** And no man after that durst ask him any question.

9-12. The question about David's son.

a. While the Pharisees were gathered together, Jesus asked them, while he taught in the temple, Saying, **What think ye of Christ? Whose son is he?**

b. They say unto him, The son of David. He said unto them, **How say the scribes that Christ is the son of David? for David himself said by the Holy Ghost, in the book of Psalms, The LORD said to my Lord, Sit thou on my right hand, till I make thine enemies thy footstool.**

c. **David therefore himself calleth him Lord; and whence is he then his son** *(Psalms 110:1)*? **And the common people heard him gladly.** And no man was able to answer him a word, neither durst any man from that day forth ask him any more questions.

**9-13. The woes upon the scribes, Pharisees, and
hypocrites!**

a. Then in the audience of all the people he said to
the multitude and unto his disciples, saying, **The scribes
and the Pharisees sit in Moses' seat: Beware of the
scribes, which desire to walk in long robes, and love
greetings in the markets.**

b. **All therefore whatsoever they bid you observe,
that observe and do; but not ye after their works: for
they say, and do not.**

c. **For they bind heavy burdens and grievous to be
borne, and lay them on men's shoulders; but they
themselves will not move them with one of their
fingers.**

d. **But all their works they do for to be seen of
men: they make broad their phylacteries, and enlarge
the borders of their garments, And love the uppermost
rooms at feasts, and the chief seats in the synagogues,
and to be called of men, Rabbi, Rabbi.**

e. **But be not ye called Rabbi: for one is your
Master, even Christ; and all ye are brethren. And call no
man your father upon the earth: for one is your Father,
which is in heaven. Neither be ye called masters: for
one is your Master, even Christ.**

f. **But he that is greatest among you shall be your
servant. And whosoever shall exalt himself shall be
abased; and he that shall humble himself shall be
exalted.**

g. **But woe unto you, scribes and Pharisees,
hypocrites! for ye shut up the kingdom of heaven
against men: for ye neither go in yourselves, neither
suffer ye them that are entering to go in.**

h. Woe unto you, scribes and Pharisees, hypocrites! for ye devour widows' houses, and for a pretence make long prayer: therefore ye shall receive the greater damnation.

i. Woe unto you, scribes and Pharisees, hypocrites! for ye compass sea and land to make one proselyte, and when he is made, ye make him twofold more the child of hell than yourselves.

j. Woe unto you, ye blind guides, which say, Whosoever shall swear by the temple, it is nothing; but whosoever shall swear by the gold of the temple, he is a debtor!

k. Ye fools and blind: for whether is greater, the gold, or the temple that sanctifieth the gold?

l. And, Whosoever shall swear by the altar, it is nothing; but whosoever sweareth by the gift that is upon it, he is guilty. Ye fools and blind: for whether is greater, the gift, or the altar that sanctifieth the gift?

m. Whoso therefore shall swear by the altar, sweareth by it, and by all things thereon. And whoso shall swear by the temple, sweareth by it, and by him that dwelleth therein. And he that shall swear by heaven, sweareth by the throne of God, and by him that sitteth thereon.

n. Woe unto you, scribes and Pharisees, hypocrites! for ye pay tithe of mint and anise and cumin, and have omitted the weightier matters of the law, judgment, mercy, and faith: these ought ye to have done, and not to leave the other undone.

o. Ye blind guides, which strain at a gnat, and swallow a camel.

p. Woe unto you, scribes and Pharisees, hypocrites! for ye make clean the outside of the cup and of the platter, but within they are full of extortion and excess.

q. Thou blind Pharisee, cleanse first that which is within the cup and platter, that the outside of them may be clean also.

r. Woe unto you, scribes and Pharisees, hypocrites! for ye are like unto whited sepulchers, which indeed appear beautiful outward, but are within full of dead men's bones, and of all uncleanness.

s. Even so ye also outwardly appear righteous unto men, but within ye are full of hypocrisy and iniquity.

t. Woe unto you, scribes and Pharisees, hypocrites! because ye build the tombs of the prophets and garnish the sepulchers of the righteous, And say, If we had been in the days of our fathers, we would not have been partakers with them in the blood of the prophets.

u. Wherefore ye be witnesses unto yourselves, that ye are the children of them which killed the prophets. Fill ye up then the measure of your fathers. Ye serpents, ye generation of vipers, how can ye escape the damnation of hell?

v. Wherefore, behold, I send unto you prophets, and wise men, and scribes: and some of them ye shall kill and crucify; and some of them shall ye scourge in your synagogues, and persecute them from city to city.

w. That upon you may come all the righteous blood shed upon the earth, from the blood of righteous Abel unto the blood of Zacharias son of Barachias, whom ye slew between the temple and the altar.

x. Verily I say unto you, All these things shall come upon this generation. O Jerusalem, Jerusalem, thou that killest the prophets, and stonest them which are sent unto thee, how often would I have gathered thy children together, even as a hen gathered her chickens under her wings, and ye would not!

y. Behold, your house is left unto you desolate. For I say unto you, Ye shall not see me henceforth, till ye shall say, Blessed is he that cometh in the name of the Lord.

9-14. The widow's offering.

a. And Jesus sat over against the treasury, and beheld how the people cast money into the treasury: and he looked up, and saw many that were rich cast in much.

b. And there came a certain poor widow, and she threw in two mites, which make a farthing.

c. And he called unto him his disciples, and saith unto them, **Verily I say unto you of a truth, That this poor widow hath cast more in, than all they which have cast into the treasury: For all they did cast in of their abundance unto the offerings of God; but she of her want did cast in all that she had, even all her living.**

9-15. Prophecy of Jerusalem destruction (A.D. 70); signs of the end of the world.

a. And Jesus went out, and departed from the temple: one of his disciples saith unto him, Master, see what manner of goodly stones and gifts and buildings are here!

b. And Jesus answering said unto him, **Seest thou these great buildings which ye behold? verily I say unto you, the days will come, there shall not be left one stone upon another, that shall not be thrown down.**

c. And as he sat upon the mount of Olives over against the temple, Peter and James and John and Andrew asked him privately, saying, Master, Tell us, when shall these things be? And what shall be the sign when all these things shall be fulfilled? and what shall be the sign of thy coming, and of the end of the world?

d. And Jesus answered and said unto them, **Take heed that no man deceive you: for many shall come in my name, saying, I am Christ; and the time draweth near: and shall deceive many, go ye not therefore after them.**

e. **And when ye shall hear of wars and rumours of wars: see that ye be not troubled: for all these things must first come to pass, but the end is not yet.**

f. **For nation shall rise against nation, and kingdom against kingdom: and there shall be famines and troubles, and pestilences** *(epidemic of disease)*; **and fearful sights and great signs shall there be from heaven; and great earthquakes shall be in divers places** *(tsunami).*

g. **All these are the beginning of sorrows. But before all of these, they shall lay their hands on you, and persecute you: for they shall deliver you up to councils to be afflicted, and shall kill you: and ye shall be hated of all nations for my name's sake; and in the synagogues ye shall be beaten, and into prisons: and ye shall be brought before rulers and kings for my name's sake, for a testimony against them.**

h. **And then shall many be offended, and shall betray one another, and shall hate one another. And many false prophets shall rise, and shall deceive many.**

i. **And because iniquity shall abound, the love of many shall wax cold. But he that shall endure unto the end, the same shall be saved.**

j. And this gospel of the kingdom must first be published and shall be preached in all the world for a witness unto all nations; and then shall the end come.

k. But when they shall lead you, and deliver you up, take no thought beforehand what ye shall speak, neither do ye premeditate what ye shall answer: but whatsoever shall be given you in that hour, that speak ye: For I will give you a mouth and wisdom, which all your adversaries shall not be able to gainsay nor resist; for it is not ye that speak, but the Holy Ghost.

l. Now the brother shall betray the brother to death, and the father the son; and the children shall rise up against their parents, and shall cause them to be put to death.

m. And ye shall be betrayed both by parents, and brethren, and kinsfolks, and friends; and some of you shall they cause to be put to death.

n. And ye shall be hated of all men for my name's sake: but he that shall endure unto the end, the same shall be saved.

o. But there shall not an hair of your head perish. In your patience posses ye your souls.

p. And when ye shall see Jerusalem compassed with armies, then know that the desolation thereof is nigh. When ye therefore shall see the abomination of desolation, spoken by Daniel the prophet, stand in the holy place, (whoso readeth, let him understand:).

q. Then let them which be in Judaea flee into the mountains: and let them which are in the midst of it depart out; and let not them that are in the countries enter thereinto. For these be the days of vengeance, that all things which are written may be fulfilled.

r. Let him which is in the housetop not come down to take any thing out of his house: Neither let him which is in the field return back to take his clothes.

s. And woe unto them that are with child, and to them that give suck in those days! for there shall be great distress in the land, and wrath upon this people.

t. And they shall fall by the edge of the sword, and shall be led away captive into all nations: and Jerusalem shall be trodden down of the Gentiles, until the times of the Gentiles be fulfilled.

u. But pray ye that your flight be not in the winter, neither on the sabbath day: For in those days shall be great tribulation, such as was not since the beginning of the Creation which God created the world to this time, no, nor ever shall be.

v. And except that the Lord had shortened those days, there should no flesh be saved: but for the elect's sake, whom he had chosen, those days shall be shortened.

w. Then if any man shall say unto you, Lo, here is Christ, or there; believe it not. For there shall arise false Christ's, and false prophets, and shall show great signs and wonders to seduce; insomuch that, if it were possible, they shall deceive the very elect.

x. But take ye heed: behold, I have foretold you all things. Wherefore if they shall say unto you, Behold, he is in the desert; go not forth: behold, he is in the secret chambers; believe it not.

y. For as the lightning cometh out of the east, and shineth even unto the west; so shall also the coming of the Son of man be.

z. For wheresoever the carcase is, there will the eagles be gathered together.

aa. And there shall be signs in the sun, and in the moon, and in the stars; and upon the earth distress of nations, with perplexity; the sea and the waves roaring; Immediately after the tribulation of those days shall the sun be darkened, and the moon shall not give her light, and the stars shall fall from heaven,

bb. And men's heart failing them for fear, and for looking after those things which are coming on the earth: for the powers of heaven shall be shaken.

cc. And then shall appear the sign of the Son of man in heaven: and then shall all the tribes of the earth mourn, and they shall see the Son of man coming in the clouds of heaven with great power and great glory.

dd. And when then things begin to come to pass, then look up, and lift up your heads; for your redemption draweth nigh.

ee. And then shall he send his angels with a great sound of a trumpet, and they shall gather together his elect from the four winds, from the uttermost part of the earth to the uttermost part of heaven.

ff. And he spake to them a parable; Behold the fig tree, and all the trees; When the branch is yet tender they now shoot forth leaves, ye see and know of your own selves that summer is near . So likewise ye, when ye see these things come to pass, know ye that the kingdom of God is nigh at hand, even at the doors.

gg. Verily I say unto you, This generation shall not pass, till all these things be fulfilled. Heaven and earth shall pass away, but my words shall not pass away.

hh. And take heed to yourselves, lest at any time your hearts be overcharged with surfeiting, and drunkenness, and cares of this life, and so that day come upon you unawares. For as a snare shall it come on them that dwell on the face of the whole earth.

ii. But of that day and hour knoweth no man, no, not the angels of heaven, neither the Son, but my Father only.

jj. But as the days of Noe were, so shall also the coming of the Son of man be. For as in the days that were before the flood they were eating and drinking, marrying and giving in marriage, until the day that Noe entered into the ark.

kk. And knew not until the flood came, and took them all away; so shall also the coming of the Son of man be.

ll. Then shall two be in the field; the one shall be taken, and the other left. Two women shall be grinding at the mill; the one shall be taken, and the other left.

mm. Watch therefore, and pray always that ye may be accounted worthy to escape all these things that shall come to pass, and to stand before the Son of man: for ye know not what hour your Lord doth come.

nn. But know this, that if the goodman of the house had known in what watch the thief would come, he would have watched, and would not have suffered his house to be broken up. Therefore be ye also ready: for in such an hour as ye think not the Son of man cometh.

oo. And in the day time he was teaching in the temple; and at night went out, and abode in the mount that is called *the mount* of Olives.

pp. And all the people came early in the morning to him in the temple, for to hear him.

9-16. The parable of the ten virgins.

a. Then shall the kingdom of heaven be likened unto ten virgins, which took their lamps, and went forth to meet the bridegroom. And five of them were wise, and five were foolish.

b. They that were foolish took their lamps, and took no oil with them: But the wise took oil in their vessels with their lamps.

c. While the bridegroom tarried, they all slumbered and slept. And at midnight there was a cry made, Behold, the bridegroom cometh; go ye out to meet him.

d. Then all those virgins arose, and trimmed their lamps. And the foolish said unto the wise, Give us of your oil; for our lamps are gone out.

e. But the wise answered, saying, Not so; lest there be not enough for us and you: but go ye rather to them that sell, and buy for yourselves.

f. And while they went to buy, the bridegroom came; and they that were ready went in with him to the marriage: and the door was shut.

g. Afterward came also the other virgins, saying, Lord, Lord, open to us. But he answered and said, Verily I say unto you, I know you not.

h. Watch therefore, for ye know neither the day nor the hour wherein the Son of man cometh.

9-17. The parable of the talents.

a. For the kingdom of heaven is as a man traveling into a far country, who called his own servants, and delivered unto them his goods.

b. And unto one he gave five talents, to another two, and to another one; to every man according to his several ability, and straightway took his journey.

c. Then he that had received the five talents went and traded with the same, and made them other five talents. And likewise he that had received two, he also gained other two.

d. But he that had received one went and digged in the earth, and hid his lord's money.

e. After a long time the lord of those servants cometh, and reckoned with them.

f. And so he that had received five talents came and brought other five talents, saying, Lord, thou deliveredst unto me five talents: behold, I have gained beside them five talents more.

g. His lord said unto him, Well done, thou good and faithful servant: thou hast been faithful over a few things, I will make thee ruler over many things: enter thou into the joy of thy lord.

h. He also that had received two talents came and said, Lord, thou deliveredst unto me two talents: behold, I have gained two other talents beside them.

i. His lord said unto him, Well done, good and faithful servant; thou hast been faithful over a few things, I will make thee ruler over many things: enter thou into the joy of the lord.

j. Then he which had received the one talent came and said, Lord, I knew thee that thou art an hard man, reaping where thou hast not sown, and gathering where thou hast not strawed: And I was afraid, and went and hid thy talent in the earth: lo, there thou hast that is thine.

k. His lord answered and said unto him, Thou wicked and slothful servant, thou knewest that I reap where I sowed not, and gather where I have not strawed: Thou oughtest therefore to have put my money to the exchangers, and then at my coming I should have received mine own with usury.

l. Take therefore the talent from him, and give it unto him which hath ten talents.

m. For unto every one that hath shall be given, and he shall have abundance: but from him that hath not shall be taken away even that which he hath.

n. And cast ye the unprofitable servant into outer darkness: there shall be weeping and gnashing of teeth.

9-18. The judgment.

a. When the son of man shall come in his glory, and all the holy angels with him, then shall he sit upon the throne of his glory: And before him shall be gathered all nations: and he shall separate them one from another, as a shepherd divideth his sheep from the goats: And he shall set the sheep on his right hand, but the goats on the left.

b. Then shall the king say unto them on his right hand, Come, ye blessed of my Father, inherit the kingdom prepared for you from the foundation of the world: For I was an hungered, and ye gave me meat: I was thirsty, and ye gave me drink: I was a stranger, and ye took me in: Naked, and ye clothed me: I was sick, and ye visited me: I was in prison, and ye came unto me.

c. Then shall the righteous answer him, saying, Lord, when saw we thee an hungered, and fed thee? Or thirsty, and gave thee drink? When saw we thee a stranger, and took thee in? or naked, and clothed thee? Or when saw we thee sick, or in prison, and came unto thee?

d. And the King shall answer and say unto them, Verily I say unto you, Inasmuch as ye have done it unto one of the least of these my brethren, ye have done it unto me.

e. Then shall he say also unto them on the left hand, Depart from me, ye cursed, into everlasting fire, prepared for the devil and his angels: For I was an hungered, and ye gave me no meat; I was thirsty, and ye gave me no drink: I was a stranger, and ye took me not in: naked, and ye clothed me not: sick, and in prison, and ye visited me not.

f. Then shall they also answer him, saying, Lord, when saw we thee an hungered, or athirst, or a stranger, or naked, or sick, or in prison, and did not minister unto thee?

g. Then shall he answer them, saying, Verily I say unto you, Inasmuch as ye did it not to one of the least of these, ye did it not to me.

h. And these shall go away into everlasting punishment: but the righteous into life eternal.

Chapter Ten
The garden of Gethsemane

10-1. The plot to kill Jesus.
a. Now the feast of unleavened bread drew nigh; which is called the passover.

b. Then assembled together the chief priests, and the scribes, and the elders of the people, unto the palace of the high priest, who was called Caiaphas.

c. After two days was the feast of the passover, and of unleavened bread: and the chief priest and the scribes sought how they might take Jesus by craft and put him to death.

d. But the chief priests consulted that they might put Lazarus also to death. Because that by reason of him many of the Jews went away, and believed on Jesus.

e. But they said, Not on the feast day, lest there be an uproar among the people; for they feared the people.

10-2. Jesus anointed at Bethany.
a. Then Jesus six days before the passover came to Bethany, where Lazarus was which had been dead, whom he raised from the dead.

b. Now when Jesus was in Bethany, in the house of Simon the leper, there they made him a supper; and Martha *(Lazarus sister)* served: but Lazarus was one of them that sat at the table with him.

c. As he sat at meat, there came Mary *(Lazarus other sister)* unto him having an alabaster box *(a type of gypsum - usually white or translucent)* of ointment of spikenard very precious; and she brake the box, and poured it on his head.

d. Then took Mary a pound of ointment of spikenard, very costly, and anointed the feet of Jesus, and wiped his feet with her hair: and the house was filled with the odour of the ointment.

e. But when some of his disciples saw it, they had indignation within themselves, saying, To what purpose was this waste of ointment made?

f. Then saith one of the disciples, Judas Iscariot, Simon's son, which should betray him, for this ointment might have been sold for more than three hundred pence, and have been given to the poor.

g. And they murmured against her. This he said, not that he cared for the poor; but because he was a thief, and had the bag, and bare what was put therein.

h. When Jesus understood it, he said unto them, **Let her alone, Why trouble ye the woman? For she hath wrought a good work upon me; against the day of my burying hath she kept this.**

i. **For ye have the poor always with you, and whensoever ye will ye may do them good; but me ye have not always. For in that she hath poured this ointment on my body, she is come afore-hand to anoint my body to the burying.**

j. **Verily I say unto you, Wheresoever this gospel shall be preached in the whole world, there shall also this, that this woman hath done, shall be spoken of for a memorial of her.**

k. Much people of the Jews therefore knew that he was there: and they came not for Jesus' sake only, but that they might see Lazarus also, whom he had raised from the dead.

l. And it came to pass, when Jesus had finished all these saying, he said unto his disciples, Ye know that after two days is the feast of the passover, and the son of man is betrayed to be crucified.

10-3. The bargain of Judas Iscariot.

a. Then entered Satan into Judas surnamed Iscariot, being one of the twelve. And he went his way, and communed with the chief priests and captains, how he might betray him unto them.

b. And said unto them, What will ye give me, and I will deliver him unto you? And when they heard it, they were glad, and promised to give him money.

c. And they covenanted with him for thirty pieces of silver. And from that time he promised, and sought opportunity to conveniently betray him unto them in the absence of the multitude.

10-4. The last passover meal.

a. Now the first day of the feast of unleavened bread, when they killed the passover, the disciples came to Jesus, saying unto him, Where wilt thou that we go and prepare that thou mayest eat the passover?

b. And he sendeth forth Peter and John, and saith unto them, **Go ye into the city and prepare us the passover, that we may eat.**

c. And they said unto him, Where wilt thou that we prepare?

d. And he said unto them, **Behold, when you are entered into the city, there shall a man meet you, bearing a pitcher of water: follow him into the house where he entereth in.**

e. **And ye shall say unto the goodman of the house, The Master saith unto thee, My time is at hand; I will keep the passover at thy house with my disciples. Where is the guestchamber, where I shall eat the passover with my disciples?**

f. **And he will show you a large upper room furnished and prepared: there make ready for us.**

g. And his disciples went forth as Jesus had appointed them, and came into the city, and found as he had said unto them; and they made ready the passover.

h. And in the evening he cometh with the twelve, and as they sat and did eat.

i. And he said unto them, **With desire I have desired to eat this passover with you before I suffer:**

j. And as they did eat, Jesus said, **Verily I say unto you, that one of you which eateth with me shall betray me.**

k. And they began to inquire among themselves, which of them it was that should do this thing. And they were exceeding sorrowful, and began every one of them to say unto him, Lord, is it I? and another said, Is it I?

l. And he answered and said, **But, behold, the hand of him that betrayeth me is with me on the table. It is one of the twelve that dippeth his hand with me in this dish, the same shall betray me.**

m. **And truly the Son of man indeed goeth, as it is written of him: but woe unto that man by whom the Son of man is betrayed! It had been good for that man if he had not been born.**

n. Then Judas, which betrayed him, answered and said, Master, is it I? He said unto him, **Thou hast said.**

o. And as they were eating, Jesus took bread, and blessed it, and brake it, and gave it to the disciples, and said, **Take, eat; this is my body which is given for you: this do in remembrance of me.**

p. **For I say unto you, I will not any more eat thereof, until it be fulfilled in the Kingdom of God.**

q. And he took the cup, and when he had given thanks, said, **take this and divide it among yourselves,** he gave it to them, saying, **Drink ye all of it:** and they all drank of it.

r. And he said unto them, **This is my blood of the new testament, which is shed for many for the remission of sins. Verily I say unto you, I will not drink henceforth of this fruit of the vine, until that day when I drink it new with you in my Father's kingdom.**

s. And there was also a strife among them, which of them should be accounted the greatest. And he said unto them, **The kings of the Gentiles exercise lordship over them; and they that exercise authority upon them are called benefactors.**

t. **But ye shall not be so: but he that is greatest among you, let him be as the younger; and he that is chief, as he that doeth serve.**

u. **For whether is greater, he that sitteth at meat, or he that serveth? Is not he that sitteth at meat? but I am among you as he that serveth.**

v. **Ye are they which have continued with me in my temptations. And I appoint unto you a kingdom, as my Father hath appointed unto me; That ye may eat and drink at my table in my kingdom, and sit on thrones judging the twelve tribes of Israel.**

10-5. First foretelling of Peter's denial.

a. And the Lord said, **Simon, Simon, behold, Satan hath desired to have you, that he may sift you as wheat: But I have prayed for thee, that thy faith fail not: and when thou art converted, strengthen thy brethren.**

b. And he said unto him, Lord, I am ready to go with thee, both into prison, and to death.

c. And he said, **I tell thee, Peter, the cock shall not crow this day, before that thou shalt thrice deny that thou knowest me.**

d. And he said unto them, **When I sent you without purse, and scrip, and shoes, lacked ye any thing?** And they said, Nothing.

e. Then said he unto them, **But now, he that hath a purse, let him take it, and likewise his scrip: and he that hath no sword, let him sell his garment, and buy one.**

f. **For I say unto you, that this that is written must yet be accomplished in me, And he was reckoned among the transgressors: for the things concerning me have an end.**

g. And they said, Lord, behold, here are two swords. And he said unto them, **It is enough.**

10-6. Washing the disciples feet.

a. Now before the feast of the passover, when Jesus knew that his hour was come that he should depart out of this world unto the Father, having loved his own which were in the world, he loved them unto the end.

b. And supper being ended, the devil having now put into the heart of Judas Iscariot, Simon's son, to betray him;

c. Jesus knowing that the Father had given all things into his hands, and that he was come from God, and went to God; He riseth from supper, and laid aside his garments; and took a towel, and girded himself.

d. After that he poureth water into a basin, and began to wash the disciples' feet, and to wipe them with the towel wherewith he was girded.

e. Then cometh he to Simon Peter: and Peter saith unto him, Lord, dost thou wash my feet?

f. Jesus answered and said unto him, **What I do thou knowest not now; but thou shalt know hereafter.** Peter saith unto him, Thou shalt never wash my feet.

g. Jesus answered him, **If I wash thee not, thou hast no part with me.**

h. Simon Peter saith unto him, Lord, not my feet only, but also my hands and my head.

i. Jesus saith to him, **He that is washed needeth not save to wash his feet, but is clean every whit: and ye are clean, but not all.**

j. For he knew who should betray him; therefore, said he, Ye are not all clean.

k. So after he had washed their feet, and had taken his garments, and was set down again, he said unto them, **Know ye what I have done to you?**

l. **Ye call me Master and Lord: and ye say well; for so I am. If I then, your Lord and Master, have washed your feet; ye also ought to wash one another's feet. For I have given you an example, that ye should do as I have done to you.**

m. **Verily, Verily, I say unto you, The servant is not greater than his lord; neither he that is sent greater than he that sent him. If ye know these things, happy are ye if ye do them.**

n. I speak not of you all: I know whom I have chosen: but that the scripture may be fulfilled, **He that eateth bread with me hath lifted up his heel against me.**

o. Now I tell you before it come, that, when it is come to pass, ye may believe that I am he.

p. Verily, verily, I say unto you, He that receiveth whomsoever I send, receiveth me; and he that receiveth me, receiveth him that sent me.

10-7. Jesus dismiss Judas.

a. When Jesus had thus said, he was troubled in spirit, and testified, and said, **Verily, verily, I say unto you, that one of you shall betray me.**

b. Then the disciples looked one on another, doubting of whom he spake. Now there was leaning on Jesus' bosom one of his disciples, whom Jesus loved.

c. Simon Peter therefore beckoned to him, that he should ask who it should be of whom he spake. He then lying on Jesus' breast saith unto him, Lord, who is it?

d. Jesus answered, **He it is, to whom I shall give a sop, when I have dipped it.**

e. And when he had dipped the sop, he gave it to Judas Iscariot, the son of Simon. And after the sop Satan entered into him.

f. Then said Jesus unto him, **That thou doest, do quickly.**

g. Now no man at the table knew for what intent he spake this unto him. For some of them thought, because Judas had the bag, that Jesus had said unto him, Buy those things that we have need of against the feast; or, that he should give something to the poor.

h. He then having received the sop went immediately out: and it was night. Therefore when he was gone out, Jesus said, **now is the Son of man glorified, and God is glorified in him.**

i. **If God be glorified in him, God shall also glorify him in himself, and shall straightway glorify him.**

j. **Little children, yet a little while I am with you. Ye shall seek me: and as I said unto the Jews, Whither I go, ye cannot come, so now I say to you.**

k. **A new commandment I give unto you, That ye love one another; as I have loved you, that ye also love one another.**

l. **By this shall all men know that ye are my disciples, if ye have love one to another.**

10-8. Second foretelling of Peter's denial.

a. Simon Peter said unto him, Lord, whither goest thou? Jesus answered him, **Whither I Go, thou canst not follow me now; but thou shalt follow me afterwards.**

b. Peter said unto him, Lord, why cannot I follow thee now? I will lay down my life for thy sake.

c. Jesus answered him, **Wilt thou lay down thy life for my sake? Verily, verily, I say unto thee, The cock shall not crow, till thou hast denied me thrice.**

10-9. The way, the truth, and the life.

a. **Let not your heart be troubled: ye believe in God, believe also in me.**

b. **In my Father's house are many mansions: if it were not so, I would have told you.**

c. **I go to prepare a place for you. And if I go and prepare a place for you, I will come again, and receive you unto myself; that where I am, there ye may be also.**

d. **And whither I go ye know, and the way ye know.** Thomas saith unto him, Lord, we know not whither thou goest; and how can we know the way?

e. Jesus saith unto him, **I am the way, the truth and the life: no man cometh unto the Father, but by me.**

f. **If ye had known me, ye should have known my Father also: and from henceforth ye know him, and have seen him.**

g. Philip saith unto him, Lord, show us the Father, and it sufficeth us.

h. Jesus saith unto him, **Have I been so long time with you, and yet hast thou not known me, Philip?**

i. **He that hath seen me hath seen the Father; and how sayest thou then, Show us the Father?**

j. **Believest thou not that I am in the Father, and the Father in me? The words that I speak unto you I speak not of myself: but the Father that dwelleth in me, he doeth the works.**

k. **Believe me that I am in the Father, and the Father in me: or else believe me for the very works' sake.**

l. **Verily, verily, I say unto you, He that believeth on me, the works that I do shall he do also; and greater works than these shall he do; because I go unto my Father.**

m. **And whatsoever ye shall ask in my name, that will I do, that the Father may be glorified in the Son. If ye shall ask any thing in my name, I will do it.**

10-10. The promise of the spirit.

a. **If ye love me, keep my commandments.**

b. **And I will pray the Father, and he shall give you another Comforter, that he may abide with you for ever; Even the spirit of truth; whom the world cannot** receive, because it seeth him not, neither knoweth him: but ye know him; for he dwelleth with you, and shall be in you.

c. I will not leave you comfortless: I will come to you. Yet a little while, and the world seeth me no more; but ye see me: because I live, ye shall live also.

d. At that day ye shall know that I am in my Father, and ye in me, and I in you. He that hath my commandments, and keepeth them, he it is that loveth me: and he that loveth me shall be loved of my Father, and I will love him, and will manifest myself to him.

e. Judas saith unto him, not Iscariot, Lord, how is it that thou wilt manifest thyself unto us, and not unto the world?

f. Jesus answered and said unto him, **If a man love me, he will keep my words: and my Father will love him, and we will come unto him, and make our abode with him.**

g. He that loveth me not keepeth not my sayings: and the word which ye hear is not mine, but the Father's which sent me.

h. These things have I spoken unto you, being yet present with you. But the Comforter, which is the Holy Ghost, whom the Father will send in my name, he shall teach you all things to your remembrance, whatsoever I have said unto you.

i. Peace I leave with you, my peace I give unto you: not as the world giveth, give I unto you. Let not your heart be troubled, neither let it be afraid.

j. Ye have heard how I said unto you, I go away, and come again unto you. If ye loved me, ye would rejoice, because I said, I go unto the Father: for my Father is greater than I.

k. And now I have told you before it come to pass, that, when it come to pass, ye might believe. Hereafter I will not talk much with you: for the prince of this world cometh, and hath nothing in me.

l. But that the world may know that I love the Father; and as the Father gave me commandment, even so I do. Arise, let us go hence.

10-11. Third foretelling of Peter's denial.

a. And when they had sung an hymn, they went out into the mount of Olives.

b. Then saith Jesus unto them, **All ye shall be offended because of me this night: for it is written, I will smite the shepherd, and the sheep of the flock shall be scattered abroad.**

c. **But after that I am risen again, I will go before you into Galilee.**

d. Peter answered and said unto him, Though all men shall be offended because of thee, yet will I never be offended.

e. Jesus said unto him, **Verily I say unto thee, That this day, even in this night, before the cock crow, thou shalt deny me thrice** (*Controversy: Matthew 26:34 said before the cock crow; Mark 14:30 said before the cock crow twice; I went with before the cock crow, see Luke 22:60-61*). Peter said unto him more vehemently, Though I should die with thee, yet will I not deny thee in any wise. Likewise also said all the disciples.

10-12. Jesus the true vine.

a. **I am the true vine, and my Father is the husbandman.**

b. Every branch in me that beareth not fruit he taketh away: and every branch that beareth fruit, he purgeth it, that it may bring forth more fruit.

c. Now ye are clean through the word which I have spoken unto you. Abide in me, and I in you. As the branch cannot bear fruit of itself, except it abide in the vine; no more can ye, except ye abide in me.

d. I am the vine, ye are the branches: He that abideth in me, and I in him, the same bringeth forth much fruit: for without me ye can do nothing.

e. If a man abide not in me, he is cast forth as a branch, and is withered; and men gather them, and cast them into the fire, and they are burned.

f. If ye abide in me, and my words abide in you, ye shall ask what ye will, and it shall be done unto you. Herein is my Father glorified, that ye bear much fruit; so shall ye be my disciples.

g. As the Father hath loved me, so have I loved you: continue ye in my love. If ye keep my commandments, ye shall abide in my love; even as I have kept my Father's commandments, and abide in his love.

h. These things have I spoken unto you, that my joy might remain in you, and that your joy might be full.

i. This is my commandment, That ye love one another, as I have loved you. Greater love hath no man than this, that a man lay down his life for his friends. Ye are my friends, if ye do whatsoever I command you.

j. Henceforth I call you not servants; for the servant knoweth not what his lord doeth: but I have called you friends; for all things that I have heard of my Father I have made known unto you.

k. Ye have not chosen me, but I have chosen you, and ordained you, that ye should go and bring forth fruit, and that your fruit should remain: that whatsoever ye shall ask of the Father in my name, he may give it to you.

l. These things I command you, that ye love one another.

10-13. The hatred of the world.

a. If the world hate you, ye know that it hated me before it hate you. If ye were of the world, the world would love his own: but because ye are not of the world, but I have chosen you out of the world, therefore the world hateth you.

b. Remember the word that I said unto you, The servant is not greater than his lord. If they have persecuted me, they will also persecute you; if they have kept my saying, they will keep yours also.

c. But all these things will they do unto you for my name's sake, because they know not him that sent me. If I had not come and spoken unto them, they had not had sin: but know they have no cloak for their sin.

d. He that hateth me hateth my Father also. If I had not done among them the works which none other man did, they had not had sin: but know have they both seen and hated both me and my Father.

e. But this cometh to pass, that the word might be fulfilled that is written in their law, they hated me without a cause.

f. But when the Comforter is come, whom I will send unto you from the Father, even the Spirit of truth, which proceeded from the Father, he shall testify of me: And ye also shall bear witness, because ye have been with me from the beginning.

g. These things have I spoken unto you, that you should not be offended. They shall put you out of the synagogues: yea, the time cometh, that whosoever killeth you will think that he doeth God service.

h. And these things will they do unto you, because they have not known the Father, nor me. But these things have I told you, that when the time shall come, ye may remember that I told you of them.

i. And these things I said not unto you at the beginning, because I was with you.

10-14. The coming of the spirit.

a. But now I go my way to him that sent me; and none of you asketh me, Whither goest thou? But because I have said these things unto you, sorrow hath filled your heart.

b. Nevertheless I tell you the truth; It is expedient for you that I go away: for if I go not away, the Comforter will not come unto you; but if I depart, I will send him unto you.

c. And when he is come, he will reprove the world of sin, and of righteousness, and of judgment: Of sin, because they believe not on me; Of righteousness, because I go to my Father, and ye see me no more. Of judgment, because the prince of this world is judged.

d. I have yet many things to say unto you, but ye cannot bear them now. Howbeit when he, the Spirit of truth, is come, he will guide you into all truth: for he shall not speak of himself; but whatsoever he shall hear, that shall he speak: and he will show you things to come.

e. He shall glorify me: for he shall receive of mine, and shall show it unto you. All things that the Father hath are mine therefore said I, that he shall take of mine, and shall show it unto you.

10-15. Jesus farewell to his disciples.

a. A little while, and ye shall not see me: and again, a little while, and ye shall see me, because I go to the Father.

b. Then said some of his disciples among themselves, What is this that he saith unto us, a little while, and ye shall not see me: and again, a little while, and ye shall see me: and, Because I go to the Father?

c. They said therefore, What is this that he saith, A little while? we cannot tell what he saith.

d. Now Jesus knew that they were desirous to ask him, and said unto them, **Do ye inquire among yourselves of that I said, A little while, and ye shall not see me: and again, a little while, and ye shall see me?**

e. Verily, verily, I say unto you, That ye shall weep and lament, but the world shall rejoice: and ye shall be sorrowful, but your sorrow shall be turned into joy.

f. A woman when she is in travail hath sorrow, because her hour is come: but as soon as she delivered of the child, she remembered no more the anguish, for joy that a man is born into this world.

g. And ye now therefore have sorrow: but I will see you again, and your heart shall rejoice, and your joy no man taketh from you.

h. And in that day ye shall ask me nothing. Verily, verily, I say unto you, Whatsoever ye shall ask the Father in my name, he will give it to you. Hitherto have ye asked nothing in my name: ask, and ye shall receive, that your joy may be full.

i. These things have I spoke unto you in proverbs: but the time cometh, when I shall no more speak unto you in proverbs, but I shall show you plainly of the Father.

j. At that day ye shall ask in my name: and I say not unto you, that I will pray the Father for you: For the Father himself loveth you, because ye have loved me, and have believed that I came out from God.

k. I came forth from the Father, and am come into the world: again, I leave the world, and go to the Father.

l. His disciples said unto him, Lo, now speakest thou plainly, and speaketh no proverb. Now are we sure that thou knowest all things, and needest not that any man should ask thee: by this we believe that thou camest forth from God.

m. Jesus answered them, **Do ye now believe? Behold, the hour cometh, yea, is now come, that ye shall be scattered, every man to his own, and shall leave me alone: and yet I am not alone, because the Father is with me.**

n. These things I have spoken unto you, that in me ye might have peace. In the world ye shall have tribulation: but be of good cheer; I have overcome the world.

10-16. The prayer to be glorified.

a. These words spake Jesus, and lifted up his eyes to heaven, and said, **Father, the hour is come; glorify thy Son, that thy Son also may glorify thee: As thou hast given him power over all flesh, that he should give eternal life to as many as thou hast given him.**

b. And this is life eternal, that they might know thee the only true God, and Jesus Christ, whom thou hast sent. I have glorified thee on the earth: I have finished the work which thou gavest me to do.

c. And now, O Father, glorify thou me with thine own self with the glory which I had with thee before the world was.

10-17. The prayer for the disciples.

a. I have manifested thy name unto the men which thou gavest me out of the world: thine they were, and thou gavest them me; and they have kept thy word.

b. Now they have known that all things whatsoever thou hast given me are of thee.

c. For I have given unto them the words which thou gavest me; and they have received them, and have known surely that I came out from thee, and they have believed that thou didst send me.

d. I pray for them: I pray not for the world, but for them which thou hast given me; for they are thine. And all mine are thine, and thine are mine; and I am glorified in them.

e. And now I am no more in the world, but these are in the world, and I come to thee. Holy Father, keep through thine own name those whom thou hast given me, that they may be one, as we are.

f. While I was with them in the world, I kept them in thy name: those that thou gavest me I have kept, and none of them is lost, but the son of perdition; that the scripture might be fulfilled.

g. And now come I to thee; and these things I speak in the world, that they might have my joy fulfilled in themselves.

h. I have given them thy word; and the world hath hated them, because they are not of the world, even as I am not of the world. I pray not that thou shouldest take them out of the world, but that thou shouldest keep them from evil.

i. They are not of the world, even as I am not of the world. Sanctify them through thy truth: thy word is truth.

j. As thou hast sent me into the world, even so have I also sent them into the world. And for their sakes I sanctify myself, that they also might be sanctified through the truth.

10-18. The prayer for the church.

a. Neither pray I for these alone, but for them also which shall believe on me through their word; That they all may be one; as thou, Father, art in me, and I in thee, that they also may be one in us: that the world may believe that thou hast sent me.

b. And the glory which thou gavest me I have given them; that they may be one, even as we are one: I in them, and thou in me, that they may be made perfect in one; and that the world may know that thou hast sent me, and hast loved them, as thou hast loved me.

c. Father, I will that they also, whom thou hast given me, be with me where I am; that they may behold my glory, which thou hast given me: for thou lovedst me before the foundation of the world.

d. O righteous Father, the world hath not known thee: but I have known thee, and these have known that thou hast sent me.

e. And I have declared unto them thy name, and will declare it: that the love wherewith thou hast loved me may be in them, and I in them.

10-19. Jesus agony in Gethsemane.

a. When Jesus had spoken these words, he went forth with his disciples, over the brook Cedron, where was a garden, into the which he entered, and his disciples.

b. And they came to a place called Gethsemane, and he saith to his disciples, **Sit ye here, while I go and pray yonder. Pray that ye enter not into temptation.**

c. And he took with him Peter and the two sons of Zebedee, James and John, and began to be sorrowful, and sore amazed, and very heavy.

d. And he came out, and went, as he was wont, to the mount of Olives; and his disciples also followed him.

e. Then saith he unto them, **My soul is exceeding sorrowful, even unto death: tarry ye here, and watch with me** (Prophecy fulfilled: *"surely he had borne our griefs, and carried our sorrows:…"* Isaiah 53:4).

f. And he was withdrawn from them about a stone's cast, and kneeled down, and prayed,

g. And he went forward a little farther, and fell on his face on the ground, and prayed, that, if it were possible, the hour might pass from him.

h. **Abba, O my Father all things are possible unto thee, if it be possible, let this cup pass from me: Father, if thou be willing, remove this cup from me, nevertheless not as I will, but as thou wilt.**

i. And he cometh unto the disciples, and findeth them asleep, and saith unto Peter, **Simon, sleepest thou? Couldest not thou watch with me one hour? Watch ye and pray, that ye enter not into temptation: the spirit indeed is willing, but the flesh is weak.**

j. And again he went away the second time, and prayed, and spake the same words saying, **O my Father all things are possible unto thee, if it be possible, let this cup pass from me: Father, if thou be willing, remove** this cup from me nevertheless not as I will, but as thou wilt.

k. **O my father, if this cup may not pass away from me, except I drink it, thy will be done.**

l. And when he returned, he found them asleep again: for their eyes were heavy, neither wist they what to answer him.

m. And he left them, and went away again, and prayed the third time, saying the same words. **O my Father all things are possible unto thee, if it be possible, let this cup pass from me: Father, if thou be willing, remove this cup from me, nevertheless not as I will, but as thou wilt.**

n. **O my father, if this cup may not pass away from me, except I drink it, thy will be done.**

o. And there appeared an angel unto him from heaven, strengthening him.

p. And being in an agony he prayed more earnestly: and his sweat was as it were great drops of blood falling down to the ground.

q. And he cometh the third time to his disciples, and saith unto them, **sleep on now, and take your rest: it is enough, the hour is come; behold, the Son of man is betrayed into the hands of sinners.**

r. And said unto them, **Rise up, let us be going; behold, he that betrayed me is at hand.**

10-20. Jesus betrayal and arrest.

a. And Judas also, which betrayed him, knew the place: for Jesus ofttimes resorted thither with his disciples.

b. Judas then, having received a band of men and officers from the chief priests and Pharisees, cometh thither with lanterns and torches and weapons.

c. And immediately, while he yet spake, cometh Judas, one of the twelve, and with him a great multitude with swords and staves, from the chief priests and the scribes and the elders of the people.

d. Jesus therefore, knowing all things that should come upon him, went forth, and said unto them, **Whom seek ye?**

e. They answered him, Jesus of Nazareth. Jesus saith unto them, **I am he**. And Judas also, which betrayed him, stood with them.

f. As soon then as he had said unto them, I am he, they went backward, and fell to the ground. Then asked he them again, **Whom seek ye?**

g. And they said, Jesus of Nazareth.

h. Jesus answered, **I have told you that I am he: if therefore ye seek me, let these go their way:** That the saying might be fulfilled, which he spake, Of them which thou gavest me have I lost none. (Prophecy Fulfilled: *"While I was with them in the world, I kept them in thy name: those that thou gavest me I have kept, and none of them is lost, but the son of perdition...".* John 17:12)

i. Now he that betrayed him gave them a sign, saying, Whomsoever I shall kiss, that same is he: hold him fast, take him, and lead him away safely.

j. And as soon as he was come, he goeth straightway to him, and saith, Hail, Master, master; and kissed him.

k. And Jesus said unto him, **Friend, wherefore art thou come? Judas, betrayest thou the Son of man with a kiss?**

l. When they which were about him saw what would follow, they said unto him, Lord, shall we smite with the sword?

m. Then came they, and laid their hands on Jesus, and took him.

n. And, behold, Simon Peter which were with Jesus, having a sword, stretch out his hand, and drew it, and struck the high priest's servant, and cut off his right ear. The servant's name was Malchus.

o. And Jesus answered and said, **Suffer ye thus far.** And he touched his ear, and healed him.

p. Then said Jesus unto Peter, **put up thy sword into the sheath: for all they that take the sword shall perish with the sword, the cup which my Father hath given me, shall I not drink it?**

q. **Thinkest thou that I cannot now pray to my Father, and he shall presently give me more than twelve legions of angels?** *(In ancient Rome a legion was 3000 to 6000 soldiers; 12 legions of angels would be at least 36,000).* **But how then shall the scriptures be fulfilled, that thus it must be?**

r. In the same hour said Jesus to the multitudes, chief priests, and captains of the temple, and the elders, which were come to him.

s. **Are ye come out, as against a thief with swords and with staves to take me?**

t. **I sat daily with you teaching in the temple, and ye stretched forth no hands against me: but the scripture must be fulfilled, this is your hour, and the power of darkness.**

u. Then the band and the captain and officers of the Jews took Jesus, and bound him.

v. But all this was done, that the scriptures of the prophets might be fulfilled. (Prophecy Fulfilled: *"He was oppressed, and he was afflicted, yet he opened not his mouth: he is brought as a lamb to the slaughter, and as a sheep before her shearers is dumb, so he openeth not his mouth."* Isaiah 53:7).

w. Then all the disciples forsook him and fled.

x. And there followed him a certain young man, having a linen cloth cast about his naked body; and the young men laid hold on him: And he left the linen cloth, and fled from them naked.

The Combined Gospel of Jesus Christ

Chapter Eleven
Jesus Trials and Crucifixion

11-1. Jesus before Jewish authorities Annas and Caiaphas (1st/2nd trials before Jewish authorities respectively).

a. And led him away to Annas first; for he was the father-in-law to Caiaphas, which was the high priest that same year; Peter followed him afar off.

b. Then they that had laid hold on Jesus, took they him, and led him away to Caiaphas the high priest's house. And with him were assembled all the chief priests and the elders and the scribes.

c. Now Caiaphas was he, which gave counsel to the Jews, that it was expedient that one man should die for the people.

d. And Simon Peter followed Jesus, unto the high priest palace, and so did another disciple: that disciple was known unto the high priest, and went in with Jesus into the palace of the high priest. But Peter stood at the door without.

e. Then went out that other disciple, which was known unto the high priest, and spake unto her that kept the door, and brought in Peter. And he went in, and sat with the servants, to see the end.

f. And when they had kindled a fire in the midst of the hall beneath in the palace, and were set down together, Peter sat down among them and warmed himself at the fire.

g. But a certain maid, the damsel that kept the door, beheld him as he sat by the fire warming himself, and earnestly looked upon him, and said unto Peter, This man was with Jesus of Galilee. Art not thou also one of this man's disciples?

h. *(Peter, 1st Denial)* And he denied him before them all, saying, Woman, I am not, I know him not, neither understand I what thou sayest.

i. And the servants and officers stood there, who had made a fire of coals, for it was cold: and they warmed themselves: and Peter stood with them, and warmed himself.

j. The high priest then asked Jesus of his disciples, and of his doctrine.

k. Jesus answered him, **I spake openly to the world; I ever taught in the synagogue, and in the temple, whither the Jews always resort; and in secret have I said nothing. Why askest thou me? Ask them which heard me, what I have said unto them: behold they know what I said.**

l. And when he had thus spoken, one of the officers which stood by struck Jesus with the palm of his hand, saying, answerest thou the high priest so?

m. Jesus answered him, **If I have spoken evil, bear witness of the evil: but if well, why smitest thou me?**

n. Now Annas had sent him abound unto Caiaphas the high priest.

o. Now the chief priests, and elders, and all the council, sought false witness against Jesus, to put him to death; But found none: for many bare false witnesses against him, but there witness agreed not together.

p. At the last came two and bare false witness against him. And said, This fellow said, I will destroy this temple of God made with hands, and within three days I will build another made without hands. But neither so did their witness agree together.

q. And the high priest arose, and stood up in the midst, and asked Jesus, saying, answerest thou nothing? what is it which these witness against thee?

r. But Jesus held his peace and answered nothing.

s. And the high priest answered and said unto him, I adjure thee by the living God, that thou tell us whether thou be the Christ, the Son of God.

t. Jesus saith unto him, **I am: nevertheless I say unto you, Hereafter shall ye see the Son of man sitting on the right hand of power, and coming in the clouds of heaven.**

u. Then the high priest rent his clothes, and saith, What need we any further witnesses? Ye have heard his blasphemy: what think ye?

v. And they all answered and said, He is guilty of death.

w. And the men that held Jesus mocked him, and smote him. And some began to spit in his face, and when they had blindfolded him, they struck him on the face, and buffeted *(a blow with the fist or hand; a heavy or repeated blow or stroke)* him, and others smote him with the palm of their hands, saying prophesy unto us, thou Christ, Who is he that smote thee?

x. And many other things blasphemously *(expressing disrespect for God or sacred things)* spake they against him.

y. *(Peter, 2nd Denial)* And Simon Peter stood and warmed himself. And when he was gone out onto the porch, after a little while another maid saw him again, and said unto them that stood by, This is also one of them, This fellow was also with Jesus of Nazareth. Art not thou also one of his disciples?

z. And again Peter denied with an oath, Man, I am not, I do not know the man.

aa. *(Peter, 3rd Denial)* And about the space of one hour after another confidently affirmed, saying, Of a truth this fellow also was with him; for he is a Galilean.

bb. And a little after, they that stood by said again to Peter, Surely thou art also one of them: for thou art a Galilean, and thy speech betrayed thee and agreeth thereto.

cc. One of the servants of the high priest *(Malchus)*, being his kinsman whose ear Peter cut off, saith, Did not I see thee in the garden with him?

dd. And Peter said, Man, I know not what thou sayest. Then began he to curse and to swear, saying, I know not the man whom ye speak.

ee. And immediately, while he yet spake, the cock crew. (Controversy: Matthew 26:74-75 *said the cock crew once after Peter denied Jesus thrice;* Mark 14:72 *indicates that the cock crowed the second time after Peter had made his third denial;* Luke 22:60-61 *said before the cock crew thou shalt deny me thrice;* John 18:27 *said Peter denied again* (the third time) *and immediately the cock crew; I went with the majority and dismissed Mark's account.)*

ff. And the Lord turned, and looked upon Peter.

gg. And Peter remembered the word of the Lord, which he said unto him, Before the cock crow, thou shalt deny me thrice. And Peter went out, and wept bitterly.

11-2. Trial before Jewish council (3rd trial before Jews).

a. And straightway in the morning, as soon as it was day. The elders of the people and the chief priests, and the scribes came together, and led him (*Jesus*) into their council (*unbound*), saying, Art thou the Christ? tell us.

b. And he said unto them, **If I tell you, ye will not believe: And if I also ask you, ye will not answer me, nor let me go. Hereafter shall the Son of man sit on the right hand of the power of God.**

c. Then said they all, Art thou then the Son of God?

d. And he said unto them, **Ye say that I am.**

e. And all the chief priests held a consultation with the elders and scribes and the whole council, took counsel against Jesus to put him to death, and they said, What need we any further witness? for we ourselves have heard of his own mouth.

f. And when they had bound Jesus, the whole multitudes of them arose, and led him away from Caiaphas unto the hall of judgment; and delivered him to Pontius Pilate the governor: and it was early; and they themselves went not into the judgment hall, lest they should be defiled; but that they might eat the passover.

11-3. The death of Judas Iscariot.

a. Then Judas, which had betrayed him, when he saw that he was condemned, repented himself, and brought again the thirty pieces of silver to the chief priests and the elders, saying, I have sinned in that I have betrayed the innocent blood.

b. And they said, What is that to us? See thou to that. And he cast down the pieces of silver in the temple, and departed, and went and hanged himself.

c. And the chief priests took the silver pieces, and said, It is not lawful for to put them into the treasury, because it is the price of blood.

d. And they took counsel, and bought with them the potter's field, to bury strangers in. Wherefore that field was called, The field of blood, unto this day.

e. Then was fulfilled that which was spoken by Jeremy the prophet, saying, And they took the thirty pieces of silver, the price of him that was valued, whom they of the children of Israel did value; And gave them for the potter's field, as the Lord appointed me. (Fulfilled Prophecy: *"And I said unto them, if ye think good, give me my price; and if not, forbear. So they weighed for my price thirty pieces of silver. And the LORD said unto me, Cast it unto the potter: a goodly price that I was prised at of them. And I took the thirty pieces of silver, and cast them to the potter in the house of the LORD."* Zechariah 11:12-13).

11-4. Jesus before Pontius Pilate (1ST trial before the Gentiles).

a. Pilate then went out into them, and said, What accusation bring ye against this man?

b. And they began to accuse him, saying, We found this fellow perverting the nation, and forbidding to give tribute to Caesar, saying that he himself is Christ a King.

c. And Jesus stood before the governor Pilate: and the governor asked him, saying, Art thou the King of the Jews?

d. And Jesus said unto him, **Thou sayest it**.

e. And when he was accused of the chief priests of many things and elders, he answered nothing. They answered and said unto him, if he were not a malefactor, we would not have delivered him up unto thee.

f. Then saith Pilate unto him, Hearest thou not how many things they witness against thee? Answerest thou nothing.

g. But Jesus yet answered nothing; insomuch that the governor marvelled greatly.

h. (***Pilate, 1st No Fault***) Then said Pilate to the chief priests and to the people, I found no fault in this man.

i. Then said Pilate unto them, Take ye him and judge him according to your law.

j. The Jews therefore said unto him, It is not lawful for us to put any man to death: That the saying of Jesus might be fulfilled, which he spake, signifying what death he should die. (Fulfilled prophecy: *"Behold, we go up to Jerusalem; and the Son of man shall be betrayed unto the chief priests and unto the scribes, and they shall condemn him to death, And shall deliver him to the gentiles to mock, and to scourge, and to crucify him; and the third day he shall rise again."* Matthew 20:18-19).

k. And they were the more fierce, saying, He stirreth up the people, teaching throughout all Jewry, beginning from Galilee to this place.

l. When Pilate heard of Galilee, he asked whether the man were a Galilaean.

m. And soon as he knew that he belonged unto Herod's jurisdiction, he sent him to Herod, who himself also was at Jerusalem at that time.

11-5. Jesus before Herod (2nd trial before the Gentiles)

a. And when Herod saw Jesus, he was exceeding glad: for he was desirous to see him of a long season, because he had heard many things of him, and he hoped to have seen some miracles done by him.

b. Then he questioned with him in many words; but he answered him nothing.

c. And the chief priests and scribes stood and vehemently accused him.

d. And Herod with his men of war set him at nought, and mocked him, and arrayed him in a gorgeous robe, and sent him again to Pilate.

e. And the same day Pilate and Herod were made friends together: for before they were at enmity between themselves.

11-6. Jesus before Pilate again (3rd trial), 2nd No Fault

a. And Pilate, when he had called together the chief priests and the rulers and the people, Said unto them, Ye have brought this man unto me, as one that perverted the people : and, behold, I, having examined him before you, have found no fault in this man touching those things whereof ye accuse him: No, nor yet Herod: for I sent you to him; and, lo, nothing worthy of death is done unto him.

b. Then Pilate entered into the judgment hall again, and called Jesus, and said unto him, Art thou the King of the Jews? Jesus answered him, **Sayest thou this thing of thyself, or did others tell it thee of me?**

c. Pilate answered, Am I a Jew? Thine own nation and the chief priests have delivered thee unto me: what has thou done?

d. Jesus answered, **My kingdom is not of this world: if my kingdom were of this world, then would my servants fight, that I should not be delivered to the Jews: but now is my kingdom not from hence.**

e. Pilate therefore said unto him, Art thou a king then?

f. Jesus answered, **Thou sayest that I am a king. To this end was I born, and for this cause came I into the world, that I should bear witness unto the truth. Every one that is of the truth heareth my voice.**

g. Pilate saith unto him, What is truth?

h. (*Pilate, 3rd No Fault*) And when he had said this, he went out again unto the Jews, and saith unto them, I find in him no fault at all.

i. Now at that feast the governor of necessity was wont to released unto the people one prisoner, whomsoever they desired.

j. And there was a notable prisoner named Barabbas, which lay bound with them that had made insurrection with him, who had committed murder in the insurrection.

11-7. Pilate, 1st attempt to release Jesus.

a. But ye have a custom, that I should release unto you one at the passover: will ye therefore that I release unto you the King of the Jews?

b. And the multitude crying aloud began to desire him to do as he had ever done unto them.

c. Therefore when they were gathered together, Pilate said unto them, Whom will ye that I release unto you? Barabbas, or Jesus which is called Christ?

d. For he knew that the chief priests had delivered him for envy.

e. I will therefore chastise him, and release him. (for of necessity he must release one unto them at the feast.).

f. But the chief priests and elders persuaded the multitude that he should rather release Barabbas unto them, and destroy Jesus.

g. And they cried out all at once, saying, not this man, Away with this man, and release unto us Barabbas, now Barabbas was a robber, and a murderer (Who for a certain sedition made in the city, and for murder, was cast into prison).

h. When he was set down on the judgment seat, his wife sent unto him, saying, Have thou nothing to do with that just man: for I have suffered many things this day in a dream because of him.

11-8. Pilate, 2nd attempt to release Jesus.

a. Pilate therefore, willing to release Jesus, spake again to them.

b. The governor answered and said unto them, Whether of the twain will ye that I release unto you? They said Barabbas.

c. Pilate said unto them, What shall I do then with him whom ye call the King of the Jews?

d. They all cried out again saying unto him, Let him be crucified, Crucify him, crucify him.

11-9. Pilate, 3rd attempt to release Jesus.

a. And the governor said unto them the third time, Why, what evil hath he done? I have found no cause of death in him: I will therefore chastise him, and let him go.

b. But they cried out the more instant with loud voices exceedingly, saying, Let him be crucified, Crucify him. And the voices of them and of the chief priests prevailed.

c. When Pilate saw that he could prevail nothing, but that rather a tumult was made, he took water, and washed his hands before the multitude, saying, I am innocent of the blood of this just person: see ye to it.

d. Then answered all the people, and said, His blood be on us, and on our children. And Pilate gave sentence that it should be as they required.

e. And so Pilate, willing to content the people, released Barabbas unto them, him that for sedition and murder was cast into prison, whom they had desired; but he scourged Jesus.

11-10. Jesus scourged and crowned with thorns.

a. Then the soldiers of the governor took Jesus and led him away into the common hall, called Praetorium, and they called together the whole band of soldiers.

b. And they stripped him, and scourged him (Fulfilled prophecy: *"But he was wounded for our transgressions, he was bruised for our iniquities: the chastisement of our peace was upon him; and with his stripes we are healed."* Isaiah 53:5) and put on him a purple robe. (Controversy: Matthew 27:28 *says a scarlet robe;* Mark 15:17 *says a purple robe;* John 19:2 *says a purple robe; so I went with the majority here).*

c. And when they had platted a crown of thorns, they put it upon his head, and a reed in his right hand: and they bowed the knee before him.

d. And began to salute him, saying, Hail, King of the Jews!

e. And they spit upon him, and took the reed, and smote him on the head, and they smote him with their hands, bowing their knees worshipped him.

f. And after that they had mocked him (*they took him to Pilate*).

11-11. Pilate, 1st No Fault after scourging and attempt to release.

a. Pilate therefore went forth again, and saith unto them, Behold, I bring him forth to you, that ye may know that I find no fault in him.

b. Then came Jesus forth, wearing the crown of thorns, and the purple robe.

c. And Pilate saith unto them, Behold the man!

d. When the chief priests therefore and officers saw him, they cried out, saying, Crucify him, crucify him.

11-12. Pilate, 2nd No Fault after scourging and attempt to release.

a. Pilate saith unto them, Take ye him, and crucify him: for I find no fault in him.

b. The Jews answered him, We have a law, and by our law he ought to die, because he made himself the son of God.

c. When Pilate therefore heard that saying, he was the more afraid; And went again into the judgment hall, and saith unto Jesus, Whence art thou?

d. But Jesus gave him no answer.

e. Then saith Pilate unto him, Speakest thou not unto me? knowest thou not that I have power to crucify thee, and have power to release thee?

f. Jesus answered, **Thou couldest have no power at all against me, except it were given thee from above: therefore he that delivered me unto thee hath the greater sin.**

11-13. Pilate, 3rd No Fault after scourging and attempt to release.

a. And from thenceforth Pilate sought to release him: but the Jews cried out, saying, If thou let this man go, thou art not Caesar's friend: whosoever maketh himself a king speaketh against Caesar.

b. When Pilate therefore heard that saying, he brought Jesus forth, and sat down in the judgment seat in a place that is called the Pavement, but in the Hebrew, Gabbatha.

c. And it was the preparation of the Passover, and he saith unto the Jews, Behold your King! *(See controversy in 11-14. i., regarding the time, under John 19:14-16).*

d. But they cried out, Away with him, away with him, crucify him.

e. Pilate saith unto them, Shall I crucify your King? The chief priests answered, We have no king but Caesar.

f. Then delivered he him therefore unto them to be crucified. And they took off the purple robe, and put his own clothes on him, and led Jesus away to crucify him.

11-14. Jesus crucified.

a. And as they led him away bearing his cross, as they came out, they found a man, who passed by, they laid hold upon one Simon, a Cyrenian, coming out of the country.

b. The father of Alexander and Rufus, and on him they laid the cross, and they compel him, that he might bear it after Jesus.

c. And there followed him a great company of people, and of women, which also bewailed and lamented him.

d. But Jesus turning unto them said, **Daughters of Jerusalem, weep not for me, but weep for yourselves, and for your children.**

e. **For, behold, the days are coming, in the which they shall say, Blessed are the barren, and the wombs that never bare, and the paps which never gave suck. Then shall they begin to say to the mountains, Fall on us; and to the hills, Cover us.**

f. **For if they do these things in a green tree, what shall be done in the dry?**

g. And there were also two other, malefactors, led with him to be put to death.

h. And when they were come unto a place called in the Hebrew Golgotha, that is to say, a place of a skull, which is called Calvary.

i. They gave him vinegar to drink mingled with gall, and wine mingled with myrrh: and when he had tasted thereof, he would not drink (Controversy: Matthew 27:34, *said it was vinegar mingled with gall;* Mark 15:23, *said it was wine mingled with myrrh. I used them all*). And it was the third hour (*9:00 am*), and they crucified him (Controversy: John 19:14-16, *said Pilate had the soldiers lead Jesus away to be crucified, at the sixth hour (12:00 am);* Mark 15:25-33, *said Jesus was nailed to the cross at the third hour (9:00 am) and there was darkness over the whole land, from the sixth (12:00 am), until the ninth hour (3:00 pm);* Matthew 27:35-45, *said he was crucified and later, at the sixth hour, until the ninth hour, there was darkness all over the land;* Luke 23:33-44, *said Jesus was crucified, and later, at the sixth hour there was darkness over all the earth, until the ninth hour. I had to dismiss John's account, based on the harmony of the other three gospels*).

j. Then said Jesus, **Father, forgive them; for they know not what they do.**

k. Then were there two thieves crucified with him, one on the right hand, and another on the left, and Jesus in the midst.

l. And the scripture was fulfilled, which saith, And he was numbered with the transgressors. (Fulfilled Prophecy: *"Therefore will I divide him a portion with the great, and he shall divide the spoil with the strong; because he hath poured out his soul unto death: and he was numbered with the transgressors; and he bare the sin of many, and made intercession for the transgressors."* Isaiah 53:12.)

m. And Pilate wrote a title, and put it on the cross. And set up over his head his accusation written, THIS IS JESUS OF NAZARETH THE KING OF THE JEWS.

n. This title then read many of the Jews: for the place where Jesus was crucified was nigh to the city: and it was written in Hebrew, and Greek, and Latin.

o. Then said the chief priests of the Jews to Pilate, Write not, The King of the Jews; but that he said, I am King of the Jews.

p. Pilate answered, What I have written I have written.

11-15. Jesus humiliated.

a. Then the soldiers, when they had crucified Jesus, took his garments, and made four parts, to every soldier a part; and also his coat: now the coat was without seam, woven from the top throughout.

b. They said therefore among themselves, Let us not rend it, but cast lots for it, whose it shall be: that the scripture might be fulfilled, which was spoken by the prophet, they parted my garments among them, what every man should take, and for my vesture they did cast lots (Fulfilled Prophecy: *"They part my garments among them, and cast lots upon my vesture."* Psalms 22:18). These things therefore the soldiers did.

c. And sitting down they watched him there; And the people stood beholding.

d. And the rulers also with them derided him, saying, He saved others; let him save himself, if he be Christ, the chosen of God.

e. And the soldiers also mocked him, coming to him, and offering him vinegar. And saying, If thou be the king of the Jews, save thyself.

f. And they that passed by railed on him, wagging their heads, and saying, Ah, thou that destroyest the temple, and buildest it in three days. Save thyself, if thou be the Son of God, and come down from the cross.

g. And saying, If thou be the king of the Jews, save thyself. Likewise also the chief priests mocking him, with the scribes and elders, said among themselves. He saved others; himself he cannot save.

h. Let Christ the King of Israel descend now from the cross, that we may see and believe. He trusted in God; let him deliver him now, if he will have him: for he said, I am the Son of God.

i. The thieves also, which were crucified with him, cast the same in his teeth. And they reviled (*abuse verbally*) him.

j. And one of the malefactors which were hanged railed on him, saying, If thou be Christ, save thyself and us.

k. But the other answering rebuked him, saying, Dost not thou fear God, seeing thou art in the same condemnation? (Controversy: Matthew 27:44 *and* Mark15:32 *said the thieves spoke negatively of Jesus.* Luke 23:40-43 *said one thief spoke on Jesus behalf; I used them all*).

l. And we indeed justly; for we receive the due reward of our deeds: but this man hath done nothing amiss (*wrong*). And he said unto Jesus, Lord, remember me when thou comest into thy kingdom.

m. And Jesus said unto him, **Verily I say unto thee, To day shalt thou be with me in paradise.**

n. Now there stood by the cross of Jesus his mother, and his mother's sister, Mary the wife of Cleophas, and Mary Magdalene.

o. When Jesus therefore saw his mother, and the disciple standing by, whom he loved, he saith unto his mother, **Woman, behold thy son!**

p. Then saith he to the disciple, **Behold thy mother!** And from that hour that disciple took her unto his own home.

11-16. Jesus death.

a. Now from the sixth hour (*12:00 am, high noon, hottest part of the day*) there was darkness over all the earth unto the ninth hour.

b. And at the ninth hour (*3:00 pm, 6 hours of hanging nailed to the cross*) Jesus cried with a loud voice, saying, **Eli, Eli, lama sabachthani?** that is to say, **My God, my God, why hast thou forsaken me?** (Fulfilled Prophecy: *"Reproach hath broken my heart; and I am full of heaviness: and I looked for some to take pity, but there was none; and for comforters, but I found none."* Psalm 69:20.)

c. Some of them that stood there, when they heard that, said, This man calleth for Elias.

d. After this, Jesus knowing that all things were now accomplished, that the scripture might be fulfilled, saith, **I thirst.**

e. Now there was set a vessel full of vinegar: And straightway one of them ran, and took a spunge, and filled it with vinegar, and put it on a reed, and put it to his mouth to drink, saying, let alone, let us see whether Elias will come to take him down. (Fulfilled Prophecy: *"They gave me also gall for my meat; and in my thirst they gave me vinegar to drink."* Psalm 69:21).

f. The rest said, Let be, let us see whether Elias will come to save him.

g. And when Jesus therefore had received the vinegar cried again with a loud voice, he said, **Father, it is finished, into thy hands, I commend my spirit**: and having said thus, he bowed his head and gave up the ghost.

h. And, behold, the sun was darkened, and the veil of the temple was rent in twain in the midst from top to bottom; and the earth did quake, and the rocks rent; And the graves were opened;

i. Now when the centurion, which stood over against him, saw that he so cried out, and gave up the ghost, he glorified God saying, Truly this man was the Son of God.

j. And they that were with him, watching Jesus, saw the earthquake, and those things that were done, they feared greatly, saying, Truly this was the Son of God.

k. And all the people that came together to that sight, beholding the things which were done, smote their breasts, and returned.

l. And all his acquaintance, and many women were there beholding these things afar off, which followed Jesus from Galilee, ministering unto him:

m. Among which was Mary Magdalene, and Mary the mother of James the less and Joses, and Salome, and the mother of Zebedee's children. (Who also, when he was in Galilee, followed him, and ministered unto him;) and many other women which came up with him unto Jerusalem.

n. The Jews therefore, because it was the preparation, that the bodies should not remain upon the cross on the sabbath day, (for that sabbath day was a high day,) besought Pilate that their legs might be broken (*to speed up death*), and that they might be taken away.

o. Then came the soldiers, and brake the legs of the first, and of the other which was crucified with him.

p. But when they came to Jesus, and saw that he was dead already, they brake not his legs: But one of the soldiers with a spear pierced his side, and forthwith came there out blood and water.

q. And he that saw it bare record, and his record is true: and he knoweth that he saith true, that ye might believe.

r. For these things were done, that the scripture should be fulfilled, A bone of him shall not be broken. (Fulfilled Prophecy: *"He keepeth all his bones: not one of them is broken."* Psalm 34:20).

s. And again another scripture saith, They shall look on him whom they pierced.
(Fulfilled Prophecy: *"And I will pour upon the house of David, and upon the inhabitants of Jerusalem, the spirit of grace and of supplications: and they should look upon me whom they have pierced, and they shall mourn for him, as one mourneth for his only son, and shall be in bitterness for him, as one that is in bitterness for his firstborn."* Zechariah 12:10).

11-17. Jesus laid in the sepulchre.

a. And now when the even was come, because it was the preparation (*Friday*), that is, the day before the sabbath (*Saturday*), there came a rich man named Joseph, an honourable counsellor, and he was a good man, and a just: who also himself was Jesus' disciple: (The same had not consented to the counsel and deed of them;) he was of Arimathaea, a city of the Jews: who also himself waited for the kingdom of God.

b. But secretly for fear of the Jews, This man came, and went in boldly unto Pilate, and begged the body of Jesus.

c. And there came also Nicodemius, which at the first came to Jesus by night (*meet Jesus about three years ago, see Para 2-14*) and brought a mixture of myrrh and aloes, about an hundred pound weight.

d. And Pilate marvelled if he were already dead: and calling unto him the centurion, he asked him whether he had been any while dead.

e. And when he knew it of the centurion, Then Pilate commanded the body to be delivered to Joseph.

f. And he (*Joseph*) bought fine linen.

g. And when Joseph had taken the body down, Then took they the body of Jesus, and wrapped it in a clean linen cloth with the spices, as the manner of the Jews is to bury.

h. Now in the place where he was crucified there was a garden; and in the garden a new sepulchre, wherein was never man yet laid.

i. There they laid Jesus in his (*Joseph*) own sepulchre, which he had hewn out in the rock, wherein never man before was laid. Because of the Jews' preparation day; for the sepulchre was nigh at hand.

j. And he *(Joseph)* rolled a great stone to the door of the sepulchre, and departed.

k. And that day was the preparation, and the Sabbath drew on.

l. And the women also, which came with him from Galilee, followed after, and beheld the sepulchre, and how his body was laid.

m. And there was Mary Magdalene, and Mary the mother of Joses, sitting over against the sepulchre.

n. And they returned, and prepared spices and ointments: and rested the sabbath day according to the commandment.

11-18. The sepulchre guarded.

a. Now the next day, that followed the day of the preparation *(The sabbath)*, the chief priests and Pharisees came together unto Pilate, saying, Sir, we remember that that deceiver said, while he was yet alive, After three days I will rise again.

b. Command therefore that the sepulchre be made sure until the third day, lest his disciples come by night, and steal him away, and say unto the people, He is risen from the dead: so the last error shall be worse than the first.

c. Pilate said unto them, Ye have a watch: go your way, make it as sure as ye can.

d. So they went, and made the sepulchre sure, sealing the stone, and setting a watch.

The Combined Gospel of Jesus Christ

Chapter Twelve
The Resurrection and Ascension of Jesus Christ

12-1. The Resurrection of Jesus Christ.

a. And when the sabbath was past (*Sunset Saturday*), Mary Magdalene, and Mary the mother of James, and Salome, had bought sweet spices, that they might come and anoint him.

b. As it began to dawn (*to begin to develop or exist*) toward the first day of the week, came Mary Magdalene and the other Mary to see the sepulchre.

c. And, behold there was a great earthquake: for the angel of the Lord descended from heaven, and came and rolled back the stone from the door, and sat upon it.

d. His countenance was like lightning, and his raiment white as snow: And for fear of him the keepers did shake, and became as dead men.

e. And many bodies of the saints which slept arose, And came out of the graves after his resurrection and went into the holy city and appeared unto many.

f. The first day (*Sunday morning*) of the week cometh Mary Magdalene early, when it was yet dark, unto the sepulchre and seeth the stone taken away from the sepulchre.

g. Then she runneth, and cometh to Simon Peter, and to the other disciple (*John*), whom Jesus loved, and saith unto them, They have taken away the Lord out of the sepulchre, and we know not where they have laid him.

h. Now upon the first day of the week, very early in the morning, they (*the other women*) came unto the sepulchre at the rising of the sun, bringing the spices which they had prepared, and certain others with them.

i. And they said among themselves, Who shall roll us away the stone from the door of the sepulchre?

j. And when they looked, they saw that the stone was rolled away from the sepulchre: for it was very great.

k. And the angel answered and said unto the women, *fear not ye: for I know that ye seek Jesus, which was crucified. He is not here: for he is risen, as he said. Come, see the place where the Lord lay.*

l. And entering into the sepulchre, and found not the body of Lord Jesus. They saw a young man sitting on the right side, clothed in a long white garment; and they were affrighted.

m. And the angel answered and said unto the women, *Be not affrighted: for I know that Ye seek Jesus of Nazareth, which was crucified: He is not here: for he is risen, as he said: behold the place where they laid him.*

n. *But go your way quickly, and tell his disciples and Peter that he is risen from the dead; and, behold, he goeth before you into Galilee; there shall ye see him, as he said unto you. lo, I have told you.*

o. And they went out quickly, and fled from the sepulchre with fear and great joy; for they trembled and were amazed:

p. And it came to pass, as they were much perplexed thereabout, behold, two men stood by them in shining garments:

q. And as they were afraid, and bowed down their faces to the earth, they said unto them, *Why seek ye the living among the dead? He is not here, but is risen: remember how he spake unto you when he was yet in*

Galilee, Saying, The Son of man must be delivered into the hands of sinful men, and be crucified, and the third day rise again. And they remembered his words.

r. And did run to bring his disciples word, neither said they any thing to any man; for they were afraid.

s. (*After hearing from Mary*) Peter therefore went forth, and that other disciple, and came to the sepulchre.

t. So they ran both together: and the other disciple did outrun Peter, and came first to the sepulchre.

u. And he stooping down, and looking in, saw the linen clothes lying; yet went he not in.

v. Then cometh Simon Peter following him, and stooping down, he beheld the linen clothes laid by themselves, went into the sepulchre, and seeth the linen clothes lie, And the napkin, that was about his head, not lying with the linen clothes, but wrapped together in a place by itself.

w. Then went in also that other disciple, which came first to the sepulchre, and he saw, and believed.

x. For as yet they knew not the scripture, that he must rise again from the dead.

y. Then the disciples went away again unto their own home. (*Peter*) departed wondering in himself at that which was come to pass.

12-2. Jesus appears to Mary and the women.

a. But Mary stood without at the sepulchre weeping: and as she wept, she stooped down, and looked into the sepulchre.

b. And seeth two angels in white sitting, the one at the head, and the other at the feet, where the body of Jesus had lain.

c. And they say unto her, *Woman, why weepest thou?* She saith unto them, Because they have taken away my Lord, and I know not where they have laid him.

d. And when she had thus said, she turned herself back, and saw Jesus standing, and knew not that it was Jesus.

e. Jesus saith unto her, **Woman, why weepest thou? whom seekest thou?**

f. She, supposing him to be the gardener, saith unto him, Sir, if thou have borne him hence, tell me where thou hast laid him, and I will take him away.

g. Now when Jesus was risen early the first day of the week, he appeared first to Mary Magdalene, out of whom he had cast seven devils.

h. Jesus saith unto her, **Mary.**

i. She turned herself, and saith unto him, Rabboni; which is to say, Master

j. Jesus saith unto her, **Touch me not; for I am not yet ascended to my Father: but go to my brethren, and say unto them, I ascend unto my Father, and your Father; and to my God, and your God.**

k. And as they *(the other women)* went to tell his disciples, behold, Jesus met them, saying, **All hail.** And they came and held him by the feet, and worshipped him.

l. Then said Jesus unto them, **Be not afraid: go tell my brethren that they go into Galilee, and there shall they see me.**

12-3. The bribing of the soldiers.

a. Now when they were going, behold, some of the watch came into the city, and showed unto the chief priests all the things that were done.

b. And when they were assembled with the elders, and had taken counsel, they gave large money unto the soldiers, Saying, Say ye, His disciples came by night, and stole him away while we slept.

c. And if this come to the governor's ears, we will persuade him, and secure you.

d. So they took the money, and did as they were taught: and this saying is commonly reported among the Jews until this day.

12-4. The women inform the disciples.

a. And (*the women*) retuned from the sepulchre, and told all these things to the eleven, and to all the rest

b. It was Mary Magdalene, and Joanna, and Mary the Mother of James, and other women that were with them, which told these things unto the apostles.

c. And their words seemed to them as idle tales, and they believed them not.

d. Mary Magdalene came and told the disciples that had been with him, as they mourned and wept that she had seen the Lord, and that he had spoken these things unto her.

e. And they, when they had heard that he was alive, and had been seen of her, believed not.

12-5. The walk to Emmaus.

a. After that he appeared in another form unto two of them *(Cleopas 12-5.(e) and Simon 12-5. (v.)*, as they walked, and went into the country.

b. And, behold, two of them went that same day to a village called Emmaus, which was from Jerusalem about threescore furlongs. And they talked together of all these things which had happened.

c. And it came to pass, that, while they communed together and reasoned, Jesus himself drew near, and went with them. But their eyes were holden that they should not know him.

d. And he said unto them, **What manner of communications are these that ye have one to another, as ye walk, and are sad?**

e. And the one of them, whose name was Cleopas, answering said unto him, Art thou only a stranger in Jerusalem, and hast not known the things which are come to pass there in these days?

f. And he said unto them, **What things?**

g. And they said unto him, Concerning Jesus of Nazareth, which was a prophet mighty in deed and word before God and all the people.

h. And how the chief priests and our rulers delivered him to be condemned to death, and have crucified him.

i. But we trusted that it had been he which should have redeemed Israel: and beside all this, to day is the third day since these things were done.

j. Yea, and certain women also of our company made us astonished, which were early at the sepulchre;

k. And when they found not his body, they came, saying, that they had also seen a vision of angels, which said that he was alive.

l. And certain of them which were with us went to the sepulchre, and found it even so as the women had said: but him they saw not.

m. Then he said unto them, **O fools, and slow of heart to believe all that the prophets have spoken. Ought not Christ to have suffered these things, and to enter into his glory?**

n. And beginning at Moses and all the prophets, he expounded unto them in all the scriptures the things concerning himself.

o. And they drew nigh unto the village, whither they went: and he made as though he would have gone further.

p. But they constrained him, saying, Abide with us: for it is toward evening, and the day is far spent. And he went in to tarry with them.

q. And it came to pass, as he sat at meat with them, he took bread, and blessed it, and brake and gave to them.

r. And their eyes were opened, and they knew him; and he vanished out of their sight.

s. And they said one to another, Did not our heart burn within us, while he talked with us by the way, and while he opened to us the scriptures?

t. And they rose up the same hour, and returned to Jerusalem, and found the eleven gathered together, and them (*the women*) that were with them.

u. And they told it unto the residue. Saying, the Lord is risen indeed, and hath appeared to Simon.

v. And they told what things were done in the way, and how he was known of them in breaking of bread. Neither believed they them.

12-6. Jesus first appearance to the ten.

a. Then the same day at evening, being the first day of the week, when the doors were shut where the disciples (*ten disciples; Judas dead and Thomas missing*) were assembled as they sat at meat for fear of the Jews.

b. And as they thus spake, came Jesus himself and stood in the midst, and saith unto them, **Peace be unto you.**

c. And unbraided them with their unbelief and hardness of heart, because they believed not them which had seen him after he was risen. (Controversy: Mark 16:14 *said he appeared to eleven, but he has to be referring to the second appearance Thomas was at, and not the first appearance, see* John 20:19-24. *This was Jesus first appearance, because the disciples were in disbelief, after hearing three accounts of people, who said they saw Jesus. Thomas must have left out after hearing Cleopas and Simon accounts of Jesus*).

d. But they were terrified and affrighted, and supposed that they had seen a spirit.

e. And he said unto them, **Why are ye troubled? And why do thoughts arise in your hearts?**

f. And when he had so said, He showed unto them his hands and his side. **Behold my hands and my feet, that it is I myself: handle me, and see; for a spirit hath not flesh and bones, as ye see me have.**

g. Then were the disciples glad, when they saw the Lord.

h. And while they yet believed not for joy, and wondered, he said unto them, **Have ye here any meat?**

i. And they gave him a piece of broiled fish, and of an honeycomb.

j. And he took it and did eat before them.

k. And he said unto them, **These are the words which I spake unto you, while I was yet with you, that all things must be fulfilled, which were written in the law of Moses, and in the prophets, and in the psalms, concerning me.**

l. Then opened he their understanding, that they might understand the scriptures. And said unto them, **Thus it is written, and thus it behooved Christ to suffer, and to rise from the dead the third day. And that repentance and remission of sins should be preached in** his name among all nations, beginning at Jerusalem. And ye are witnesses of these things.

m. And, behold, I send the promise of my Father upon you: but tarry ye in the city of Jerusalem, until ye be endued with power from on high.

n. Then said Jesus to them again, **Peace be unto you: as my Father hath sent me, even so send I you.**

o. And when he had said this, he breathed on them, and saith unto them, **Receive ye the Holy Ghost: Whosoever sins ye remit, they are remitted** (*pardon or forgive*) **unto them; and whosoever sins ye retain, they are retained.**

12-7. Jesus second appearance to the disciples.

a. But Thomas, one of the twelve, called Didymus, was not with them when Jesus came. The other disciples therefore said unto him, We have seen the Lord.

b. But he said unto them, Except I shall see in his hands the print of the nails, and put my finger into the print of the nails, and thrust my hand into his side, I will not believe.

c. And after eight days again his disciples were within, and Thomas with them: then came Jesus, the doors being shut, and stood in the midst, and said, **Peace be unto you.**

d. Then saith he to Thomas, **Reach hither thy finger, and behold my hands; and reach hither thy hand, and thrust it into my side: and be not faithless, but believing.**

e. And Thomas answered and said unto him, My Lord and my God.

f. Jesus saith unto him, **Thomas, because thou hast seen me, thou hast believed: blessed are they that have not seen, and yet have believed.**

g. And many other signs truly did Jesus in the presence of his disciples, which are not written in this book.

h. But these are written, that ye might believe that Jesus is the Christ, the Son of God; and that believing ye might have life through his name.

12-8. Jesus third appearance to the disciples.

a. After these things, Jesus showed himself again to the disciples at the sea of Tiberias; and on this wise showed he himself.

b. There were together Simon Peter, and Thomas called Didymus, and Nathaniel of Cana in Galilee, and the sons of Zebedee (*James and John*), and two other of his disciples.

c. Simon Peter saith unto them, I go a-fishing. They say unto him, We also go with thee.

d. They went forth, and entered into a ship immediately; and that night they caught nothing.

e. But when the morning was now come, Jesus stood on the shore: but the disciples knew not that it was Jesus.

f. Then Jesus saith unto them, **Children, have ye any meat?** They answered him, No.

g. And he said unto them, **Cast the net on the right side of the ship, and ye shall find.**

h. They cast therefore, and now they were not able to draw it for the multitudes of fishes.

i. Therefore that disciple whom Jesus loved saith unto Peter, It is the Lord. Now when Simon Peter heard that it was the Lord, he girt his fisher's coat unto him, (for he was naked,) and did cast himself into the sea.

j. And the other disciples came in a little ship; (for they were not far from land, but as it were two hundred cubits,) dragging the net with fishes.

k. As soon then as they were come to land, they saw a fire of coals there, and fish laid thereon, and bread.

l. Jesus saith unto them, **Bring of the fish which ye have now caught.**

m. Simon Peter went up, and drew the net to land full of great fishes, and hundred and fifty and three: and for all there were so many, yet was not the net broken.

n. Jesus saith unto them, **Come and dine.**

o. And none of the disciples durst ask him, Who art thou? Knowing that it was the Lord.

p. Jesus then cometh, and taketh bread, and giveth them, and fish likewise. This is now the third time that Jesus showed himself to his disciples, after that he was risen from the dead.

12-9. Jesus questions Peter.

a. So when they had dined, Jesus saith to Simon Peter, **Simon, son of Jonas, lovest thou me more than these?** He saith unto him, Yea, Lord; thou knowest that I love thee. He saith unto him, **Feed my lambs.**

b. He saith to him again the second time, **Simon, son of Jonas, lovest thou me?** He saith unto him, Yea, Lord; thou knowest that I love thee. He saith unto him, **Feed my sheep.**

c. He saith unto him the third time, **Simon son of Jonas, lovest thou me?** Peter was grieved because he said unto him the third time, Lovest thou me? And he said unto him, lord, thou knowest all things; thou knowest that I love thee. Jesus saith unto him **Feed my sheep.**

d. **Verily, verily, I say unto thee, When thou wast young, thou girdedst thyself, and walkedst whither thou wouldest: but when thou shalt be old, thou shalt stretch forth thy hands, and another shall gird thee, and carry thee whither thou wouldest not.**

e. This spake he, signifying by what death he should glorify God *(Peter was crucified with his arms and legs stretched forth. Out of respect for Jesus crucifixion, he asked to be crucified upside down on the cross).* And when he had spoken this, he saith unto him, **Follow me.**

f. Then Peter, turning about, seeth the disciple whom Jesus loved following; which also leaned on his breast at supper, and said, Lord, which is he that betrayed thee?

g. Peter seeing him saith to Jesus, Lord, and what shall this man do? Jesus saith unto him, **If I will that he tarry till I come, what is that to thee? Follow thou me.**

h. Then went this saying abroad among the brethren, that that disciple should not die: yet Jesus said not unto him, He shall not die; but, If I will that he tarry till I come, what is that to thee?

i. This is the disciple which testifieth of these things, and write these things: and we know that his testimony is true. *(Here John is telling us, that this is his testimony. Jesus truly loved all his disciples, just like he loves all of us).*

12-10. Jesus final commands to the disciples.

a. Then the eleven disciples went away into Galilee, into a mountain where Jesus had appointed them. And when they saw him, they worshipped him: but some doubted.

b. And Jesus came and spake unto them, saying, **All power is given unto me in heaven and in earth. Go ye therefore into all the world, and preach the gospel to every creature, and teach all nations.**

c. Teaching them to observe all things whatsoever I have commanded you. He that believeth and is baptized shall be saved; but he that believeth not shall be damned.

d. Baptizing them in the name of the Father, and of the Son, and of the Holy Ghost.

e. And these signs shall follow them that believe; In my name shall they cast out devils; they shall speak with new tongues;

f. They shall take up serpents; and if they drink any deadly thing, it shall not hurt them; they shall lay hands on the sick, and they shall recover.

12-11. Jesus ascension.

a. The Former treatise have I made, O Theophilus, of all that Jesus began both to do and teach.

b. Until the day in which he was taken up, after that he through the Holy Ghost had given commandments unto the apostles whom he had chosen:

c. To whom also he showed himself alive after his passions by many infallible proofs, being seen of them forty days, and speaking of the things pertaining to the kingdom of God:

d. And he led them out as far as to Bethany. And, being assembled together with them, commanded them that **they should not depart from Jerusalem, but wait for the promise of the Father, which, saith he, ye have heard of me.**

e. For John truly baptized with water; but ye shall be baptized with the Holy Ghost not many days hence.

f. When they therefore were come together, they asked of him, saying, Lord, wilt thou at this time restore again the kingdom of Israel?

g. And he said unto them, **It is not for you to know the times or the seasons, which the Father hath put in his own power.**

h. **But ye shall receive power, after that the Holy Ghost is come upon you: and ye shall be witnesses unto me both in Jerusalem, and in all Judaea, and in Samaria, and unto the uttermost part of the earth.**

i. And after the Lord had spoken these things, while they beheld. He lifted up his hands, and blessed them.

j. And it came to pass, while he blessed them, he was taken up into heaven; and a cloud received him out of their sight. **And, lo, I am with you always, even unto the end of the world. Amen.** And sat on the right hand of God.

k. And while they looked steadfastly toward heaven as he went up, behold, two men stood by them in white apparel;

l. Which also said, *Ye men of Galilee, why stand ye gazing up into heaven? This same Jesus, which is taken up from you into heaven, shall so come in like manner as ye have seen him go into heaven.*

m. And they worshipped him, and returned to Jerusalem with great joy:

n. And there are also many other things which Jesus did, the which, if they should be written every one, I suppose that even the world itself could not contain the books that should be written. Amen.

12-12. Matthias chosen to replace Judas.

a. Then returned they unto Jerusalem from the mount called Olivet, which is from Jerusalem a sabbath day's journey.

b. And when they were come in, they went up into an upper room, where abode both Peter, and James, and John, and Andrew, Philip, and Thomas, Bartholomew, and Matthew, James the son of Alphaeus, and Simon Zelotes, and Judas the brother of James.

c. These all continued with one accord in prayer and supplication, with the women, and Mary the mother of Jesus, and with his brethren.

d. And in those days Peter stood up in the midst of the disciples, and said, (the number of names together were about an hundred and twenty,). Men and brethren, this scripture must needs have been fulfilled, which the Holy Ghost by the mouth of David spake before concerning Judas, which was guide to them that took Jesus.

e. For he was numbered with us, and had obtained part of this ministry. Now this man purchased a field with the reward of iniquity, and falling headlong, he burst asunder in the midst, and all his bowels gushed out.

f. And it was known unto all the dwellers at Jerusalem; insomuch as that field is called in their proper tongue, Aceldama, that is to say, The field of blood.

g. For it is written in the book of Psalms, Let his habitation be desolate, and let no man dwell therein: and his bishopric let another take.

h. Wherefore of these men which have companied with us all the time that the Lord Jesus went in and out among us. Beginning from the baptism of John, unto that same day that he was taken up from us, must one be ordained to be a witness with us of his resurrection.

i. And they appointed two, Joseph called Barsabas, who was surnamed Justus, and Mathias.

j. And they prayed, and said, Thou, Lord, which knowest the hearts of all men, show whether of these two thou hast chosen. That he may take part of this ministry and apostleship, from which Judas by transgression fell, that he might go to his own place.

k. And they gave forth their lots; and the lot fell upon Matthias; and he was numbered with the eleven apostles.

12-13. The gift of the Holy Spirit.

a. And (*the disciples*) were continually in the temple, praising and blessing God. Amen.

b. And when the day of Pentecost was fully come, they were all with one accord in one place. And suddenly there came a sound from heaven as of a rushing mighty wind, and it filled all the house where they were sitting.

c. And there appeared unto them cloven tongues like as of fire, and it sat upon each of them. And they were all filled with the Holy Ghost, and began to speak with tongues, as the spirit gave them utterance.

d. And they went forth, and preached everywhere, the Lord working with them, and confirming the word with signs following. Amen.

Appendix A

Authors of the Gospel of Jesus Christ: Matthew, Mark, Luke, and John. God does not force man hand to act on his behalf. God provided the inspiration from above to these four men. They utilized that inspiration, coupled with their own God given talents and knowledge, to tell the story of Jesus Christ life on earth. Divinity and humanity acted together to produce the Gospel of Jesus Christ. The Gospel is the earthly life story of Jesus Christ.

Matthew: Matthew, or Levi, son of Alphaeus, lived in Capernaum. He was a publican or tax collector. Jesus Christ choose him as one of his twelve disciples. He is called Levi by the gospel of Mark and Luke. Early historical testimonies have ascribes this Gospel to Matthew. It was probably published before the destruction of Jerusalem in A.D. 70, because there is no reference to this prophetic event occurring. Some have indicated his gospel was written approximately A.D. 64.

Unlike most of the other Apostles, he was not a fisherman. He was skilled in writing and statistics revolving around numbers. These talents were valuable to him, in recording the genealogy of Jesus Christ, and writing the beginning Gospel of the New Testament. Tax collectors are accustomed to being exact, orderly, and neat. Perhaps this is what Jesus saw in him, when he was chosen. His narration of Jesus Christ life story is not done chronologically, but facts are group topically.

Matthew cleverly starts his book with a genealogy of Jesus. Many would consider this portion of the book insignificant and will show little interest in reading or studying it. On the contrary, it is of utmost importance, and provide the linkage of the Old Testament with the New Testament. It also establish the prophetic royal bloodline of the promise Messiah (*Christ* is a Greek translation of the world *Messiah*), by tracing his lineage back to Abraham. Abraham had received the promise of the Messiah through his seed by God. God reiterated this promise to King David of the same blood line as Abraham.

He links the old with the new again by quoting fulfillment of prophecy. He links the Old Testament prophecy from the prophets, with the life of Jesus, through the use of the word fulfilled more than any other Gospel writer. His gospel is distinctively different from the other three gospels. After Jesus Christ ascension; Matthew became a missionary of the Gospel. He laid down his life for the Lord and died a martyr in Ethiopia. His apostolic symbol is represented by three money bags, depicting his former occupation of a tax collector, before Jesus called him as a disciple.

Mark: John Mark was not one of the chosen twelve disciples, however, he was closely associated with them from the beginning. He lived in Jerusalem. He initially began working alongside Paul and Barnabas, before becoming closely associated with Peter.

It is apparent that Mark wrote this Gospel for the church at Rome, shortly after the death of Peter. Eusebius, in his *Church History* , quoted Papias of Hierapolis, who wrote the *Interpretations of the Lord's Sayings* about A.D. 150: *"Mark having become the interpreter of Peter, wrote down accurately everything that he remembered, without however recording in order what was either said or done by Christ."* Mark's Gospel is solely based upon the eye-witness accounts of Simon Peter coupled with the inspiration of the Holy Spirit. Peter taught him under the inspiration of the divine Holy Spirit.

The crazy Emperor Nero, martyred Simon Peter by crucifixion, about A.D. 64. Four years later Emperor Nero committed suicide, which ended the Julio-Claudian dynasty. Titus conquest and destruction of Jerusalem and the Temple was in A.D. 69-70. Mark gospel assumes that the city of Jerusalem and the temple is still standing. Mark gospel was probably written approximately A.D. 57. Some religious scholars have indicated that it was the first gospel written.

Human nature is more attentive to action, and Mark Gospel provides more drama, than any of the other three Gospel writers. He gives the most detailed account of the activity revolving around the life of Jesus Christ. He only provides a sample of the parables, very little personal reflection of sermons, and display a small tolerance for dialogue. He splice together scenes and defy any structure or outline.

Approximately 90 percent of Mark's content appear in the other three Gospels. He wraps up the life story of Jesus Christ with far less words than the other three Gospels. It is the only Gospel that can be read and understood as a novel. It does not accurately follow the chronology of Jesus' life.

Luke: Luke the physician, was not one of the chosen twelve disciples. From a second century tradition (The Muratorian Canon) it is believed that the Gospel "was compiled by Luke the physician, when, after Christ's ascension, Paul had taken him to be with him." Once Luke became converted into the church, he accompanied Paul on missionary trips. Paul speak of Luke in three of his letters with great affection. Paul called Luke his companion *(II Tim. 4:11; Phil. 24)* and the beloved physician *(Col 4:14)*. During Paul third journey at Philippi about A.D. 57-58, Luke was with him again.

Upon returning with Paul to Jerusalem (Paul arrested and imprisoned in Caesarea for two years) is where many scholars believe he collected the information to complete this Gospel. Access to other disciples, Mary, and the Palestinian Christian community would have provided the material needed to complete this Gospel. He was with Paul in Rome before his death and the scriptures records the passionate words that he spoke concerning his close associate; "Only Luke is with me" *(2 Tim. 4:11)*.

A settled conclusion of New Testament scholarship is that Luke used the Gospel of Mark as one of his sources, thus requiring a date after Mark's Gospel, about A.D. 60. Many have concluded that Luke had an earlier form of his Gospel about A.D. 58 based upon his contact with the "eye witnesses and ministers of the word" *(Luke 1:2)*. He later encountered Mark and others sources, which he used in compiling his "orderly account."

As a physician has a caring heart for his patient, Luke writing displays a true sense of detail and thoroughness for the subject he is writing about. His writing are among some of the world classic of literature. He was a gifted writer, and the stories he recorded have won their place among the classic of literature: the Good Samaritan, the Lost Son, the Rich Man and Lazarus.

John: Although the book does not name the writer, he is indicated as "the loved disciple" *(John 13:23; John 21:20, 23, 24)*. The testimony of the ancient church is to the effect that this is John, the son of Zebedee. Irenaeus is the chief witness. Some scholars have questioned whether one who was unschooled and inexperience *(Acts 4:13)* could have written such a work. Time, motivation, and the enablement of the Spirit ought not to be underestimated in evaluating the ability of John and the overcoming of handicaps. He is responsible for writing the Gospel of John, I John, II John, III John, and Revelation. Identified as the loved disciple. Many moderns prefer to hold that an unknown disciple is the actual author of this Gospel, even though most of the material may well go back to John as its source. But this is a needless exchange of a known for an unknown.

According to Christian tradition, John spent the latter years of his life at Epheus, where he carried on a ministry of preaching and teaching, as well as writing. From this point he was exiled to Patmos in the reign of the Emperor Domitian. His Gospel seems to presuppose a knowledge of the Synoptic tradition and for this reason should be placed last in the series, approximately A.D. 86.

Some have put it even later. The discovery in Egypt of fragments of the Gospel, which have been dated from the first half of the second century, requires the writing of the Gospel within the limits of the first century.

He spoke again, says John, and this time the Word took the form of a man, Jesus Christ. John's book tells the story of that Word who became flesh.

It's clear from the first few paragraphs that John broke sharply from the style of Matthew, Mark, and Luke. The other Gospel writers focused on events, following Jesus through the bustling marketplaces and villages.

Unlike them, John assumed readers knew the basic facts about Jesus. Instead of focusing on facts, he mulled over the profound meaning of what Jesus had said and done. John apparently had lots of time for reflection.

In his first sentence, John highlights Christ's nature. There are no Christmas scenes here: no stable, shepherds, or wise men. John tells nothing of Jesus' birth or youth. He introduces him as the adult Son of God. After an eloquent prologue, John the Baptist is shown, humbly pointing to Jesus, as the one "preferred before me, whose shoe's latchet I am not worthy to unloose" *(John 1:27)*.

In Summary: Matthew a disciple, some religious scholars believe he wrote his book approximately A.D. 64. It is composed of 28 Chapters, 1,071 verses, and c. 23,684 words.

Mark not a disciple, some religious scholars believe he wrote his book approximately A.D. 57. They also believe his gospel was the first to be written. It is composed of 16 Chapters, 678 verses, and c. 15,171 words.

Luke not a disciple, some religious scholars believe he wrote his book approximately A.D. 60. It is composed of 24 Chapters, 1,151 verses, and c. 25,944 words.

John a disciple, some religious scholars believe he wrote his book approximately A.D. 86. It is composed of 21 Chapters, 878 verses, and c. 19,099 words.
The four gospels combined consists of 89 Chapters and 3778 verses, and c. 83,898 words.

In comparison, The Combined Gospel of Jesus Christ book (minus the introduction and appendixes), consists of 12 Chapters, 238 paragraphs with sub-alphabets, and Chapter headings c. 75,035 words. That a reduction of 77 Chapters, and 8,863 words, you will have to read.

Appendix B

Biblical prophecy regarding Jesus Christ life, before he descended. Listed below are 12 Old Testament prophecies, and their New Testament fulfillment. The High Priest and Chief Priest had these scriptures from the prophets. Jesus stood up in the synagogue, and read from their book of the prophet Esaias (Elijah) *(Isaiah 61:1-2; Luke 4:17-19)*; the scripture that he fulfilled. The Jews knew of the prophetic scripture concerning Jesus Christ, as evident by *Luke 24:44* and *John 7:42*.

Prophetic Scripture	Subject	Scripture Fulfilled
Therefore the Lord himself shall give you a sign; Behold, a virgin shall conceive, and bear a son, and shall call his name Im-man'-u-el. *Isaiah 7:14*	**Will be born of a virgin**	And in the sixth month the angel Gabriel was sent from God unto a city of Galilee, named Nazareth, To a virgin espoused to a man whose named was Joseph, of the house of David; and the virgin's name *was* Mary. And the angel said unto her, Fear not, Mary: for thou hast found favor with God. And, behold, thou shalt conceive in thy womb, and bring forth a son, and shalt call his name JESUS. *Luke 1:26-27; 30-31.*

Prophetic Scripture	Subject	Scripture Fulfilled
But thou, Bethlehem Ephratah, *though* thou be little among the thousands of Judah, yet out of thee shall he come forth unto me *that is* to be ruler of Israel; whose goings forth *have been* from of old, from everlasting. *Micah 5:2*	**Born in Bethlehem**	And Joseph also went up from Galilee, out of the city of Nazareth, into Judea, unto the city of David, which is called Bethe-lehem, (because he was of the house and lineage of David;) To be taxed with Mary his espoused wife, being great with child. And she brought forth her firstborn son, and wrapped him in swaddling clothes, and laid him in a manger; because there was no room for them in the inn. *Luke 2:4-5, 7*
I gave my back to the smiters, and my cheeks to them that plucked off the hair: I hid not my face from shame and spitting. *Isaiah 50:6*	**Spat upon and smitten**	Then did they spit in his face, and buffeted him; and others smote *him* with the palms of their hands, *Matthew 26:67*
He was oppressed, and he was afflicted, yet he opened not his mouth: he is brought as a lamb to the slaughter, and as a sheep before her shearers is dumb, so he openeth not his mouth. *Isaiah 53:7*	**Silent to accusations**	And Pilate asked him again, saying, Answerest thou nothing? behold how many things they witness against thee. But Jesus yet answered nothing; so that Pilate marvelled. *Mark 15:4-5*

Prophetic Scripture	Subject	Scripture Fulfilled
All they that see me laugh me to scorn: they shoot out the lip, they shake the head, *saying*, He trusted on the LORD that he would deliver him: let him deliver him, seeing he delighted in him. *Psalm 22:7-8*	Scorned and mocked	And the people stood beholding. And the rulers also with them derided *him*, saying, He saved others; let him save himself, if he be Christ, the chosen of God. *Luke 23:35*
They gave me also gall for my meat; and in my thirst they gave me vinegar to drink. *Psalm 69:21*	Given vinegar and gall	They gave him vinegar to drink, mingled with gall: and when he had tasted *thereof*, he would not drink. *Matthew 27:34*
I may tell all my bones: they look and stare upon me. They part my garments among them, and cast lots upon my vesture. *Psalm 22:17-18*	Soldiers gambled for his vesture (coat)	And they crucified him, and parted his garments, casting lots: that it might be fulfilled which was spoken by the prophet, They parted my garments among them, and upon my vesture did they cast lots. And sitting down they watched him there; *Matthew 27:35-36*

Prophetic Scripture	Subject	Scripture Fulfilled
He keepeth all his bones: not one of them is broken. *Psalm 34:20*	**No bones broken**	Then came the soldiers, and brake the leg of the first, and of the other which was crucified with him. But when they came to Jesus and saw that he was dead already, they brake not his legs: For these things were done that the scripture should be fulfilled, A bone of him shall not be broken. *John 19:32-33, 36*
And I will pour upon the house of David, and upon the inhabitants of Jerusalem, the spirit of grace and of supplications: and they shall look upon me whom they have pierced, and they shall mourn for him, as one mourneth for *his* only *son*, and shall be in bitterness for him, as one that is in bitterness for *his* firstborn. *Zechariah 12:10*	**Pierced in his side**	But one of the soldiers with a spear pierced his side, and forthwith came there out blood and water. *John 19:34*

Prophetic Scripture	Subject	Scripture Fulfilled
And he made his grave with the wicked, and with the rich in his death; because he had done no violence, neither *was any* deceit in his mouth. *Isaiah 53:9*	**Buried with the rich**	When the even was come, there came a rich man of Ar-im-a-the'-a, named Joseph, who also himself was Jesus' disciple: He went to Pilate, and begged the body of Jesus. Then Pilate commanded the body to be delivered. And when Joseph had taken the body, he wrapped it in a clean linen cloth, And laid it in his own new tomb, which he had hewn out in the rock: and he rolled a great stone to the door of the sepulchre, and departed. *Matthew 27:57-60*
For thou will not leave my soul in hell; neither will thou suffer thine Holy One to see corruption. *Psalm 16:10* But God will redeem my soul from the power of the grave: for he shall receive me. Selah. *Psalm 49:15*	**To be resurrected**	And he saith unto them, Be not affrighted: Ye seek Jesus of Nazareth, which was crucified: he is risen; he is not here: behold the place where they laid him. But go your way, tell his disciples and Peter that he goeth before you into Galilee: there shall ye see him, as he said unto you. *Mark 16:6-7*

Prophetic Scripture	Subject	Scripture Fulfilled
Thou hast ascended on high, thou hast led captivity captive: thou has received gifts for men; yea, *for* the rebellious also, that the LORD God might dwell among them. *Psalm 68:18*	**Jesus Christ ascension**	Wherefore he saith, When he ascended up on high, he led captivity captive, and gave gifts unto men. *Ephesians 4:8*

Appendix C

Commandments. What about the ten commandments, should they be followed? God created the heavens (earth), moon, stars, (*Psalm 8:3/Hebrews 1:10*) man, and woman (*Genesis 2:7, 21, 22*) with his own finger/hands. God also created the law, in which the man and woman he created, was to abide by during their tenure on earth. God wrote his law on two tables of stone with his own finger (*Exodus 31:18*). The law written on two stone tablets is symbolic of God strength, and the enduring nature of the law he wrote.

Let's take a look at what the bible says regarding the ten commandments of God in *Exodus 20:1-17*.

1. AND GOD spake all these words, saying,

2. **I am the LORD thy God, which have brought thee out of the land of Egypt, out of the house of bondage.**

3. (1st Commandment) **Thou shalt have no other gods before me.**

4. (2nd Commandment) **Thou shalt not make unto thee any graven image, or any likeness *of any thing* that is in heaven above, or that is in the earth beneath, or that *is* in the water under the earth:**

5. **Thou shalt not bow down thyself to them, nor serve them: for I the LORD thy God *am* a jealous God, visiting the iniquity of the fathers upon the children unto the third and fourth *generation* of them that hate me;**

6. And showing mercy unto thousands of them that love me, and keep my commandments.

7. (3rd Commandment) **Thou shalt not take the name of the LORD thy God in vain; for the LORD will not hold him guiltless that taketh his name in vain.**

8. (4th Commandment) **Remember the Sabbath day, to keep it holy.**

9. **Six days shalt thou labour, and do all thy work:**

10. **But the seventh day** *is* **the sabbath of the LORD thy God:** *in it* **thou shalt not do any work, thou, nor thy son, nor thy daughter, thy manservant, nor thy maidservant, nor thy cattle, nor thy stranger that** *is* **within thy gates:**

11. **For** *in* **six days the LORD made heaven and earth, the sea, and all that in them** *is*, **and rested the seventh day: wherefore the LORD blessed the sabbath day, and hallowed it.**

Note: God numbered the days and gave man authority to name them. Listed below are the names man came up with (*Emphasis applied to the First and Seventh Day*). First day-Sunday, means the day of the *Sun,* by the old Teutonic people. Recognize as a day of worship by Europe, in the A.D. 300's, because Jesus resurrected on the First Day. It is a man made law/doctrine. Second Day-Monday; Third Day-Tuesday; Fourth Day-Wednesday; Fifth Day-Thursday; and Sixth Day-Friday. The Seventh Day-Saturday was named by the Anglo-Saxons for the Roman god Saturn. It is God, our creator, Holy Sabbath day. It is kept by Jews, Adventists, and some Christians.

Please refer to the ten points listed below regarding God's Fourth Commandment, before we go to the Fifth:

1. After God had created man, he ended his work, and rested. *"Thus the heavens and the earth were finished, and all the host of them. And on the seventh day God ended his work which he had made. And God blessed the seventh day, and sanctified it* (Set it aside for sacred use, made it holy)*: because that in it he had rested from all his work which God created and made" (Gen 2:1-3).* It is evident by this scripture, that this commandment existed, at the beginning of creation.

2. God starts off the Fourth Commandment with a key word, that word is **_Remember (to retain in the mind)_**. God being Alpha and Omega, the beginning and the end, the first and the last *(Rev 22:13)*, knew that at some stage throughout man's history on earth, he would forget his Sabbath Day. We are living that history today. How many religious bodies obey this commandment today?

3. The fourth commandment is extremely vital, because by keeping it, we recognize God as our creator. It is the very first commandment that God instituted on earth, after he had created Adam on the sixth day *(Gen. 1:26; 2:1-3)*. God worked six days and rested the seventh day and made it holy for us to worship him on. When you recognize and worship him on the day he sanctified *(Make holy)*, you are sending a sign to God, that you recognize him as your creator and God, by following his example at creation. You work from the first to the sixth day. At sunset on the sixth day, until sunset on the seventh day, you rest and worship God, on his holy Sabbath Day.

You are now linked to God, by your symbolic act of **worshipping him, on the day he set aside for that purpose.** Refer to the scriptures below for reproof. *"...Verily my Sabbaths ye shall keep: for it is a sign between me and you throughout your generations; that ye may know that I am the LORD that doth sanctify you."* Exodus 31:13. *It is a sign between me and the **children of Israel for ever**: for in six days the LORD made heaven and earth, and on the seventh day he rested, and was refreshed."* Exodus 31:17.

4. All of us that believe in the Gospel of Jesus Christ, become baptized, and obey God's holy commandments, are considered a child of Israel. Nationality has no bearing here, because Jesus died for all mankind. In heaven, the righteous throughout perpetual generations and nationalities, that have ever existed on the earth, will be split into the twelve tribes of Israel, in New Jerusalem.

Jesus made the following statement to his disciples, at the last passover meal, he had with them, in the upper room. *"And I appoint unto you a kingdom, as my Father hath appointed unto me; That ye may eat and drink at my table in my kingdom, and sit on thrones judging the twelve tribes of Israel."* Luke 22:29-30. All human beings on earth that worship Jesus on the sabbath day are Jews. My definition of **JEWS** are: **J**esus **E**arthly **W**orshipper'**S**. The saved will be listed under one of the twelve tribes of Israel. Salvation is of the Jews as stated by Jesus in *John 4:22.*

5. We all must understand that in heaven the angels also worship Jesus, but they are not called Jews, because they are not from the earth. *"And again, when he bringeth in the firstbegotten into the world, he saith, And let all the angels of God worship him."* Heb. 1:6.

6. *"Whosoever therefore shall break one of these least commandments, and shall teach men so, he shall be called the least in the kingdom of heaven: but whosever shall do and teach them, the same shall be called great in the kingdom of heaven."* Matthew 5:19.   You don't think Jesus knew about the fourth commandment, and how man would teach others, to disobey this commandment. Considering our present day situation, what other commandment would the scripture above apply to, other than the Fourth Commandment. It is the only commandment that is broken on a weekly basis by millions of Christians unaware. *"Whosoever shall keep the whole law, and yet offend in one point, he is guilty of all."* James 2:10.

7. *"But in vain they do worship me, teaching for doctrines the commandments of men."* Matthew 15:9. Worshipping on any other day that was not sanctified for worship, is to do so in vain, said Jesus himself. Here is a prophetic statement and warning to the world from our Lord. The order by man to worship on the First day of the week, instead of the Seventh day, is a doctrine of man, not of God. It has no biblical foundation to support it.

8. Didn't the Sabbath day worship end at the cross? *"Let no man therefore judge you in meat, or in drink, or in respect for an holyday, or of the new moon, or of the sabbath days:."* Colossians 2:16. If you begin reading Chapter 2, from verses 14-16, you will see that this is referring to the law of Moses. Moses law contained the ordinances and ceremonial law governing the sacrificial system and the priesthood. These ceremonies and rituals, foreshadowed the cross, and ended at the cross, with Jesus Christ death. **Worship of God on the Sabbath day will never cease.**

9. God took this matter one final step forward. He stated that in his holy city of New Jerusalem, the inhabitants of earth that are saved, will worship him on every **Sabbath day**, and every new moon. *"For as the new heavens and the new earth, which I will make, shall remain before me, saith the LORD, so shall your seed and your name remain. And it shall come to pass, that from one new moon to another, and from one sabbath to another, shall all flesh come to worship before me, saith the LORD."* Isaiah 66:22-23. He ordained it at creation, and kept it during his tenure on earth. He is telling us, that it will be kept in New Jerusalem on the new earth.

10. Many point to *Acts 20:7* as justification for worshipping on the First day of the week. The verse speaks of Paul who was a missionary. Paul traveled abroad, spreading the gospel of Jesus Christ, and did not show up at every place on the Sabbath Day. He did keep the Sabbath Day. Refer to the following scriptures concerning Paul observance of the Sabbath Day: *Acts 13:14-18, 27, 43-46* and *Acts 15:21; 17:1-2; 18:1-4.*

Don't be fooled, worship God on the day, he set aside for this purpose, so your worship want be in vain. If you didn't know before, he winked *(Acts 17:30)* at it, and did not hold it against you. But now you know, and from this point, if you continue to break this commandment, it becomes sin to you. During Jesus tenure on earth. Many worshippers of God, to include the high priest, chief priest, and many Jews were caught off guard. Due to their ignorance and failure to carefully study the scriptures, they sent the son of God, to the Gentiles slaughter house to be beaten and crucified on the cross.

The reason for you keeping the Sabbath is because of God's commandment and Jesus example while on earth. You should not be concerned as much about what Paul did as you should be about what Jesus did. Jesus died for our sins and he kept the Sabbath Day (*Luke 4:16, 31*).

12. (5th Commandment) **Honour thy father and thy mother: that thy days may be long upon the land which the LORD thy God giveth thee.**

13. (6th Commandment) **Thou shalt not kill.**

14. (7th Commandment) **Thou shalt not commit adultery.**

15. (8th Commandment) **Thou shalt not steal.**

16. (9th Commandment) **Thou shalt not bear false witness against thy neighbour.**

17. (10th Commandment) **Thou shalt not covet thy neighbour's house, thou shalt not covet thy neighbour's wife, nor his manservant, nor his maidservant, nor his ox, nor his ass, nor any thing that is thy neighbour's.**

Do we really need to keep the Ten Commandments of God? Let's review five points regarding this question:

1. Jesus during his tenure on earth reiterated the ten commandments on various occasions: *"Thou knowest the commandments, Do not commit adultery, Do not kill, Do not steal, Do not bear false witness, Defraud not, Honour thy father and mother."* Mark 10:19.

2. God ten commandments, written with his finger, are everlasting. *"The works of his hands are verity and judgment; all his commandments are sure. They stand fast for ever and ever, and are done in truth and uprightness."* Psalms 111:7-8.

3. You are not saved by the law, you are saved by grace through faith. No one has ever been saved by the law since creation, they have all been saved by God's gift of grace. That will prevent anybody from boasting, concerning their keeping of the law, over anybody else. *Ephesians 2:8, 9.* The law must be kept, because it points out sin, and that is what you will be judged by. *"...for by the law is the knowledge of sin."* Romans 3:20. *"So speak ye, and so do, as they that shall be judged by the law of liberty."* James 2:12. *"...The wages of sin is death...."* Romans 6:23. *"...Fear God, and keep his commandments: for this is the whole duty of man."* Ecclesiastes 12:13.

4. Get on the straight and narrow path by believing in the gospel of Jesus Christ. Getting baptized for remission of sins, and start living a Christian life by following the Ten Commandments. Fear God of what will happen, if you do not follow the law of the Ten Commandments. The fear is eternal damnation in hell fire. By doing so, it is God's grace through your faith in him, that will save you. Jesus made this statement during his tenure on earth *"If ye love me, keep my commandments."* John 14:15.

5. Always keep this scripture in mind from Jesus. *"He that hath my commandments, and keepeth them, he it is that loveth me: and he that loveth me shall be loved of my Father, and I will love him, and will manifest myself to him."* John 14:21.

Appendix D

Disciples. During Jesus three year ministry he had many disciples. There were only 12 disciples that he choose to be with him, whom he named apostles. One of them betrayed him and was replaced by the disciples with Matthias. Jesus value them so much, that he decided to name the twelve foundations of the walls of New Jerusalem, after them *(Rev 21:14)*. They are all listed in the following scriptures and below: *Matthew 10:2-4; Mark 3:16-19; Luke 6:14-16; and Acts 1:13; 26.*

__Andrew:__ Son of Jonas and the brother of Peter. He was a disciple of John the Baptist *(John 1:35, 40)*. He introduced his brother Peter to Jesus *(John 1:40-42)*. He lived in Capernaum and Bethsaida. Tradition has him dying in a town called Patra that was in Achaia, Greece.

Through his spreading of the gospel, Governor Aepeas' wife was converted to Christianity. Aepeas' was very upset, especially when his brother also became a Christian. Andrew was confined and condemned to death through crucifixion.

He begged that his cross be different than Jesus. Therefore, he was crucified on a X-shaped cross. He was formerly a fisherman. His apostolic symbol is two crossed fish, better known as Saint Andrew's cross.

__Bartholomew:__ Introduced to Jesus by Philip *(John 1:45-51)*. His first name was Nathanael. Jesus called him an Israelite indeed in whom there is no guile *(John 1:47)*. He lived in Galilee in a city called Cana.

Tradition have him dying a martyr in India by the flaying of knives, while he was alive. Three parallel knives is his apostolic symbol.

James, son of Zebedee and Salome, brother of the disciple John. Jesus surname these brothers Boanerges "sons of thunder". He was a fisherman that preached in Judea and Jerusalem.

One of three often chosen by Jesus to accompany him. Herod had him killed with the sword in A.D. 44 *(Acts 12:1, 2).* He was the first apostles to become a martyr, and is represented by the apostolic symbol of three shells, because of his pilgrimage beside the sea.

James, son of Alphaeus, brother of Judas (not Iscariot). Religious scholars credit him with writing the Epistle of James.

He ministered in Egypt and Palestine and was killed in Egypt. Traditionally speaking, James died a martyr, and his body was sawed in pieces. His apostolic symbol is represented by the saw.

John, son of Zebedee and Salome, for more information concerning John, see Appendix A.

Judas, brother of James, son of Alphaeus or Cleophas and Mary. Brother of James, son of Alphaeus. He was also called Thaddaeus and Lebbaeus. He lived in Galilee and ministered in Persia and Assyria.

He preached the Gospel all around and was killed at Arafat with arrows. He was a fisherman and a missionary, therefore, his apostolic symbol is a ship.

Judas Iscariot, lived in Kerioth of Judah. He was the treasurer. He betrayed Jesus for 30 pieces of silver. He hanged himself, and was replaced by the disciples, with **Matthias**.

Matthew the publican, son of Alphaeus. For more information on Matthew, see Appendix A.

Peter, son of Jonas, brother of Andrew. He was a fisherman that lived in Capernaum and Bethsaida. He was married and the main spokesman of the disciples. Religious scholars ascribe the I and II Peter to him.

Christ called Peter his rock upon which he would build his Church. Peter was one of the three Jesus told to accompany him on numerous occasions, such as the Transfiguration and Gethsemane.

He denied Jesus three times before the cock crowed. He died a martyr and was crucified. He requested to be crucified upside down to show respect for the Lord. His apostolic symbol is a cross upside down with crossed keys.

Philip, was from Bethsaida. He was one of the first disciples that Jesus said to "Follow me."

Philip died in Hierapolis by hanging and requested that his body be wrapped in papyrus instead of linen. He did not want his body to be treated with the same respect as the Lord. His apostolic symbol is a basket, due to the role he played in feeding the five thousand.

Simon Zelotes, lived in Galilee. He was probably a fisherman. He was a zealot that was converted to a Christian follower of Jesus.

Tradition have him dying as a martyr, and his apostolic symbol is a fish, lying on a bible.

Thomas, lived in Galilee. He has an alias of "doubting Thomas", because he could not believe until he seen and felt. It was Thomas that Jesus told to put his hands in his nail print and spear print to increase his faith.

He died a martyr by a spear at Mt. St. Thomas in India. His apostolic symbol is a group of spears, stones, and arrows.

Jesus told the disciples at the last supper, that they would sit on thrones in his kingdom, judging the twelve tribes of Israel *(Luke 22:29-30)*.

Appendix E

Earth: *"It is he that sitteth upon the circle of the earth."* Isaiah 40:22. **God is truly awesome!!!**

"He... hangeth the earth upon nothing." **Job 26:7**

Take a good look at the picture of our giant celestial spaceship, that was taken from out in space, isn't she magnificent. *"In the beginning God created the heaven and the earth."* Genesis 1:1. Earth manifest as of 14:35 GMT, 08 Jun 09, was 6,785,207,318 human inhabitants, traveling through space. God placed us on the surface, and not inside the Earth, so we can view his glorious creation. We log 595 million miles each year as we orbit the sun. For comfort, he surrounded us with 78% Nitrogen, 21% Oxygen, and 1% of other gases. To keep us pinned down, he added gravity. You do not need seat belts for this ride.

The USA call a person who travels out in space inside a spaceship an *astronaut* (Russians use the name *cosmonaut* and the French call them *spationaute*). God calls the creatures that he created and placed in charge of his planet called earth, man and woman (humans) *(Genesis 1:1, 27; 2:22)*. After bringing earth into existence. God calibrated the traveling speed at 66,629 mph (107,229 km/h) and gave it direction to make a complete revolution around the sun every 365 ¼ days. In comparison, the top flying speed of a jumbo jet (Boeing 747/8) is 650.83 mph; the space shuttle travel in orbit around the earth at a top speed of 17,500 mph. As the earth flew, it was also giving a command to rotate on her invisible axis, at a speed of about 1,000 mph. She was commanded to complete a full rotation about every 24 hours, providing 12 hours for the day, and night equally. She was also ordered to tilt on her axis at 23.45 degrees towards the great light for seasons *(Genesis 1:14-16)*.

God hath established the earth to last for ever *(Psalm 78:69)*. Unlike many of us, earth has obeyed the orders of the creator with incredible precision, since the day he established it. Earth is where we will all live and die *(with the exception of those who will never die)*. Only three from the earth are now in heaven, with the exception of those that were resurrected with Jesus. Once the world come to an end, we will be called at the First, or Second Resurrection from the dead. The righteous of the First Resurrection will get a 1000 year (millennium) vacation to God the Father home in heaven. After the millennium, Jesus and the righteous will return to Earth, with the Holy City of New Jerusalem, for the Second Resurrection. The wicked that are raised will burn to ashes in the Lake of fire *(Malachi 4.3)*. Jesus Christ will renew the face of the Earth, and she will be forever inhabited by the righteous.

The Hubble Space Telescope (HST)

The HST orbiting the earth with eyes open to the universe.

About the HST: It is named in honor of Edwin Hubble, an astronomer, who stated that the Milky Way was not the only Galaxy. Launched on April 24, 1990 with the space shuttle *Discovery mission (STS-31)* and released into orbit April 25, 1990. It orbits 353 miles (569 km) above the surface of the earth and weighs 12 tons (11 metric tons) and has a diameter of 14 feet (4.2 meters). It contains two mirrors; a primary mirror at 7.9 feet (2.4 meters) wide; a secondary mirror at 1 foot (30 centimeters) wide. The HST travels at a speed of 17,500 miles per hour (28,000 kilometers per hour) and complete its orbit around the earth every 97 minutes.

The HST is actually a flying spacecraft, that requires several support systems to allow it to operate in orbit around the earth. The support systems are the housing, computers, two solar arrays for power, and communication antennae.

Housing (HST makeup): It was created with a skin of multi-layered insulation (MLI), that protects it from temperature fluctuations of more than 100 degrees Fahrenheit, during each trip around the earth. Underneath the MLI is a lightweight aluminum shell that provides an external structure to the spacecraft. It is the location of the optical systems and science instruments.

The optical system is supported by a truss that measures 210 in (5.3m), with a length of 115 in (2.9m) in diameter. The truss is made of graphite epoxy and weighs 252 lbs (114 kg). Graphite epoxy is the same material that is used in bicycles, golf clubs, and tennis racquets. It is strong, lightweight, and stiff, which enables it to resist expanding in the extreme temperatures of space.

Computers: It has several computers and microprocessors in the body and in each science instrument that runs all the subsystems onboard. Two of the computers that girdle the waist directs the show.

Two solar arrays: The solar arrays are two thin wing, blue solar arrays. They are responsible for providing electricity to run the computers, radio transmitters, and the telescope's scientific instruments. Each ray has a solar cell blanket that converts the solar rays received from the sun, into 2,800 watts of electricity. Some of the converted energy is stored into onboard batteries and is used when the HST needs to operate while it's blanketed from sunlight by earth shadow. The loss of direct sunlight, occurs about 36 minutes, out of each orbit of 97 minutes. A fully charged battery will sustain the HST for normal science operation for five orbits or 7.5 hours.

Communication antennae: The HST is a giant robotic computer in space that is controlled by the Space Telescope Science Institute (STSI) flight operations, located in Baltimore, Maryland. The people at the STSI send and receive detailed instructions through the four antennae, and command the HST on what to do, and when to do it.

Communication is made possible through one of the five Tracking and Data Relay Satellite (TDRS), in various locations in the sky. During time of the satellite visibility with HST, through line of sight, scientists can interact directly with the satellite and make changes to fine tune HST observation. A planned observation is done in advance and do not require satellite assistance via TDRS. The observation from that command is stored in a special date recorder, and transmitted during satellite visibility with TDRS. God has finally increased man knowledge enough, so he can look into his infinite creation.

The Space Shuttle flying the Hubble Space Telescope into orbit.

Sometimes I wander as people, whether some of us are crazy, stupid, ignorant, dumb, or as God will say, stiffnecked (Exodus 33:3, 5). I say that because, who in their right mind, would make the following statement: *"The HST formed itself from the ground, flew into outer space, and started orbiting the earth. While orbiting, it started taking pictures, and sending them back to earth."*

Nobody in their right mind would believe that, because we all know, that man created the HST with his own fingers, and flew it into outer space, and set it on its orbital path around the earth. It is also man that gives commands from the ground, to control HST on when and where to take pictures. HST reacts to the commands, based on the computers (brains) that man installed in it, before it was launched.

God is telling us through HST to open up your eyes and your mind and see the similarity. The operation of the HST demonstrates, how it could be possible, for there to be a superior being, that controls the universe. A God that created the earth and the sun to provide the solar energy to sustain the earth. Earth has obeyed it's command, since its creation, by God's own fingers.

Wake up, and see the comparison, and the light, that God is shinning, before your eyes. By the way, I haven't seen anything coming out of the water, and changing from an ape to a man, since I have been born. However, on the contrary, I have seen a lot of people having babies that looks like them (Genesis 1:27). God is a creative genius and the heavens are now declaring his glory and infinite Kingdom through the lens of HST. Take a look.

The Universe

During 1995, the Hubble Space Telescope took this picture of more than 1,500 galaxies in a tiny region of the sky called Hubble Deep Field.

"God created the heaven...he made the stars also." Gen. 1:1, 16.

Hubble Deep Field
Hubble Space Telescope · WFPC2

Here was only a tiny piece of the universe selected for viewing. Location for this viewing was between the handle and the dipper of the Big Dipper, which is part of the constellation Ursa Major. Galaxies consist of millions and possibly billions of stars. All galaxies differ in size and shape, therefore, their capacity for the amount of stars they contain are different.

The Milky Way Galaxy

Our Milky way Galaxy is a spiral galaxy, similar to the Spiral Galaxy (M101) pictured above. The galaxies are composed of gases, dust particles, and stars. The largest ones hold hundreds of billions of stars. These gigantic areas of cosmic matter are not scattered around the universe; they are grouped together into large arrangement of galaxies, which are called clusters.

Scientist estimate there are about 100 billion galaxies that form clusters, which are grouped into super clusters. Even though they are enormous, these super clusters barely fill the universe, and there is plenty of empty space left between them. Using the most powerful telescope available, astronomers have already observed millions of galaxies.

Up until the 20th century, astronomers believed that the universe contained just a single galaxy: The Milky Way. They observed some fuzzy spots in space, which they called nebulas, but otherwise ignored them. In 1924, American astronomer Edwin Hubble observed that these fuzzy spots were, in fact, other galaxies. Hubble's discovery completely changed our understanding of the universe.

Galaxies are sorted into three main groups: spiral galaxies, elliptical galaxies, and irregular galaxies. Our neighbor the Andromeda galaxy is also a spiral galaxy. The Milky Way Galaxy is made up of more than 100 billion stars similar to the sun. Many who have their own solar system. Below is a view of our Solar System located within the Milky Way Galaxy.

Our Solar System

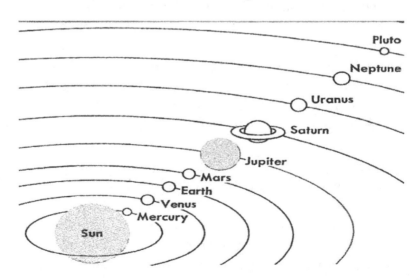

Our Solar System consists of nine planets that rotates around the sun. Our planet Earth is the **third** planet from the sun. Our sun is a star that always shine.

Our sun is surrounded by a procession of nine fascinating planets (celestial bodies). As they move together through the universe, they are kept on course by the Sun's force of attraction. Scientist estimate there are billions of galaxies in our universe. It is my firm belief, that God did not create this glorious magnificient universe, for us alone. Jesus came to save the planet, that was lost in the Garden of Eden. Our sun is just one of the hundreds of billions of stars that shines in the universe. These little points of lights that we call stars are actually gigantic furnaces that produces enormous quantities of light and heat.

What will Jesus Christ glorious return be like?

Like the Eskimo Nebula (NGC 2392) or the Sombrero Galaxy (M104) above?

Our sun has a lot of company in the Milky Way Galaxy.

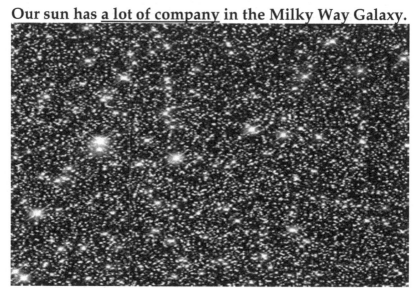

Above is a sky full of glittering stars. The HST peered into the Sagittarius Star Cloud, and viewed a narrow dust free region, inside our Milky Way Galaxy, for this picture.

Below are listed ten fascinating quotes, from the King James Version of the bible. Some of these scriptures are prophetic. They were written before man was ever able to look into the heavens, with powerful ground telescopes, and the Hubble Space Telescope.

1. *"And he brought him forth abroad, and said, Look now toward heaven, and tell the stars, if thou be able to number them: and he said unto him, So shall thy seed be."* Genesis 15:5. When God made this statement to Abram, later renamed Abraham by God, he was speaking from an Alpha and Omega standpoint. He knew that the Hubble Space Telescope, and every other telescope he gives man the knowledge to build, will never be able to number the stars in his magnificent universe.

2. *"That in blessing I will bless thee, and in multiplying I will multiply thy seed as the stars of the heaven, and as the sand which is upon the sea shore; and thy seed shall possess the gate of his enemies;."* Genesis 22:17. Here God is speaking to Abraham after he had demonstrated his faith, by preparing to slay his promised son Isaac with a knife. God let us know that the number of his stars in heaven are as the sand is upon the sea shore. We have now learned through the Hubble Space Telescope that this prophetic statement is incredibly accurate.

3. *"When I consider thy heavens, the work of thy fingers, the moon and the stars, which thou hast ordained;."* Psalm 8:3. David is letting us know, that God created all the celestial bodies with his own fingers.

4. *"There is one glory of the sun, and another glory of the moon, and another glory of the stars: for one star differeth from another star in glory."* 1 Corinthians 15:41. We have learned that all the planets in our solar system are different as well as the suns we have studied. It is apparent that God created all his celestial bodies different, just like he did with you and I.

5. *"Praise ye him, sun and moon: praise him, all ye stars of light."* Psalm 148:3. All of God celestial bodies gives respect to their creator. We are part of a gigantic family of celestial stars and planets that all praised their creator God.

6. *"For the stars of heaven and the constellations thereof shall not give their light: the sun shall be darkened in his going forth, and the moon shall not cause her light to shine."* Isaiah 13:10.

Isaiah refers to the actions of the stars and constellations during the end time. Note how constellations are indicated here, before we started peering out into the universe and naming them.

7. *"Canst thou bind the sweet influences of Pleiades, or loose the bands of Orion?"* Job 38:31. Here God is speaking to Job out of a whirlwind. God demand many questions of Job, like this one. Here God has named one of the many constellations in the universe.

8. *"Seek him that maketh the seven stars and Orion, and turneth the shadow of death into the morning, and maketh the day dark with night: that calleth for the waters of the sea, and poureth them out upon the face of the earth: The LORD is his name:."* Amos 5:8.

Currently we have named 88 constellations in the sky. The Greeks and the Romans are credited with naming two-thirds of them. The constellation Orion named by God is composed of seven bright stars as the scripture prophetically indicated. Betelgeuse is a red super giant star located in the shoulder of Orion. It has a diameter 650 times that of our sun and shines with a luminosity 60,000 times that of our sun. Rigel is a blue super giant star located at Orion's ankle (knee). It is made up of two smaller stars that orbits it to form a triple star system. The hunter's belt is composed of three stars name Alnitak, Alnilam, and Mintake. The outline of the seven stars represents the hunter Orion, which is one of the easiest and most spectacular constellation you can see in the sky. It is full of young stars and many nebulaes (similar to the Eskimo nebula on page 305). Orion is the son of the god of the sea in Roman and Greek mythology. In Greek mythology Orion indicated he could kill any living creature. He was bitten and killed by a scorpion, which is identified by the constellation Scorpio. These two enemy constellations are located at opposite ends of the night sky. It appear as though they are running from each other, because Orion sets as Scorpio rises.

Hubble Space Telescope with eyes open, as it orbits the earth

9. *"For thou hast said in thine heart, I will ascend into heaven, I will exalt my throne above the stars of God: I will sit also upon the mount of the congregation, in the sides of the north:."* Isaiah 14:13. Here God is speaking regarding Lucifer fall from Heaven. Scripture below indicates, that above all the stars in heaven, is God sanctuary of Heaven, wherein lies his exalted throne *(Psalm 8:1; 57:5, 11)*.

10. *"He telleth the number of the stars; he calleth them all by their names."* Psalm 147:4. We have estimated billions upon billions of stars in the universe by the Hubble telescope. God through his infinite wisdom and knowledge, knows the exact number of all the stars he created. In addition, he has a name for everyone of them, just like he named our planet earth. He also know each one of us by name *(Revelation 17:8)*, along with the number of hairs that are on our head *(Matthew 10:30)*. God is truly awesome and worthy of our praise!

Now let's summarized what we have learned so far, based on the knowledge of the HST and science:

1. **Universe:** is everything that exist in the heavens above, including our earth. All of the celestial bodies found in space. Using the most powerful telescopes, astronomers have already accounted for over a million galaxies. Scientists estimate there is at least 100 billion galaxies in the universe.

2. **Galaxies:** consist of millions and probably billions of stars (suns) inside each galaxy. They all differ in size and capacity to hold stars.

3. **Milky Way:** Is the name of the galaxy our solar system belongs to. There are millions of stars in our Milky Way Galaxy (see page 306).

4. **Solar System:** Is our family of nine planets that rotates around our sun (star). We do not know how many planets rotates around some of the other stars in our Milky Way Galaxy.

5. **Stars:** In our solar system we have one star (sun).

6. **Planets:** We have nine planets that rotate around our sun (star).

7. **Earth:** Is the name of our planet and spaceship. Based on our current knowledge of the universe, they are billions of planets in the universe.

What an incredible magnitude of love! Words probably do an injustice to what Jesus did. There are no real words that can express or put into context the depth of God's love for us. Especially when we consider the facts as we know them now. He came to earth and died for our sins, so that we could have an opportunity to inherit eternal life, aboard our magnificent spaceship called earth.

If you were a member of a family that had 16 kids, you probably would not feel special to your Mother or Father. Unless you were extremely smart, talented, or athletically gifted. Now think of God as having billion upon billion of kids, yet he felt that we were so special, that he was willing to allow his only begotten son to die for us.

Also think of his son, who created the earth and us, who was willing to leave his heavenly throne and come down to earth and die for us. But more importantly than that, realize that both the Father and the son, knew the manner of persecution Jesus would suffer. They knew the kind of death he would die, to redeem us back to his Father.

Jesus knew he would be nailed to a cross, suspended between heaven and earth, before dying. He also knew he would be laid in the tomb until the third day. The knowledge of that degree of pain and suffering is what brought about so much of the agony and passion, which he was experiencing, in the garden of Gethsemane. Yet he continued and drunk of the cup and completed his mission. He redeemed us back to God, and offers salvation, for all who believe his story.

He will be coming back again, with a host of angels, all around him. His brightness will slain the wicked dead.

The spiral galaxy NGC 7742

Appendix F

Flying. Before a butterfly can take flight from an egg, it must go through four stages of *complete* metamorphosis (Greek-means to transform). Listed below are the comparison of a butterfly metamorphosis, with that of a saved Christian.

Stages 1

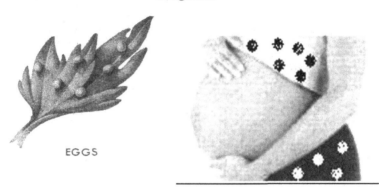

EGGS

Egg: Lays an egg on a leaf, waiting to hatch into a Larva.

Pregnancy: Through the pleasurable experience of sexual intercourse a man and a woman posses two thirds of the ability to procreate life. The woman posses the egg, that is fertilized by the man during sexual intercourse. God posses the other one third. Without his involvement in the pleasurable experience of procreation, the couple cannot procreate life. *"Thou art worthy, O Lord, to receive glory and honour and power: for thou hast created all things, and for thy pleasure they are and were created."* Revelation 4:11. God send his spirit (*the power of life*) to complete the conception. *"Thou sendest forth thy spirit, they are created: and thou renewest the face of the earth."* Psalm 104:30.

LARVA

Larva: After 3 months, the egg hatch into a larva, this is a crawling fuzzy caterpillar. It does not at all resemble the butterfly that laid the egg. Colors of the larva ranges from brown, yellow, and green. The larva eats a lot and grows rapidly. The skin is sheered several times and it remains in this stage for a month.

Birth: After 9 months, the baby is born. It learns how to crawl, walk, and run. The baby resemble it's earthly parents, however, it does not resemble the angels in heaven. Humans on earth colors range from black, brown, red, yellow, white, etc. The baby grows to adulthood and is exposed along the way to a host of earthly temptations. The adult learns about its heavenly creator and the Gospel of Jesus Christ. The adult believes the Gospel of Jesus Christ and exercise that belief by being baptized. Hopefully the adult will follow the commandments and live a Christian life until death.

Stages 3

PUPA (CHRYSALIS)

Pupa (Chrysalis): The larva finds a good location to pupate. It attach itself to a plant or other object. It weaves a pattern of silk there and grabs hold of it with its rear prolegs. It begins transformation into a quiet and stiff motionless object called a *chrysalis.* Pupa (Chrysalis) is a very quiet time. There is no eating going on inside the body, however, the legs, wings and body of a mature insect is developing. The change can take anywhere from ten days to eight months.

Death: After life is complete on earth and the appointment with death has been met (*"And as it is appointed unto men once to die, but after this the judgment."* Hebrews 9:27). God retrieve his spirit from the body (*"Then shall the dust return to the earth as it was: and the spirit shall return unto God who gave it."* Ecclesiastes 12:7). The human spirit is judged in heaven and a verdict is rendered. (*"And I saw the dead, small and great, stand before God; and the books were opened: and another book was opened, which is the book of life: and the dead were judged out of those things which were written in the books, according to their works."* Revelation 20:12). The body is placed in a casket and buried. The body is transformed back to dust.

Stages 4

ADULT

Butterfly: At the end of the pupal stage, the pupa skin splits open, The once crawling caterpillar, moves out of its pupa shell and now has a new body, beautiful wings, and is now flying. A full metamorphosis is complete.

A New Creation: Jesus told the disciples before he ascended into heaven to *"Go ye into all the world, and preach the gospel to every creature. He that believeth and is baptized shall be saved; but he that believeth not shall be damned."* Mark 16:15-16. If at your judgment (Romans 14:10), Jesus made the verdict that you will be saved (*"For God so loved the world, that he gave his only begotten Son, that whosoever believeth in him should not perish, but have everlasting life."* John 3:16). When Jesus returns at the first resurrection, he will give a shout of the archangel. The graves of the righteous dead will crack open and the transformation stage will be set for the saved.

At the first resurrection, after the last trumpet sound from the angel, the righteous dead body will be transformed in a moment or a twinkling of a eye *(1 Corinthians 15:52).*

God will spare his righteous from the fiery pits of hell. *"…weeping may endure for a night, but joy cometh in the morning."* Psalm 30:5. *"For this corruptible must put on incorruption, and this mortal must put on immortality."* 1 Corinthians 15:53. Righteous will be as the angels are in heaven *(Mark 12:25)*. *"But they that wait upon the LORD shall renew their strength; they shall mount up with wings as eagles."…* Isaiah 40:31.

After the transformation, the righteous dead shall be caught up into the clouds of glory *(1 Thessalonians 4:16)*. Then those that are righteous and are remaining on the earth, that had never taste of death, will be caught up into the clouds of glory *(1 Thessalonians 4:17)*. The heavenly train will fly to heaven, to meet God the Father. They will remain in heaven for 1,000 years, this is called the millennium period. After the millennium, the heavenly host will return to earth, for the second resurrection of the wicked. They will raise with mortal and corruptible bodies, awaiting their final death, with the devil and his angels in eternal hell fire and brimstone. This is the second death and the Battle of Armageddon. After the wicked have burned to ashes, Jesus will renew the face of the earth. The righteous will live out eternity on earth.

Some people have a hard time conceiving that if they are saved, they will be able to fly with wings. The similarity of the metamorphosis of a butterfly to a Christian are incredibly similar. It is an earthly example of what a Christian will go through. It is though God is putting it right in our face and on the smallest scale (insect). It is though he is saying, see how this can be possible if you believe. Wake up and see this light God is shining.

Appendix G

Guide. The quick reference guide will assist you in quickly referring to a subject, or checking the combined scriptures of this book for correction. When the front part of a scripture is being used it will be identified as (FP). The back part of a scripture will be identified as (BP). The combined scriptures were taken from the King James Version of the Bible.

Chapter Two: Jesus Baptism.

Chapter Three: Early Galilean Ministry.

Chapter Four. Middle Galilean Ministry.

Chapter Five. Closing Galilean Ministry.

Chapter Six. Jesus heals the man born blind.

Chapter Seven. Jesus raises Lazarus from the dead.

Chapter Eight. The parable of the lost son

Chapter Nine. Prophecy of Jerusalem destruction (A.D. 70); and signs of the end of the world.

Chapter Ten. The garden of Gethsemane.

Chapter Eleven. Jesus trials and crucifixion.

Chapter Twelve. The Resurrection and Ascension of Jesus Christ

Bibliography

Doubleday & Company, Inc. *The World Book Encyclopedia.* Chicago, IL:
   Field Enterprises Educational Corporation., 1976
Nichol, Francis D. *Seventh Day Adventist Bible Commentary.* Hagerstown, MD:
   Review and Herald Publishing Association, 1980
Gutzke, Manford G. *Holy Bible Master Reference Edition.* Nashville, TN.:
   Royal Publishers, Inc., 1968
Yaucey, Philip and Stafford, Tim. *The Student Bible King James Version.* Grand Rapids, MI:
   Zondervan Publishing House., 1996

Internet Addresses

The Space Telescope Science Institute. *Images and Press Releases.* April 4, 2001.
   <http://oposite.stsci.edu/pubinfo/pictures.html>.
The Space Telescope Science Institute. *Highlights and Regular Features.*
   <http://hubblesite.org/>.
National Aeronautics and Space Administration. *National Space Science Data Center.* September 1, 1994.
   <http:/nssdc.gsfc.nasa.gov/photo_gallery/photo gallery.html>.

Photo Credits

National Aeronautics and Space Administration. *National Space Science Data Center.* September 1, 1994.
   <http:/nssdc.gsfc.nasa.gov/photo_gallery/photo gallery.html>.
Hubble Heritage Team (AURA/STScI/NASA/ESA).

A memorial of Mary

Jesus commanded, **"...Wheresoever this gospel shall be preached in the whole world, there shall also this, that this woman hath done, be told for a memorial of her."** Matthew 26:13.

Now when Jesus was in Bethany, in the house of Simon the leper, there they made him a supper; and Martha served: but Lazarus was one of them that sat at the table with him. As he sat at meat, there came Mary unto him having an alabaster box of ointment of spikenard very precious; and she brake the box, and poured it on his head. Then took Mary a pound of ointment of spikenard, very costly, and anointed the feet of Jesus, and wiped his feet with her hair: and the house was filled with the odour of the ointment.

Jesus said, **"For in that she hath poured this ointment on my body, she did it for my burial."** Matthew 26:12. (see pages 212-214, 10-2).